FOUR AFRICAN
POLITICAL SYSTEMS

FOUR AFRICAN POLITICAL SYSTEMS

Christian P. Potholm
Vassar College

PRENTICE-HALL, INC., Englewood Cliffs, New Jersey

To Sandrahene, who lived it

13–329599–0

Library of Congress Catalogue Card Number: 74–102931

Current printing (last digit):
10   9   8   7   6   5   4   3   2   1

PRINTED IN THE UNITED STATES OF AMERICA

Prentice-Hall International, Inc., London
Prentice-Hall of Australia, Pty. Ltd., Sydney
Prentice-Hall of Canada, Ltd., Toronto
Prentice-Hall of India Private Limited, New Delhi
Prentice-Hall of Japan, Inc., Tokyo

Preface

Four African Political Systems arose from a perceived need to bring African political phenomena into the study of comparative politics and political theory, and to analyze several African governments on a comparative basis. Although a plethora of monographs on single countries, continental studies, and micro and single-factor studies of Africa have appeared during the last decade, there have been few attempts to analyze four or five African political systems with a single theoretical framework. This has been due in part to the scarcity of data and to the relatively short time African states have had to develop meaningful political patterns. However, the accumulation of data has now proceeded far enough to allow a second generation analysis of at least some African states; and political systems have appeared in Africa that are relevant not only to the study of politics in Africa but also to comparative politics and political theory generally.

The book is designed to provide African material for courses that deal with comparative politics and political development. For this reason we have included a major chapter that introduces "The African Context." It is also hoped that *Four African Political Systems* will be used in courses that deal exclusively with Africa to introduce theoretical material and to place African material in a broader analytical framework.

The political systems included in this work were chosen on the basis of two criteria: that there be sufficient primary and secondary material already available, and that they be political typologies with relevance beyond their own boundaries. Thus, South Africa, while to a certain extent unique, nevertheless has relevance for the remaining colonial areas and is an interesting example of a multiparty system that is markedly undemocratic. Somalia, on the other hand, was for nearly a decade a vibrant, multiparty democracy whose grinding poverty and significant accomplishments in the area of political development combined to offer a substantial amendment to several major assumptions of developmental theory. It also continues to cast into sharp relief the factors necessary to sustain polyarchal decision making and is thus of major significance for the nine African states which, despite the recent erosion of democratic tendencies on a continental-wide basis, contain considerable democratic elements.

The Ivory Coast exhibits the characteristics of a modernizing oligarchy and a tendency toward the "no party" state, two important political patterns prevalent in West and Central Africa. Tanzania, with its accent on democratic politics within a single-party framework, .is currently without imitators but may become a model for those political systems throughout the world that desire mass participation and polyarchal decision-making, but must keep these within certain well-defined limits. In terms of relevant typologies and prominent patterns, I should have liked to include an African military regime, but lack of data and the difficulties of determining the course of decision making within these systems forced me to rule out such analysis at this stage.

These portraits of the political systems of South Africa, Tanzania, Somalia, and the Ivory Coast are not designed to be definitive country studies but rather, interpretive essays based on existing works. The four political systems are compared on the basis of decision-making, systemic capabilities, and goal formation. Because of the synthetic nature of much of the work, I have called upon a large number of scholars whose competence lies in the areas of political development and comparative politics or the individual systems under review. I am most grateful for their comments and suggestions. The work, where it succeeds, owes a great debt to their participation.

David Baldwin, Peter Smith, Howard Erdman, and Andrew Leddy read the chapters on political development and the conceptual framework. James Fernandez, Richard Taylor, and Jerry Frost commented upon "The African Context," which was first presented as a paper at the Royalton College Institute (summer 1968). Leonard Thompson, Douglas Wheeler, and Pierre van den Berghe dealt with South Africa, while Henry Bienen, Anthony Rweyemamu, and John Rensenbrink reviewed the section on Tanzania; Alphonso Castagno, Jr., and Abdulahai Hagi, Somalia; and Victor DuBois, Barbara Lewis, and William Foltz, the Ivory Coast. Scholarship is definitely a collective enterprise.

Throughout the writing of this work, Howard Bliss of Vassar College was of incalculable help. As a loyal friend, perspicacious scholar, and helpful colleague, he carefully read and commented upon each page as it was written and rewritten. His encouragement as well as his caution were of great benefit to the entire process. I am also most grateful for the excellent assistance rendered by the staff of Prentice-Hall, in particular Stan Evans, James Murray, Roger Emblen, and Ann Sickles, and for the many incisive observations provided by William Foltz and Aristide Zolberg, who read the completed work.

I should also like to thank the Research Committees of Vassar and Dartmouth for their generous support, and my research assistants, Dennis Young, Robert Bull, Nancy Rice, and Gig Babson. Dottie Schleipman and Elizabeth Blair helped in typing various chapters, while Mildred Tubby completed the final draft. Mrs. Tubby's meticulous care and consistent diligence made her a joy to work with.

C.P.P.

Hanover, N.H., 1968
Poughkeepsie, N.Y., 1969
Legon, Ghana, 1969

Contents

ix

CHAPTER I

A Conceptual Framework
for Comparative Politics

In an attempt to compare African political systems with each other and with non-African political systems, a meaningful conceptual framework is necessary. Such a framework ought to enable one to compare such diverse entities as Chile and Malaysia, Chad and Belgium, Great Britain and Mauritius, and to examine political systems far removed in time and space. For much of the 19th and early 20th centuries, political scientists did not find it necessary or even desirable to develop conceptual frameworks capable of analyzing different political forms and their change. Thus, many studies of the period were descriptive, noncomparative, essentially monographic in character, heavily oriented toward constitutions and formal institutions. With the vast proliferation of political units, the emergence of new political forms such as Fascism and Communism, and an increased incidence of revolutionary politics, the need for explicit modes of analysis became clear.

Heavily influenced by contemporary concerns and discoveries in sociology, economics, and psychology, the study of comparative politics has increasingly concentrated upon a search for common denominators that will enable political scientists to compare meaningfully the numerous political entities in existence today, as well as the larger number of political systems found in the complex and rich history of mankind. It is upon some of these common denominators that we wish to focus in this chapter.

We begin by an examination of the term *political system*. As used in this book, a political system is essentially a demand-processing, image-projecting, goal-seeking entity, embedded within an international environment. As such, it may be regarded as a group of mutually influencing variables of a social, economic, and political character that interact over a period of time. It may thus be thought of as both an analytical construct and an empirically observable structure. A political system is made up of people who place demands upon it, recognize its control or authority over them (in certain defined areas at least), support it and, on occasion, oppose it. In order for it to continue to exist, the political system as a whole must satisfy some demands, moderate others, and ignore still others. It must rally support from within the societal groups it governs and decide which of these groups have the more legitimate demands and/or the most useful supports. In some political systems, for example, the support of the military or the bureaucracy may be crucial; in others, that of the organized church or the trade unions. The political system is the sum of its institutions, sources of legitimacy, discernible structures, personnel, and laws which, taken with the way it functions, produces its image. The composite of all these elements is what we mean by Uganda or Mexico, Songhay or the Holy Roman Empire.

The ways in which the political system meets the demands placed upon it and elicits the supports it needs to survive and maintain itself determine, in large part, the way the rest of the world looks at the entity in question. This image is of great importance both in reflecting and in influencing the way in which the political system copes with its international and domestic environments. A good portion of this image stems from the goals that the system espouses. These goals are multiple and may be those of the population at large, interests of certain socio-economic groups within the country, desires of the leadership personnel within the political structure itself, or a combination of all three. These goals are in the process of constant mutation although broadly speaking, they may be categorized as active or passive (in terms of the system's intent) and realistic or chimerical (in terms of the system's capabilities).

In general, a political system will be held to be more or less comparable to a nation state, although there are some important qualifications to this equation. One way in which a political system may differ from a nation state is in the area of boundaries (1) between the political system and the society in which it is embedded, and (2) between one political system and another. Under existing international law and common usage, a state in the international community is recognized as having control over a certain geographical area with defined borders. Yet the political system may or may not correspond to the state. For example, the Danish political system and the recognized territory of Denmark coincide. If one looks at the Republic of Somalia, however, one finds that the psychological and political boundaries of the Somali political system exceed the present territorial limits of the state of Somalia. The large numbers of Somalis living outside its borders and the porous nature of its frontiers call into question the validity or usefulness of ipso facto equating the Somali state with the Somali political system. Once having said this, however, one should be quick to point out how difficult it is to define the political and psychological boundaries with any accuracy. At the same time, it does seem to be a fact of international life that one political system may overlap the territorial boundaries of another. This is particularly true in Africa. Because of the artificial and haphazard territorial boundaries inherited from the colonial period, many African states lack ethnic, economic, or geographical unity and political systems are not always coterminous with existing states. As this volume will demonstrate, theoretical and definitional problems notwithstanding, political systems in Africa illustrate difficulties of major proportions in the area of boundaries that must be taken into account in an analysis of these political systems. The interpenetration of various political systems within a particular geographical area, therefore, may well explain not only "interstate" activity, but also aspects of "domestic" politics as well.

Our comparison of political systems in general and of African political systems in particular will thus concentrate upon establishing four major categories of inquiry which take into account the unity of the political system and the way in which international politics impinge upon that system. These areas of investigation will include (1) participation in the decision-making process of the political system, (2) capability analysis (the ability of the political system to organize its human and natural resources and to implement its goals), and (3) the goals chosen and their relation to the international environment. In the next chapter, we shall deal with (4) political development (or the changing styles and structures of domestic and international decision making).

Participation in the Political System

The political system of a particular area is simultaneously embedded in two environments: one domestic, one international. The domestic environment may involve a single cultural group or society (as in the case of Norway), or a series (as in India). The political system is both conditioned by the society (or the societies) and capable of altering it (or them). Although these processes of mutual interaction may occur simultaneously, we can point to instances in which society seems to have directed the evolution of a political system (19th century Great Britain) and cases in which the political system radically reordered the society and the economic structure (the Soviet Union in the 1930's). It should also be noted that in certain political forms, ranging from simple hunting bands to advanced totalitarian systems, the boundaries between the society and the political system become blurred. This phenomenon was seen most clearly in the political "coordination" of all aspects of life in Nazi Germany.[1]

One comprehensive but rewarding way to come to grips with a political system and its society is to analyze participation in its decision-making process. For when we speak of this "nation" or that "state," we are often referring to individual human actors who decide upon goals and policies. In short, who makes the decisions; how, when, and why? Who articulates the demands, who provides the supports, who makes the decisions—these are crucial questions that enable us to focus on the heart of the political process. Are the demand formulators and decision-makers individuals or groups? If, as is likely

[1] Hanna Arendt, *The Origins of Totalitarianism* (New York: Harcourt, Brace & World, 1951).

in complex societies, they are groups, what are their socio-economic backgrounds, their age-sex composition, their ethnic or racial origins? Are they associational or ascriptive in character, well organized or amorphously constituted, political or nonpolitical in orientation? Equally important, are they more or less independent and able to influence the political parties and/or the government, or are they controlled by either of these? Are the groups that dominate the society also dominant in the formal governmental structure? Are important groups left out of the decision-making process altogether? We dwell on interest groups in order to accent the wide variety of their forms and composition and to indicate that an understanding of the decision-making process depends upon an examination of these groups—from church organizations to trade unions, from cultural and ethnic societies to linguistic or occupational associations, from the military to public corporations to political clubs. Broadly speaking, a political party may also be considered an interest group or a combination of such organizations and much of the conflict resolution within a society may take place among or within political parties.[2]

Africa itself offers some interesting variations on traditional party politics, ranging from a nonparty state (Ethiopia) to a single-party state (Liberia), a multiparty arrangement with one dominant party (Kenya) to a multiparty, historically regime-alternating system (South Africa). Although analysis of party politics will be an important aspect of our study of African political systems, excessive focus upon the formal political arrangements within an area may well hinder an accurate assessment of the total political process. Thus, in examining the political systems of Somalia, Tanzania, the Ivory Coast, and South Africa, we shall study both the formal and informal aspects of the political decision-making process.

This is of course a large order, for when one deals with the decision-making process in its entirety, one is often overwhelmed by the vast amount of data that could be analyzed. Whenever data can be quantified or systematically arranged, it becomes more manageable and the behavioral wing of political science has developed a method—or more accurately, a set of methods—which have proven worthwhile, particularly in the study of elections and in the development of pre-

[2] For a conflict-oriented study of elites and counterelites, see Harold Lasswell's seminal *Politics: Who Gets What, When, How* (New York: McGraw-Hill Book Company, 1963).

dictive models.[3] Wherever possible, we shall use these new techniques and approaches, particularly in terms of economic data gathering and categorization of aggregate voting behavior. It should be noted at the outset, however, that there are major difficulties which prevent their widespread applicability to the politics of the underdeveloped world.[4] Obviously, if there are no parties, or no elections, voter profile analysis is of little use; if one is not allowed access to internal governmental messages, it is difficult to test and evaluate communications theory. We cannot, however, wait for some future date when the data will be available and the methods operative (and many political scientists would say that, even if these conditions were met, we still might not have the answers to the most relevant questions). We must examine the evidence available—whether quantitative or qualitative—and proceed to tentative conclusions about the nature and efficacy of individuals, interest groups, and political systems. The questions we have posed are difficult to answer and we cannot be totally sure of our ability to pinpoint precisely decision-makers at each and every turn of the process, but patterns are discernible.

In addition to discovering who makes the political decisions, we will consider how and why they do so. How do the interest groups attempt to actualize their demands? What is their power and influence? Are there large and important groups that are political in character? Do they attempt to use formal institutions such as parliaments or national assemblies? And, if so, what are their channels of access to the political structure? Do they pursue their goals openly and within the existing ethos of the system, or do they use secret operations outside the institutional structure? The AFL-CIO in the United States, for example, generally supports the Democratic Party and has not attempted to create a Labor Party. Conversely, the Broederbond in South Africa, working secretly and informally, has, on occasion,

---

[3] We are not suggesting, of course, that the behavioral contributions lie only in the areas of voter analysis or economic models but, rather, that in the African context their approaches seem thus far to have yielded the most noticeable results. For an overview of traditional and behavioral contributions to the study of Africa, the reader should consult Robert A. Lystad (ed.), *The African World: A Survey of Social Research* (New York: Frederick A. Praeger, 1965).

[4] In some areas, however, data is becoming available. See *East African Survey of Federation, Political Leaders, Labour Legislation and Newspaper Reliability* (1962) and *Comparative Change in Public Opinion 1964–1966* (1966) by the Marco Public Opinion Polls (Nairobi: East African Printing Co., 1967).

challenged the very nature of the parliamentary system. Considerations of this type are of great importance in assessing the nature of both the group and the political system as a whole, for the willingness or unwillingness of various interest groups to stay within the norms of the existing system often depends upon the responsiveness of the system itself. This characteristic of a regime may change through time. In the United States, for example, some exponents of Negro rights have in recent years taken to extralegal activities to dramatize the plight of the Negro and to call into question the very character of the political system. This suggests that the political system of the United States is responsive enough to allow for some progress (at least to offer the hope of change), but not responsive enough to prevent mounting levels of frustration caused by the fact that the gap between the promise and the delivery of equal status is not diminishing rapidly enough.

The ultimate aims of the interest group that is seeking access to the decision-making process and those of the ruling elite are also of great import. Does the Communist Party of France expect to attain a majority of voter support in order to eventually rule within the legal framework of the Fifth Republic or does it plan to ultimately supplant that framework? An appraisal of an interest group's ultimate concerns or ideology is important not only to the students of politics but to its practitioners as well. When faced with a powerful, antagonistic interest group, the existing elite must often decide whether it should draw members of that group into the ruling body (whether party central committee, cabinet, or junta) in order to turn its demands into supports. The leadership is likely to base its decisions on (1) whether it feels it can keep the new elements in check and (2) whether the group in question is willing to work within the existing system on the basis of shared authority. Such an assessment must also take into account the basic power configurations of the system. According to Robert Dahl and Charles Lindblom, a useful way of assessing the power configuration of a system is to characterize it as hierarchical (in which the leaders control the nonleaders), polyarchal (in which the nonleaders control the leaders), or bargain oriented (in which the leaders control each other).[5] Although this classifica-

---

[5] Robert A. Dahl and Charles E. Lindblom, *Politics, Economics and Welfare* (New York: Harper & Row, Publishers, 1963), p. 22.

tion will prove a bit too rigid for our assessment of Tanzania, Somalia, the Ivory Coast, and South Africa, it is nevertheless a useful point of departure.

The basis on which the existing leadership makes decisions will be dealt with more fully in the next chapter when we shall examine the style of decision making (autocratic, pragmatic, etc.) as well as the relation between the political power structure and the societal and economic interest groups. At this point, however, we should note that, even when in opposition to the ruling elites, vibrant interest groups perform an essential function by viewing the societal realities and providing informational feedback and counterinfluences, thus indicating policy alternatives.[6] Often, if the interest groups are made inoperative or are so tightly controlled in terms of ideology or leadership by the political authorities that their beneficial aspects are lost, the entire political system suffers. To illustrate, the government of Ghana under Kwame Nkrumah initially made excellent use of interest groups (both independent and within the Convention People's Party) to aid in policy formation. By 1962–63, however, the highest political authorities had subverted or banned the non-CPP groups, severely altered the internal communications channels within the CPP, and begun to ignore international feedback. The result was that crucial decisions were made in what amounted to an informational vacuum and the regime gradually divorced itself from the realities of its domestic and international environments.

Nor is overresponsiveness to interest groups conducive to economic and political development (although the political system as such is more likely to endure by being overresponsive than by its opposite). Evidence from the underdeveloped world indicates that certain interest groups such as the military and the bureaucracy often make extensive demands upon the political system seeking to develop its human and natural resources and that these demands are satisfied at the expense of the society as a whole. An even more extreme case is represented by the *librum veto*, an unusual right reserved for the nobles in 18th century Poland whereby any noble could veto any proposal of the king. Not surprisingly, this political system disintegrated, and the territory of the country was divided during the latter

---

[6] Karl W. Deutsch, *The Nerves of Government* (Glencoe, Ill.: The Free Press, 1963).

part of the 18th century among Prussia, Russia and Austria. In later chapters, we shall look at this phenomenon by comparing the percentage of gross national product spent on welfare and medical care to that spent on governmental salaries and military budgets. As Réné Dumont has pointed out in his perspicacious work, *False Start in Africa*, civil servants in Senegal and the Cameroun "earn" in 1½ months what a peasant earns in a lifetime.[7] The political systems in question seem to be overreacting to certain interest groups, although what is dysfunctional with regard to the total development of the country may be functional in terms of insuring the longevity of the regime controlling the political system.

As these examples indicate, steering a course between a lack of feedback and a distortion of the purposes of that feedback is difficult. Yet it can be done. The government of Tanzania has provided strong political direction from the center to curb the potential dysfunctional elements within such groups as the Tanganyikan Federation of Labor, the military, bureaucracy, and students by subordinating their demands for rewards to the more general needs of the society as a whole for development and welfare. To have done this without diminishing the beneficial aspects of vibrant interest groups or disturbing a rational, open-ended decision-making process based on accountability to the population as a whole is one of the major reasons why Tanzania merits our attention.

The above statements indicate that in order to fully assess the decision-making process in a particular political system, it is necessary to make a series of value judgements, not only about the means but also about the ends of the system. In much the same fashion, one should judge the meaningfulness of participation in that system. The "participation revolution" in this century has not only broadened the participation in the decision-making process in many cases, but also led political leaders to claim this participation even when it is not present.[8] With such diverse entities as Canada, Mauritania, and North Korea, purporting to be "democratic," a good deal of confusion has arisen. Further, in attempting to assess the validity of participa-

[7] Réné Dumont, *False Start in Africa* (New York: Frederick A. Praeger, 1967), p. 81.

[8] The "participation revolution" and its implications have been dealt with most successfully in Gabriel A. Almond and Sidney Verba, *The Civic Culture* (Princeton: Princeton University Press, 1963).

tion, statistics are of little help by themselves. If 97% of the people eligible to vote in country X turn out to approve a single slate of candidates what is signified? Does it indicate that the government's extractive and regulative capabilities are high or does it mean that participation is meaningful and worthwhile? Probably the former, for some analysts have pointed out that low participation may be a sign that the political system is functioning smoothly, and argued that it. is only in times of great stress and heightened anxiety that partici- pants are likely to view their vote as critical.[9] Still, one could argue that the sheer act of voting provides at least some kind of identifica- tion with the regime even if one votes for a prearranged slate. At the very least, therefore, we may conclude that mere levels of participation do not tell us very much about the meaningfulness of that participa- tion and that without additional information and analysis, the figures are of only marginal significance.

Nor does an examination of the formal institutions or constitu- tional arrangements enable us to tell, a priori, whether a decision- making process is "democratic." A single-party setup may involve a good deal of internal democracy and widespread participation in the selection of candidates and ideology. This may be particularly true if local branches of that party exercise authority as interest groups and pragmatically assess alternative policies. A single-party regime may, of course, contain none of these elements and provide little participation and less democracy. The same is true of a multiparty system, however. We have often assumed that we can tell at a glance whether a regime is democratic or not, whether participation is meaningful or not, simply by looking at the institutions involved, the separation of powers among the legislature, the judiciary, and the executive, and the existence of multiple parties. South Africa clearly enjoys the institutional apparatus and the constitutional framework for democracy, but few objective observers would categorize the South African political system as democratic.

This brief discussion of the decision-making process has indicated the large number of variables involved in a political system and how difficult it is to assess the decision-making process in the abstract. We have outlined a series of categories that may tell us where to

---

[9] Seymour M. Lipset, *Political Man* (Garden City, N.Y.: Doubleday & Com- pany, Anchor edition, 1960), p. 195.

look, but do not enable us to predict the workings of the system with-out further examination and without taking into account both the capabilities foundation and the goal orientation of that system.

Capabilities of the Political System

In comparing disparate political systems, another useful category of analysis is the area of *capabilities* or the ability of the decision-makers to implement their goals. This aspect of the conceptual framework owes much to the orientation inspired by the structural-functional approach of sociologist Talcott Parsons. Subsequently applied to political systems by Gabriel Almond, James Coleman, and more recently by G. Bingham Powell, it has provided a useful way of systematically collecting data about the process by which states attain their goals.[10] Although some of the structural-functional concepts have been al-tered, rearranged, and expanded here (and the subsequent section on the goals of the political system stands as a reaction to some of the difficulties of a purely structural-functional approach), these notions have proven of value in comparing markedly different political sys-tems.

When we refer to the capabilities of a political system, we are in effect attempting to measure the performance of that political entity in organizing and utilizing its human and natural resources in order to accomplish the goals of the decision-makers. This activity involves many ingredients, for the capabilities of a system reflect not only the authority apparatus or the discernible structure of institutions which aid in goal achievement, but also the process by which the system uses its influence internally and externally. When taken together, what will be termed the regulative, extractive, distributive, rejuvenative, and symbolic capabilities represent the political system's collective capacity for action. Although we shall be referring to the regulative capacity and the symbolic capability as if they were separate cate-gories, it should be borne in mind that they are interdependent, inter-

[10] See especially Talcott Parsons, *The Social System* (New York: The Free Press, 1951); and Talcott Parsons and Edward Shils (eds.) *Toward a General Theory of Action* (Cambridge: Harvard University Press, 1951); and more re-cently, Gabriel A. Almond and James S. Coleman (eds.), *The Politics of De-veloping Areas* (Princeton: Princeton University Press, 1960) and Gabriel A. Almond and G. Bingham Powell, *Comparative Politics: A Developmental Ap-proach* (Boston: Little, Brown and Company, 1966).

acting, and in a state of flux so that we are able to achieve only a generalized representation of reality. Nevertheless, by examining the institutional framework and the resources available we should be able to discern the ability of decision-makers to achieve their goals. When coupled with an investigation of the decision-making process and the goal selection hierarchy, capability analysis will enable the reader to grasp the fundamentals of a wide variety of political systems.

REGULATIVE CAPACITY

The regulative capacity of a political system is its ability to control the actions of its populace and to influence its membership to behave in certain ways. The amount of regulation necessary to preserve the political entity and to achieve its goals differs from system to system, depending upon the nature of its environment: the type of society involved, the choice of goals, and the levels of social, economic, and political development attained. As will be seen, the existence of powerful centrifugal forces in some of the newer African states clearly indicates the need for a strong regulative capacity, particularly in the area of integration. As used here, *integration* is taken to denote commitment to the political system as a whole rather than to local or regional authorities, and, as Myron Weiner has pointed out, may have territorial, national, ideological, behavioral, and mass-elite aspects.[11] More recently, Claude Ake has indicated that consensus among elite decision-makers is perhaps of more importance than these categories of integration if the political system is to endure. If the elites of a variety of societies and regions support the system as a whole, a wide spectrum of territorial or value malintegration may be tolerated.[12]

The regulative capacity may be analyzed in a variety of ways. In our examination of African political systems, we shall be looking at the formal apparatus of regulation, the legal system and its enforcement. A good deal may be learned from the kinds of laws promulgated and enforced as well as from the punishments prescribed. For example, if the leaders of a political system fear its collapse or disintegration, treason will be broadly defined and punished by death, whereas

[11] Myron Weiner, "Political Integration and Political Development," *The Annals* (March, 1965) Vol. 359: 52–64.
[12] Claude Ake, *A Theory of Political Integration* (Homewood, Ill.: Dorsey Press, 1967).

in a more secure system, or at least one perceived to be more secure, the same crime may be far more narrowly defined and seldom enforced by capital punishment. Crime rates, too, may be of significant aid in ascertaining the regulative capacity, but a close examination of this problem is essential for an accurate assessment. In South Africa, the present government is content to tolerate a high incidence of crime in the African urban areas. At first glance this might be an indication of a low regulative capability and a sign of serious difficulty. Yet, the widespread occurrence of civil crime is balanced by a much lower rate of political crime. In terms of the maintenance of the political system in existence at the present time, a high rate of civil crime may actually be beneficial: it helps to sublimate African frustration with the situation, turning it away from political avenues and by providing a lucrative outlet; it encourages a variety of societal groups such as the Indians, Chinese, and Malays to look to the European authorities for protection; and it increases the willingness of Europeans to accept increasingly repressive measures against the Africans. In addition to an examination of the legal framework, we shall analyze the size, composition, and orientation of the police force. and the role of the army, if any, in internal supervision.

We shall also investigate the ways in which the leaders of the political system regulate society by the use of economic measures, information dissemination, force, and political action. The use of economic incentives and curbs is an essential ingredient of the regulative capacity of a system. The more positive aspects of this process (i.e. rewards) will be dealt with under the heading of the distributive capability, but there are a large number of devices and techniques which may be more properly discussed under the regulative capacity. The government may set the price of goods or services, create or destroy money, set tax and investment rates, enforce public and private savings, and regulate levels of employment. Even in a market economy, the government may seek to regulate the activities of individuals, groups, even society as a whole.

Information, too, is used by the government to encourage and discourage certain types of activities. Propaganda and the entire process of symbolic manipulation are obvious facets of this process and will be examined in some detail under the heading symbolic capability. At this point, it should simply be noted that the release of information concerning "foreign invasion," "traitors," and "imperialist" and "communist" plots is often used by the leaders of the political system to produce a desired course of action and to curb dissent.

In addition to the formal and informal law enforcement process and the dissemination of information, the political leadership may utilize local political groups such as village committees, block leaders, and action groups. These may be members of the national political party, a government bureaucracy, or associational groups and are used to induce certain modes of behavior. Often the political action groups are used to augment existing regulative agencies and to perform a wide variety of tasks on the local level. In Mali, for example, until recently village committees served to encourage political socialization and state service, and to insure adherence to the existing legal norms. On a national level, the political authorities may seek to control or supplant certain interest groups by the use of political techniques. Often the government attempts to replace the army with a popular militia which is often characterized by lower professional ability but greater ideological commitment to the goals of the regime. This pattern of attempted replacement has not proven very successful as indicated by recent events in Guatemala, Indonesia, Ghana, Algeria, Congo (Brazzaville), Mali, and Iraq, for the army has often reacted by replacing the political authority itself. A more effective method of regulating and maintaining its ideological "purity" would seem to be infiltration and control of the army from within as the political authorities have done in the Soviet Union, North Vietnam, and Guinea.

The use of political action groups is closely related to the broader category of the use of force to regulate behavior. As A. R. Radcliffe-Brown and others have quite rightly pointed out, the ultimate authority of a political organization is connected with the use, or at least the possibility of using physical force.[13] Since all political systems have a series of legal and ethical norms, penalties for their violation, and the use of force to insure adherence to them, we shall be more interested in the ways in which force is used. To illustrate, when the Czarist regime in the 1900's needed to use force to control various types of political activity, launched armed attacks upon demonstra-

---

[13] A. R. Radcliffe-Brown and E. E. Evans-Pritchard, *African Political Systems* (London: Oxford University Press, 1940), p. xiv.

tors, large scale arrests, and the like. In terms of the regulative capability, the use of force was of less importance than the haphazard and careless manner in which it was applied. In this case, a declared revolutionary, Josef Stalin, was arrested eight times, managed to escape six times, and was released twice. If we compare this use of force with that employed by the German political system from 1933 to 1945 or even the Russian political system from 1923 to 1956, we find that in the latter instances force seems to have been applied more often. We might conclude, therefore, that it was not the amount of physical coercion that put the political system in danger of collapse, but the consistent misapplication of that force.

The decision-makers of the political system, then, by the use and the threat of force, by the release of information, by economic activity, and by the legal framework and enforcement of laws seek to control the population under their jurisdiction and to regulate its behavior.

EXTRACTIVE CAPABILITY

The extractive capability of a political system is its ability to tap its human and natural resources in terms of production, collection, and utilization of these resources. The size of a country's population and its inherent richness are of great importance in determining a nation's capacity to attain its goals and, hopefully, are a factor in a realistic formation of those goals. In general, the larger, healthier, more educated and highly organized the population, the more powerful will be that country. A large population, or a rapidly growing one, is not in itself a handicap to international power; in fact, it is an asset of some magnitude if the resource base of the country and its technological development are able to insure the utilization of that population. However, if the population of a country is often on the brink of starvation, illiterate and ill, the political system in question simply will not have the same opportunity to utilize that population. A political system wishing to maximize its power will therefore seek not only to control its population, but to enrich it as well. Its leaders will seek to feed, clothe, educate, and organize it so that the time, effort, and wealth of the population may be utilized by the political authority. The political system must develop an extractive apparatus, or bureaucracy, to insure this.

In fact, the development of such a bureaucracy is often crucial to economic development, and some writers have suggested that an efficient and effective bureaucracy is a prerequisite for modernity.[14] In terms of human resources, the ability of a political system to develop a healthy, educated, organized population is an index of its extractive capability. Conversely, the amount of wastage caused by malnutrition, inadequate education, poor opportunity, or alienation is an important area of comparison which is not limited to the underdeveloped world. Irrespective of the profound moral implications involved in the "final solution" to the Jewish "problem" in Germany during the Third Reich, the waste of resources represented by the destruction of 6 million Jews was enormous and lowered the system's extractive capability. In the United States as well, a pattern of unused resources may be observed. Because 20 million Negroes have often been discriminated against and denied equal educational and occupational opportunities, the United States is less powerful than it would be if the talents and energies of this portion of the population were developed and utilized. Similar examples can be drawn from the experience of Indians in Latin America, certain castes in India, and many ethnic groups in sub-Saharan Africa.

The ways in which the political system is able to employ its population, then, provides a useful point of departure for examining the ability of that system to extract the effort and wealth necessary to achieve its goals. In much the same fashion, the leaders of a political entity must also seek to develop its natural resources. If, as in the case of Japan or Great Britain, it lacks resources, it must utilize its human and technological assets in order to acquire them, either by trade or conquest. In the developing world, the problem often centers around the formation of capital. Many African countries, for example, are rich in natural resources. Mauritania has over 125 million tons of high grade iron ore and a billion tons of usable ore.[15] Gabon, Spanish Sahara, Guinea, Ghana, Liberia, Congo (Kinshasa), and South Africa are likewise richly endowed to such an extent that an adequate natural resource base is present (although population levels may be very low). Currently, however, the indigenous capital necessary to develop these resources is not available, as many African countries

[14] For an extensive analysis of the problem of political development and economic growth, see A. F. K. Organski, *The Stages of Political Development* (New York: Alfred A. Knopf, 1967), pp. 3–120 and C. E. Black, *The Dynamics of Modernization* (New York: Harper & Row, Publishers, 1966).

[15] Alfred G. Gerteiny, *Mauritania* (New York: Frederick A. Praeger, 1967), p. 179.

have an annual domestic capital formation of less than $30 million or barely enough for one medium sized plant. The leaders of these countries have attempted to compensate for this lack of internal capital by the use of foreign aid and "human investment." The aid available from foreign sources is notoriously undependable and the results of the "human investment" programs in the Ivory Coast, Mali, Guinea, and the Malagasy Republic are, to date, highly mixed. In addition, most African countries' dependence upon one or two primary products further inhibits the ability of the political system to develop its resources, both human and natural. On balance, a low extractive capability is a prevalent feature of most political systems in sub-Saharan Africa.

The extractive capability will be appraised in a variety of ways, including the percentage of taxes assessed compared to the percentage of taxes collected and the amount of force necessary to insure collection. In the African context, the existence of a common language is also an important indication of the extractive capability. Clearly the problems of coordinating sixty or seventy languages complicate the educational and occupational processes. It can generally be stated that the political system that is able to rely on a single language (such as Tanzania's use of Swahili or Rwanda's Kinyarwanda) has an advantage. The literacy rate is often cited as a useful index of the extractive capability, but it is perhaps best examined in conjunction with an employment profile chart in order to indicate the needs of the political system in terms of trained manpower and its ability to absorb that manpower. The economic structure of a political system is also an important index of the extractive capability and includes the size of markets, the population, their purchasing power and the like. If the economy is balanced, with multiple products and an industrial base, it is less likely to be exposed to the vicissitudes of international economic changes than is a monocrop, nonindustrialized economy. Striking examples of the difficulties of monocrop economy may be found in West Africa where peanuts provide 85% of export revenue in Gambia, Senegal, and Mali and cocoa 60% in Ghana.

DISTRIBUTIVE CAPABILITY

A third category of analysis which is useful in comparing disparate political systems is the distributive capability or the ability of the system to reward its members by the allocation of goods, services, and status. This allocation may be handled directly by the political authorities (as in a command economy) or indirectly by adding inputs into the pricing mechanism (in a market economy). Diverse political systems at different stages of development may accent different types of rewards. As John K. Galbraith has so lucidly pointed out, the American system has, in recent years, accented the allocation of status in addition to goods.[16] In the Soviet Union the use of services, such as a party car or vacation facilities, plays a more important role than that of physical ownership. In examining the distributive capacity of a political system, we are concerned with the basis for allocation: who gets what, when, how, and why? Are the rewards of the system allocated on the basis of talent, merit, and service or on the basis of ascription? Are certain groups excluded or do others obtain a disproportionate share of the rewards?

In addition to these judgements concerning the equitable or inequitable allocation of rewards, the country's resource base and the extractive capability of the political system are also critical factors for, broadly speaking, the more goods and services the political leadership has at its disposal, the more opportunity it will have to reward. Sweden or Canada has more physical rewards, quantitatively and qualitatively, than the political systems of Chad or Nepal or Guatemala. The growth rate of the economy and the perception of that growth are important factors to consider as well. If a variety of groups within the country view the economic pie as "fixed" or not expanding, competition for the shares of it is likely to be more intense than if the economic rewards are viewed as growing. Often in this context groups feel that the system is based on a kind of zero-sum game in which for someone to win (or be rewarded) someone else must lose. That such a view of the distributive capacity of a particular system may prove highly disruptive and damage the political system as a whole has been amply documented by Kalman Silvert in his analysis of Argentina.[17]

In terms of quantitative measures of the distributive capability, we shall examine the percentage of the system's gross national product

---

[16] J. K. Galbraith, *The Affluent Society* (Boston: Houghton Mifflin Company, 1958) and *The New Industrial State* (Boston: Houghton Mifflin Company, 1967).

[17] K. H. Silvert, "The Costs of Anti-Nationalism: Argentina," in *The Expectant People*, K. H. Silvert (ed.) (New York: Random House, 1963), pp. 347–372.

spent on welfare services, medical care, social security, and the like. Per capita income figures may also be utilized although they are an imperfect index unless broken down into socio-economic groups within a particular system. In the case of South Africa, even if we accept the government's own figures, African per capita income for 1966 was $220, while that of the Colored community amounted to $605 and that of the Europeans $3650. These figures are all the more meaningful if compared to those of other political entities in Africa, for they indicate that, while the African per capita income is clearly low relative to the other population groups within South Africa, it is high in terms of other parts of the continent. Generally speaking, the more wealth at the disposal of the political system the greater the opportunity for the leaders of that country to compensate for low capabilities in other categories. In the South African case, a repressive political structure is endured by many Africans, including nearly a million Africans from outside the borders of the Republic, at least in part because of the economic advantages. The political systems of Kuwait or Libya may likewise be said to have both a weak symbolic capacity and an unimpressive regulative capacity but, because of the vast wealth derived from oil production and the perception that this cornucopia is increasing and will continue to be shared, these systems have a strong distributive capacity. The political leadership can thus "buy off" dissident elements within the country and, equally important, would-be predators in the international environment. On the other hand, Guinea, which has weak extractive and distributive capabilities, must rely upon a strong ideological value system, "threats" from abroad, and consensual leadership in order to survive. Thus a weak distributive capability or an inequitable distribution of the rewards available may well circumscribe the limits of political action, influence the process of goal selection, and, occasionally, threaten the very existence of the regime in question.

REJUVENATIVE CAPABILITY

Because the internal and external environments of the political system are constantly changing and because the regulative, extractive, and distributive needs of the system are more or less continuously in a state of mutation, the political system as a whole must be able to change as well if it is to survive. The ability of the political system to reinforce itself, to maintain and alter its institutions, structures, and processes, and to replenish its personnel may be referred to as its rejuvenative capability. Although the political entity must constantly face the demands for adaptation from its external, interstate environment, we are here primarily concerned with the internal aspects of the problem and shall concentrate upon the processes of political socialization and recruitment, the problems of informational inputs, and the institutionalization of change.

Political socialization, the process by which the members of a political system are civically educated and inculcated with the values of the system, is of great importance. What we generally call nationalism is often little more than a set of learned responses to certain symbols.[18] These responses are taught in both formal and informal ways. There may be classes in civics, the learning of a pledge of allegiance, exposure to the history of the entity, and promulgation of laws, decrees, and constitutions. More importantly, the entire life experience of the individual may or may not reinforce the formal teachings of the political system. Racial minorities, rural populations, and the poor often have a set of learning experiences that run counter to the professed values and procedures of the system. In the underdeveloped world, where attachments are primarily local to begin with, the central authority must take consistent and specific steps to inspire allegiance to the system, and the symbols of nationhood must be deeply inculcated if the individual is to maintain his belief in the system in the face of electoral fraud, capricious law enforcement, rapacious tax collectors, or insensitive army garrisons. The process of political socialization is closely connected with the symbolic capability of the system and is mentioned here simply to indicate the educational aspects of the rejuvenative process.

Although it is also part of the participation process, political recruitment is an important ingredient in the maintenance of the political system. In examining the different political systems in Africa, we shall look at the ways in which the political authorities—whether kings, presidents, or generals—recruit personnel for the bureaucracies, the armed forces, and the law enforcement agencies. Staffing the bureaucracy of the government, for instance, is a continual problem for its leaders. As in the case of the distributive capability, the reader

---

[18] Boyd C. Shafer, *Nationalism: Myth and Reality* (New York: Harcourt, Brace & World, 1955) and R. Dawson and K. Prewitt, *Political Socialization* (Boston: Little, Brown and Company, 1969).

should seek the basis of recruitment and appointment. Are the personnel chosen on the basis of merit, ethnic or linguistic background, expertise, loyalty, intelligence and education, or a combination of all of these? Many African political systems are often alleged to base recruitment upon ethnicity, in that a major tribe tended to dominate the administration (such as the Ewe in Togo, the Ibo in Nigeria, the Baganda in Uganda, and the Baluba in the Congo). We shall examine this problem in some detail in the chapter on the African context, but it should be noted that the recruitment and operation of the bureaucracy are often critical determinants in the survival of the political system. If talented, energetic, committed to the political system rather than to individual rulers, and recruited on a more or less equitable basis, the bureaucracy may enable the political system to survive major problems. The Roman bureaucracy during the period of emperor alteration and the Indian Civil Service of the present are specific examples of this. The lack of trained and dedicated manpower in the administration is often staggering, however, particularly in the newer nations. Tanzania, for example, which is seeking to Africanize its bureaucracy, will not attain this goal until at least 1980.[19]

In addition to their method of recruiting personnel, political systems may also be compared on the basis of their ability to absorb and utilize new information that arises domestically and internationally. This inflow of information and its utilization is of such importance that Karl Deutsch in his development of communications theory has connected the self-destruction of a political system with "the process of self closure," or the shutting off of outside information.[20] Depending upon the state of the political system, relatively small amounts of information may greatly affect it. In addition, the impact of any information depends upon its force and content, the receptivity of the decision-makers, and the level at which the information enters the system. In order to survive, the political system must accept a stream of information, process it in a rational way, and utilize it in the decision-making process. If the information is transmitted improperly (i.e., with excessive distortion), or if it is not

<hr/>

[19] Idrian N. Resnick, "Manpower Development in Tanzania," *The Journal of Modern African Studies* (1967) Vol. 5, No. 1: 107–123.

[20] Karl W. Deutsch, "Communications Models and Decision Systems," *Contemporary Political Analysis*, James C. Charlesworth (ed.) (New York: The Free Press, 1967).

utilized by decision-makers, the impact on the political system may be pernicious. During 1964 and 1965, for example, a series of signals were transmitted to the Nigerian political authorities concerning societal difficulties and the increasing malintegration in the body politic. These included an increase in the rates of violence against political figures, an intensification of vitriolic racial and ethnic propaganda, a series of markedly fraudulent elections, and the inability of the regulative agencies to curb the disorders. The decision-makers chose to ignore the implications of these signals until the situation had deteriorated beyond control. Additional input of regulative forces, such as the army, were delayed until racial pogroms and migrations had taken place on such a scale that the maladies of the society had spread to the army itself. As a result of ignoring or misusing information, the Nigerian political system entered into a stage of widespread devolution characterized by rebellion of the Eastern Region. It remains to be seen whether these difficulties can be overcome and the Nigerian system integrated again.

In order to maintain itself then, a political system must insure the collection, more or less unaltered transmission, and rational assessment of information in the decision-making process. In judging the system's capabilities in this area, attention should be paid to the sources of information (does the government encourage dissent, either publicly or privately, as a corrective source of information?), the channels of informational flow (does the information reach the decision-makers on a regular basis or is it collected randomly and haphazardly?), and the purity of information transmission (because of the need to simplify and organize the vast amounts of information coming into even the most modest political system, the collection agencies usually edit it, but does the editing process distort the information to such an extent that its usefulness is obviated?). Finally, one should examine the utilization of information: do the decision-makers attempt to use the information in helping them reach goals and allocate resources, or merely to justify existing policies?

The ability to process information and to insure its effective utilization is directly related to an additional aspect of the rejuvenative capability, the ability of the political system to change not only its personnel but its institutions and processes as well. Given the dynamic nature of the internal and external environments, change is essential to survival. Some political systems have the institutions and value orientation to change slowly but continuously and fundamentally (Sweden), while others exhibit more radical but sporadic and quicker changes (France). Still others have indicated a marked inability to adjust to a new internal environment (Czarist Russia) or a changed external environment (Japan during the late 1930's and early 1940's). We may judge a political system on its ability to institutionalize change, to rearrange and alter itself, as well as by the society and economic structure which it controls. In the course of our investigations, we shall term these changes functional or dysfunctional "depending upon whether they increase or decrease the possibility of the future successful functioning of the system, and particularly of its future learning performance." [21]

There are several indicators of the ability of a political entity to change in a functional fashion. One is a consistent pattern of dissent protection. This has often been mistakenly assumed to require formal opposition groups, whereas in reality, by protecting dissent within a single party, a regime may well be less vulnerable to centrifugal forces within the system. Another indication of adaptability is the existence of institutional avenues for alteration of the system without changing the entire system, as the constitutional amendment procedure in the United States. The ability of a political system to provide for orderly change will be the central feature of the sections of the next chapter dealing with political development, but it should be remembered that the capacity for change is closely connected with the entire spectrum of systemic capabilities. If the political system has strong regulative and extractive capabilities and is responsive to the demands of the most important interest groups within its jurisdiction, it can be less flexible and still survive, at least for a time. In much the same fashion, in the international environment a powerful country can make many mistakes and adapt slowly (Great Britain as the most powerful country in the 19th century was able to "muddle through") while a weaker political system does not have the same margin of error (Egypt in the 19th century and Great Britain in the 20th).

SYMBOLIC CAPABILITY

A final category of capability analysis is that of the symbolic capability, or the image, domestic and international, that

---

[21] Karl W. Deutsch, *The Nerves of Government*, p. 221.

the system projects. In essence, the symbolic capability is a reflection, not only of the regulative, extractive, distributive, and rejuvenative capabilities and their interaction, but also of the decision-making process and its goal orientation. When we refer to the credibility of the political authority, we are referring to its symbolic capability, its believability, the acceptance of the decision-maker's authority to issue and enforce commands. At the heart of the political process lies the notion of legitimacy. We often refer to the legitimacy of a political system or regime, implying that there is a set of attitudes and values associated with it which support the political authority. Max Weber in his pioneering work outlined three ideal types of legitimacy.[22] To sketch these ideal types briefly, there is a *traditional* legitimacy based on an ascriptive society, family and clan ties, a correlation between birth and wealth, the sanctity of tradition, and often a connection with religious or mystical forces. An example of this would be the Spanish Monarchy in the 16th century (although it can exist in modern societies as well). Weber also felt that there is a *charismatic* type of legitimacy fostered by personal magnetism, courage, toughness, self-righteousness, and dedication to the normative patterns established by the leader. Cuba under the regime of Fidel Castro would exemplify this pattern of legitimacy. Finally, Weber outlined a *rational legal* form of legitimacy where the political system is based upon law, experience, merit, and achievement. We could mention present-day Switzerland in this connection. To Weber's three types, one could add further variations, most notably, a negative form of legitimacy based on apathy, resignation, fear, and lack of information and hope such as one finds presently in Haiti under the government of Dr. François Duvalier.

In terms of the symbolic capability, these ideal types represent points of departure rather than fixed categories, for it seems far less fruitful to fit individual political systems into one or another of these categories than to recognize that the legitimacy underpinnings of a particular system are likely to include elements from all four types or that one type of authority may change into another. That legitimacy may rest on a variety of foundations is seen in the case of the Ivory Coast. For much of the present population, the president Félix

---

[22] Max Weber, *The Theory of Social and Economic Organization*, Talcott Parsons (ed.) (New York: Oxford University Press, 1947).

Houphouët Boigny represents a traditional authority rather like a powerful chief or king. He is to others, a charismatic leader with a regime based upon a strong mass party, the *Parti Démocratique de la Côte d'Ivoire*, and an ideology strongly resembling capitalism. At the same time, the Ivory Coast has a more or less rational legal structure and advancement in society based upon merit as well as ascription.

The types of legitimacy that support a particular system help us to understand the process by which the population identifies with the central authority. Levels of identification with the political system and appraisal of individual decision-makers may be measured by attitudinal surveys as well as by discernible activity. In many political systems, however, these may be difficult to obtain, and in their absence it is necessary to rely on more indirect and perhaps negative indices, such as the number of political prisoners, exiles, and refugees, increased rate of symbol flow from the political authority, and the resort to violence by opponents and adherents of the political system. In addition to using their regulative, extractive, and distributive powers to enhance identification, the leaders of a political system seek to encourage support for its chosen goals by increasing group solidarity. This may be done in a variety of ways: by national campaigns to raise production, by increased propaganda concerning commonalty, or by international activity. One traditional method of attempting to increase identification is the creation or exaggeration of a foreign threat.

On occasion leaders may attempt to increase solidarity by going to war. For example, in the months immediately prior to the Civil War, the leaders of the United States government were actively contemplating a proposal by Secretary of State William H. Seward that the United States declare war on Spain and France over their involvement in Mexico in order to unify the nation. It is worth noting that the connection between a foreign war and increased national solidarity is often tenuous and dependent upon the successful outcome of that war. The government of Russia on two occasions, 1905 against Japan and 1914 against Germany, attempted to promote identification with the central authority through this tactic but because of international defeats, actually encouraged the very dysfunctional elements it was seeking to control.

As has been indicated, the symbolic capability is perhaps the most difficult of the capacities to measure. At the same time, it is an important area of concern, and we shall be examining problems it occasions in some detail with reference to the difficulties raised by the process of nation building. The basis of identification with the central authority, the alienation of certain groups, and the attempts of the political system to project a favorable image will then be analyzed with regard to South Africa, the Ivory Coast, Somalia, and Tanzania.

Capability analysis thus provides a valuable portion of the conceptual framework for comparing different political systems removed from one another by time and space. It is not predictive theory, but it provides categories of analysis for an attempt to assess what particular political systems have been able to do in the past, seem to be doing in the present, and may be able to do in the future.

Goals of the Political System

Having in mind the central actors in the political process and their assets and liabilities, we are better equipped to judge and compare the goals of a particular government and/or the entire political system. When we speak of these goals we are, in effect, talking about the goals of the principal decision-makers within that system even though we often personify the political system by stating "Brazil wants" or "Australia needs." Although we shall be discussing the goals of major groups within the society or societies under the jurisdiction of the political system in our examination of the decision-making process, we are here concentrating on those expressed and/or pursued by the principal decision-makers whose authority to set and attain goals is recognized by the system as a whole.

It is our belief that political scientists ought to pass judgement upon the goals of a particular political system just as they attempt to evaluate the means (in terms of effectiveness or ineffectiveness) used to attain those goals. One major difficulty with the structural-functional approach is its bias toward stability or equilibrium and its tendency to equate the survivability of a political system with success. While political scientists ought to evaluate the ability of a political system to maintain itself and to achieve its goals, they should also assess the *desirability* of that particular political system enduring or attaining its goals. To illustrate: because some observers of the South

African situation since 1948 have felt that the present political system is immoral, inequitable, and pernicious, they have concluded that its capabilities are weak and its chances for survival over time are small. In point of fact, the present political regime in South Africa has been enormously effective in achieving the goals set by the agricultural and industrial elite within the European community. In addition, South Africa dominates the political and economic climate of Africa south of the Zambezi, and its influence clearly extends far beyond its geographical borders. As will be shown, its regulative, extractive, and symbolic capabilities are very strong so that as a political system, it seems destined to endure for the foreseeable future. We would err as political scientists if we did not recognize these facts, but we would also err, as scholars and as human beings, if we did not pass judgement on the desirability of the goals sought by South Africa and other political systems.

Therefore, we shall examine the goals of four African political systems, bearing in mind that these goals are multiple and changing and that they are, in essence, the goals of the principal decision-makers during a given time period. Goal analysis will also enable us to bridge the gap between the domestic political activity of a system and its international role. For example, economic development may be a high priority goal of a particular political system. The selection of economic development will induce changes in the regulative, extractive, and distributive capabilities of the political system and, if the goal is attained, may enable the system to play a larger international role. The international environment itself often influences the choice of goals as well as limits the possibilities of their being attained. Much depends upon international power configurations, the political system's place in the power ensemble, and the ideological superstructure or global ethos. If the international system is essentially bipolar (that is with two major powers), the political entity will not have the same degree of maneuverability as it would if the international system were diffuse (power dispersed among a large number of entities) or bloc (several combinations of powerful entities). Likewise, the heterogeneity or homogeneity, ideologically speaking, of the international environment may structure the choice of goals. For example, the maintenance of the slave trade was a possible goal for a variety of political systems in the 17th century but is far less plausible today.

Likewise, the physical control of overseas territory was a widely held goal among European political systems in the late 19th century, while today it is a priority item in but a few instances.

The literature of international relations is rife with analyses of the international goals of nations and states. Hans Morgenthau has stressed the goal of power; Raymond Aron, "power, glory and idea"; while K. J. Holsti is more generally concerned with core values, middle and long range goals.[23] A. F. K. Organski suggests "power, wealth, cultural welfare and peace" and then lists a set of antinomies which cut across these: absolute vs. competitive, unified vs. divergent, national vs. humanitarian, long range vs. specific, actual vs. stated, status quo vs. change.[24] Yet very little in the literature of comparative politics is devoted to internal goals. Even when goals are suggested, there is often a parochial ring to them:

> . . . values such as democracy, equality, freedom and security. They are relevant because they are instrumental to a variety of other values, because they are highly ranked by many of us, and because they are the source of much of the controversy over the desirability of alternative politico-economic techniques. Every reader might construct a slightly different list of relevant values, but the values discovered in this chapter are values that most Americans and Western European readers would also put on their lists.[25]

One would also want to add that these are probably the ultimate goals of many non-Europeans as well, but given the present difficulties in most of the developing world, there are perhaps other goals—such as survival and economic development—that precede these.

We have attempted to establish a hierarchy of goals articulated and believed to be sought by many decision-makers in a wide variety of political systems. Having established a comprehensive, but by no means exhaustive list, we shall attempt to separate the stated goals

[23] Hans J. Morgenthau, *Politics Among Nations* (New York: Alfred A. Knopf, 1960), pp. 38–86; Raymond Aron, *Peace and War* (Garden City: Doubleday and Co., 1966), pp. 71–94; and K. J. Holsti, *International Politics* (Englewood Cliffs, N.J.: Prentice-Hall, 1967), pp. 124–154.

[24] A. F. K. Organski, *World Politics* (New York: Alfred A. Knopf, 1961), pp. 51–77.

[25] Robert A. Dahl and Charles E. Lindblom, *op. cit.*, p. 25.

from those that are actually pursued and then to examine both the sets of goals and the desirability of attaining them for South Africa, the Ivory Coast, Somalia, and Tanzania.

(1) *Survival*   Perhaps the most universally articulated and pursued goal of political systems is survival or the endurance of the system as an entity. Although one must carefully distinguish between the survival of a regime and the survival of the political system, survival is probably the basic core value shared by all political systems.

(2) *Freedom*   In the sense of freedom from control by others, this rather loose term is often articulated as a major systemic goal. Given the interdependent and interpenetrable character of the global system, however, freedom must be regarded as a relative term involving lesser or greater room for political and economic maneuver. In this sense, freedom is often a function of a nation's power and wealth, for a small, weak country may find it difficult to be as relatively free from influence and coercion as will a rich, powerful entity. Many of the pronouncements concerning "neocolonialism" rampant among the new nations indicate the desire to attain this goal.

(3) *Stability*   As a goal of a political system, stability may be taken to mean an attempt to preserve the existing political structure and its societal and economic underpinnings. The French political system in the 18th century seems to have set this as a primary goal. Given the dynamics of international politics, in order to achieve stability over a long period of time, it is necessary to limit or prevent outside influences from upsetting the status quo, and this may prove most difficult to accomplish.

(4) *Political Development*   The phrase political development is widely and variously used. In the context of goal orientation, it is taken to mean a propensity to change and an accent on flexibility. As actualized, political development may be exemplified by a willingness to enter into a federation with other units (such as Senegal and Mali in 1960, and Prussia and various south German states in 1870) or more commonly, a willingness to develop a rational decision-making process.

(5) *Economic Development* As measured by an increase in the gross national product and the per capita income as well as by changes in the economic structure (subsistence to cash economy, rural to city migration, industrialization), economic development is a widely held goal. This goal may have profound political ramifications, for, as Seymour Lipset has indicated, there seems to be a discernible relation between citizen wealth and political satisfaction.[26]

(6) *Welfare* The physical and psychological well-being of the citizens of a political system may also be pursued by governmental policy. It is used to mean socialism in the broadest sense of the term and involves health care, social security, unemployment compensation, famine relief, and educational opportunities. In terms of its actualization, it may be measured by the percentage of governmental revenues spent on these services, particularly on a per capita basis.

(7) *Democratic Decision Making* Although this is often referred to as a characteristic of a particular political system, it may also represent an attempt to make the system, in Dahl's terms, polyarchal so that in the decision-making process no one citizen counts for more than any other. This is, of course, an ideal seldom achieved but, in terms of direction, differs markedly from an accent on a hierarchical or bargaining process. "Democratic" is a difficult concept to define particularly when it is often coupled with seemingly antagonistic terms (as in the "democratic autocracy" of Mauritania). In this study, it will be taken to mean the choice of leaders by the nonleaders, regardless of the institutional format of the political system.

(8) *Command Decision Making* Based on the notion that political power ought to remain in the hands of an elite, this goal clearly differs from the values invoked in (7), for an attempt to increase or decrease the command aspects of decision making is likely to have an opposite effect on this democratic decision-making process.

[26] Seymour M. Lipset, *Political Man* (Garden City, N.Y.: Doubleday & Company, 1960), pp. 25–63. The reader is encouraged to examine these findings in light of the distributive capacity of the system involved and the population's perception of that capability.

In the case of the African systems under study, we shall attempt to break the command orientation down into its social, political, and economic aspects and, if these are mixed, to ascertain which of these is the most crucial.

(9) *International Objectives* Broadly speaking, the above goals may be considered domestic even though some, such as freedom and survival, clearly have interstate ramifications. The category of international objectives is included in order to deal with goals that are primarily oriented toward the international environment. These might include international prestige (Ghana in the early 1960's sacrificed many of its domestic goals in an attempt to achieve international prestige), international influence (China's involvement in Burma during the 1950's), and international conquest (Japan's relations with the Philippines, China, and Indonesia during World War II).

The above list includes the major categories of widely articulated and pursued goals. Decision-makers in a great variety of political systems have stressed them in speeches, constitutions, policy statements, party manifestos, and diplomatic correspondence. It is quite clear, however, that some of these goals are in opposition to each other, particularly at a specific moment in time, so that all cannot be pursued simultaneously and/or with equal vigor. Political and economic development may well be threats to stability; welfare costs cannot be invested in armaments. Survival may be in competition with democratic or command decision making. Political development may conflict with freedom or independence, particularly if a federation or union is to be considered.

In dealing with the goal orientation of political systems, we are faced with two analytical problems: (1) to separate the stated goals from those actually pursued, and (2) to arrange the goals of particular political systems on the basis of priorities. In both cases our criteria will be the allocation of resources—personnel, capital, and time—to each goal; for at some point decision-makers decide which projects shall be undertaken and what resources allotted. There will be some instances of overlap in that capital devoted to arms production may be designed to insure international survival or internal stability or both. In cases of ambiguity, we shall attempt to decorticate the various strands of activity and their ramifications. The results of this approach are often surprising. Many political systems that claim to be socialist, for example, in point of fact devote a smaller proportion of their national budgets to welfare schemes and control a smaller percentage of the system's modes of production than many political systems which deny their socialist orientation.[27]

For each of the four African political systems under consideration, we shall conclude with a set of goal hierarchies. As will be demonstrated, South Africa has subordinated welfare and political development to racial control and societal stability. Conversely, Tanzania has established freedom and democratic decision making as more essential goals than economic development, but has placed economic development ahead of most welfare concerns. Somalia has accented polyarchal decision making over welfare and until recently international concerns over economic development. The Ivory Coast appears to stress economic development even at the expense of lessened freedom, stability over political development, and welfare above international concerns.

In addition to an assessment of a system's priorities, a close examination of goal competition and the process of resource allocation should provide us with valuable insights into the political system as a whole and should enable us to indicate the effectiveness or lack of effectiveness of the process by which each political system attempts to ascertain its position with regard to the goals and the possibility of attaining each one. We should not, however, overemphasize rational progress toward each goal or logical selection of goal hierarchies:

> All too often, policy is the product of random, haphazard or even irrational processes and events. Equally often it is the result of deadlocked judgements, and uneasy compromise formula. Often what appears on the surface as a nation's settled course of action may be due to indecision, unwillingness or inability to act. It may be no policy at all but simply a drift with events.[28]

American involvement in Vietnam and the course of race relations in the United States during the 1940's and 1950's would seem to

[27] Charles W. Anderson, Fred von der Mehden, and Crawford Young, *Issues of Political Development* (Englewood Cliffs, N.J.: Prentice-Hall, 1967), pp. 220–235.

[28] Paul Seabury, *Power, Freedom, and Diplomacy: The Foreign Policy of the United States of America* (New York: Random House, 1963), p. 5.

exemplify this. It should be noted, however, that the assessment of drift and indecision in the decision-making process or irrationality in the pursuance of goals does, in fact, tell us a good deal about the political system.

We have endeavored to establish three major areas of concern for comparing disparate political systems. By examining the decision-making process, the capabilities present or programmed to attain the goals selected, and the goals themselves, one should be able to come to meaningful and worthwhile conclusions concerning a wide variety of political entities. And one should then be able to judge each system not only on the basis of efficiency and responsiveness but also with regard to the types of goals chosen and the desirability of their attainment both for the individual system and the international environment as a whole. Before turning to the African political systems, however, it remains for us to outline the complicated process of political development and to discuss the important factors operative in the African context.

BIBLIOGRAPHY

Charlesworth, James (ed.), *Contemporary Political Analysis* (New York: The Free Press, 1967).

Dahl, Robert, *Modern Political Analysis* (Englewood Cliffs, N.J.: Prentice-Hall, 1963).

Easton, David, *A Framework for Political Analysis* (Englewood Cliffs, N.J.: Prentice-Hall, 1965).

—— *The Political System: An Inquiry into the State of Political Science* (New York: Alfred A. Knopf, 1953).

Eckstein, Harry, and David Apter (eds.), *Comparative Politics* (New York: The Free Press, 1963).

Lasswell, Harold, *Politics: Who Gets What, When, How* (New York: McGraw-Hill Book Company, 1963).

Lipset, Seymour M., *Political Man* (Garden City, N.Y.: Doubleday & Company, 1960).

Macridis, Roy, *The Study of Comparative Government* (New York: Random House, 1955).

CHAPTER II

Political Development:
an Overview

The last decade has seen a vast proliferation of articles and books devoted to the general phenomena associated with modernization and the more particular aspects of political development. Because political development and modernization have a good deal of relevance for the study of political systems in Africa, this chapter is designed to focus upon their most salient features. Despite the variety of approaches to modernization in this literature, there seems to be general agreement that modernization is a holistic process involving a large number of social, economic, and political variables. Before we focus precisely on the development within four African political systems we shall outline three broad stages of societal development—traditional, transitional, and modern—in order to give the reader convenient points of reference. We should, of course, bear in mind that these stages are arranged on a continuum spectrum rather than in rigidly separate categories. Just as it is difficult to distinguish the precise point at which yellow becomes orange or orange becomes red, so it is often a formidable task to separate developed from developing political systems. We should also recognize that these are essentially ideal types—composites produced by analytical simplification—and that, in reality, specific political systems are almost always mixed in character. Finally, it should be remembered that progression from one stage to another is by no means assured.

Stages of Societal Development

A traditional society or polity is characterized by strong primordial attachments. The family, extended family, and the clan are the social units of importance. Kinship, whether patrilineal, matrilineal, or ambilineal, is the primary basis for social integration and socio-economic standing. Birth determines status, for the society as a whole is static, often rigidly stratified according to class or caste. Social mobility is minimal. Custom is all important. The ethos of the society is likely to be other-world oriented and concerned with magic, religion, and the separation of objects into categories of the sacred and the profane.

The economic life of the community is closely tied to subsistence agriculture or animal husbandry. Control of land is vital and often monopolized by a single class or ethnic group. Although there may be some division of labor and an occasional incidence of handicraft manufacturing, there is generally a low level of technology. Physical infrastructure for an industrial economy (such as roads, bridges, harbors, and railroads) is lacking. The cash sector of the economy is small or nonexistent. If labor is organized, it is by class, caste, or guild. Population increases slowly because the high birth rates of this stage are almost matched by high death rates. Illiteracy is high, perhaps 90%, while urbanization is low, often under 10%. Life expectancy may not exceed 30 years.

On the political plane, the central political authority is weak for the individual village and clan leaders are often autonomous. There are few national political institutions, and political activities are minimal in scope and sporadic in operation. Decisions are made by elites and political participation is limited. Legitimacy is based upon traditional norms. What interest groups exist are primarily ascriptive in character. There is a small professional army and a tiny bureaucracy. On balance, the capabilities of the central political authority are weak. In terms of regulation, the commands of the government are seldom efficacious beyond the capital city or the kin group of the traditional leaders. What regulation exists is often limited to specific groups at specific times. The central authority has an on-going problem of curbing dissident elements, whether regional, ethnic, or political.

Even the extractive capacity, although on occasion strong in comparison to the other capabilities, is weak. Conscription is intermittent, conducted on a feudal basis, and often carried out by force. Because of the low levels of health, wealth, and literacy, the population is not a rich source of strength. Often the only talent that can be extracted is labor. Although the taxes levied are often onerous, the percentage that actually reaches the political center is quite low, for the administrative structure is both ineffective and corrupt. In much the same fashion and for much the same reasons, the distributive capability is low as well. Wealth and land are concentrated in the hands of a very few, and what distribution there is takes place on an inequitable basis, often beyond the control of the central political authority. The symbolic capability of the center is minimal. There are few national symbols and little knowledge of, let alone faith in, the political decision-makers.

In terms of rejuvenative ability, the situation is less clear. Barring extensive outside influences and the traumatic shocks of induced modernity, a political system based upon a traditional society may be able to exist for a long period of time yet, political socialization lacks meaning on the national level, political recruitment is generally ascriptive, and the informational flow necessary for efficient change is lacking, suppressed, or ignored. Thus any major intrusion from outside the political system is likely to threaten its very existence, for it is at best a fragile and tenuous creation.

A transitional society, on the other hand, is a society in flux. There are changing demographic, economic and political patterns, increasing technology, and profound attitudinal changes. The primacy of the central political authority is asserted as it acquires sovereignty and is recognized by a widening group of constituents as the supreme legal authority with the right to decree or legislate laws and then enforce them for the entire area under its jurisdiction. The composition of the political elite changes as its members are drawn from a wider set of socio-economic backgrounds. Increasingly complex political structures develop, and existing institutions may take on different and more specific functions. Political subgroups are increasingly integrated into the polity. Pressure groups multiply and become associational in character, although kinship groupings and ethnic organizations may continue to play important political roles. Labor unions develop as increasingly marked occupational differentiation and greater economic mobility occur. Political parties may appear as elements of the masses are drawn into the political process.

The impact of all these changes on individuals within the society is striking. Instead of being totally oriented toward the traditions of the past, individuals may internalize their own norms and become inner-directed, relying upon what David Riesman has called "a psychological gyroscope." [1] Whether we term this process "detribalization," "Westernization," "emancipation," or "defeudalization," the individual's entire frame of reference may shift as he becomes achievement oriented. Primordial sentiments and local attachments are replaced by more contemporary and wider identifications (although it should be remembered that a dual orientation may result). Corresponding demographic changes are startling. Perhaps 25% of the population becomes urbanized and, with the introduction of new health aids, greater awareness of disease patterns, and better nutrition, the death rate declines and the life expectancy increases to over 40 years. For a period of perhaps several generations, however, the birth rate continues at the high level associated with a traditional society. The result is a marked increase in population, perhaps 3% a year.

In the economic sphere, changes are extensive. People begin to switch from agricultural pursuits to nonagricultural activities. The cash sector of the economy increases rapidly. Industrialization becomes widespread, physical infrastructure increases. Per capita income rises. Capital accumulation for reinvestment becomes a central concern, whether directed by a governmental agency or a private entrepreneurial class. Capital investment rises from 5–10% to nearly 25% a year and the approach to economic development chosen by the political authority is of primary importance. A. F. K. Organski has evolved three major political typologies that are distinguished by their approach to capital formation: bourgeois or capitalist, Stalinist or repressive, and syncretic or the combination of industrial and agricul-

[1] For an interesting view of the impact of modernization on individuals and societies, see David Riesman, *The Lonely Crowd* (New Haven, Conn.: Yale University Press, 1961). [See the bibliography at the end of this chapter for the more standard works on modernization and political development.]

tural elites to prevent the new economic groups from gaining political power.[2] Irrespective of the political forms that accompany it, economic development is a slow, often bloody process. In terms of human suffering, the Enclosure Acts, the collectivization of the kulaks, general industrialization, and the American Civil War represent the high prices paid for economic development.[3] Violence and deferred consumer rewards seem to be universal accompaniments of the process.

During the transitional stage, the capabilities of the existing political systems may improve rapidly. Increasing numbers of people come under the jurisdiction and control of the central political authority. Industrialization and economic development increase the extractive base and often support an expanded army and bureaucracy. Rewards, whether of status, money, or education, are more equally distributed. Political socialization on the national level increases. Literacy climbs above 20%; communications improve. Yet this very process of increasing exposure to modernity may threaten the political authority. With greater access to information, the populace may demand more and more rewards. Unless the symbolic capability of the political system improves markedly, groups within the society may demand more than the government can deliver. Pressures develop within society for increased welfare, medical care, and educational opportunity.

Admittedly there is a kind of evolutionary bias to these statements: the problems of society may be so great and the political system so impotent that a revolution is called for. If the government is not able to provide strong identification patterns and cannot convince the population that it must work for the development of the country as a whole, the political system may disintegrate. Thus, the transitional society, while offering increased capabilities, also presents the political system with heightened pressures and its hour of maximum danger.

A modern society also exhibits a discernible pattern. High levels of literacy, industrialization, and urbanization are apparent. Society is complex. Individuals are required to play a variety of roles.[4] Communications are extensive—in the United States, for example, at the

---

[2] See especially "The Politics of Industrialization" in A. F. K. Organski, *The Stages of Political Development* (New York: Alfred A. Knopf, 1965).

[3] C. E. Black, *The Dynamics of Modernization* (New York: Harper & Row, Publishers, 1966), pp. 157–167.

[4] While institutions and political roles tend to specialize in this stage, individual roles increase as citizen X is expected to act as a worker, church-goer, politician, military figure, and head of a household all within a short period of time.

present time there are one and one-half radios per person. Demographic patterns change again. The birth rate declines and the death rate, after its precipitous drop during the transitional state, levels off. With advances in medical technology, life expectancy may exceed 60 years while mortality patterns change. Cancer, heart disease, and arterioschlerotic difficulties replace malaria, tuberculosis, gastritis, and pneumonia as major killers since individuals now live long enough to die from diseases of advanced age.

Occupational configurations change as well. After the initial stages of rapid industrialization, the percentage of wage earners in industrial occupations levels off, the percentage devoted to agricultural pursuits declines still further, and the percentage of workers involved in the service industries continues to increase. In a modern society, irrespective of the organization of its economic system or its political superstructure, consumption increases. Reflecting the increasing affluence, rates of litter increase sharply. The political system dispenses on the order of 7% of its gross national product to provide the benefits of welfare (in the advanced societies of Western Europe, this figure may be doubled).

Society as a whole is dominated by associational groups. Its ethos is relative, secular, and pragmatic. The basic tenets of the scientific revolution, the interrelationship of cause and effect, and the empirically verifiable nature of the common sensical world are accepted. The polity is integrated geographically, physically, and emotionally. The central political authority is recognized as the ultimate arbiter in the secular affairs of the society. There is a greater articulation of demands by groups within society and greater receptivity to those demands in the political elites. Participation in politics becomes more widespread. The regulative capacity is strong and secure, penetrating into the lower levels of society on a more or less continuous basis. The extractive capability is enhanced. There is universal military conscription. Most of the taxes assessed are collected. The bureaucracy, or more accurately, the bureaucracies swell to meet the increasing load of tasks necessary to sustain and regulate the society and the political system. Symbols are national in character, and political recruitment is continuous, rationally conducted, and open-ended. Political socialization, or the process of civil education, becomes widespread. The political system is able to change with regularity and ease, to rejuvenate itself as necessary. Yet, even in this stage the political system should not be regarded as a finished product. For if it cannot adapt to the new demands of a changing environment, revolutionary blowup may result, irrespective of the level of development already attained.

These roughly outlined stages of societal change represent convenient points of departure for our examination of political development. Just as societies shift emphasis in their orientation and dynamics, just as individuals play different roles at different stages of their development, so too, political systems undergo changes that reflect a variety of conditions. The responses of the political elite to changes and their ability to function effectively in a variety of situations may be thought of as corresponding to societal change, although there is no necessary, direct correlation between the two.

In fact, we have included these two three-stage models in discrete categories precisely because they do not always coincide in reality. Often the political system is in one stage of development while the society it governs is in another, or different sectors of the same country are in different stages simultaneously. It is often this heterogeneity that makes the problems of nation building enormous. In many African countries the situation was exacerbated when just prior to independence the colonial authorities attempted to impose the model of a stage three or developed political system on a mixed traditional-transitional society. Even in those instances where exogenous inputs worked for a while, the political system disintegrated when the leaders ignored the discrepancies between it and the society. In this regard, it is important to realize that despite the neat categories of development outlined in this chapter, development does not progress unilinearly but rather in fits and starts, and that development of a political system in particular may be slowed down, halted, even reversed. As will be seen, many observations on political and societal development have been overly optimistic, not only in terms of the rapidity, but also in terms of the longevity of such development. Our analysis of South Africa, Tanzania, Somalia, and the Ivory Coast will indicate the need for caution in assessing the permanency of political development.

Characteristics of Political Development

How do we identify political development? Is it possible to speak with authority about political system X's development or Y's devolution? There are few qualitative and quantitative features of political systems that enable us to designate them as primitive, developing, or developed.[5] These terms may be thought of as corresponding to the traditional, transitional, and modern stages of society, although societal and economic development may not coincide with political development. Assessing the degree of political development, however, is more difficult than a similar judgement of the society or the economic structure, for the notion "political modernity" involves such value clusters as "flexibility" and "rationality." We simply cannot quantify these characteristics as we can per capita income or literacy rates.

We use the term "primitive" advisedly to mean any political system or society generally characterized by the following assemblage of attributes: small scale (seldom more than 100,000 persons), preliterate, possessing minimal technology, and exhibiting intermittent political activity.[6] It should be remembered, however, that primitive political systems perform the same functions as larger, more elaborate, more differentiated systems. They provide a basic legal and societal order, process demands and elicit supports, establish decisions that are enforceable, and finally, set goals. The simplicity and sporadic nature of the decision-making process, the limited numbers of goals espoused, and the generally weak capabilities of such systems should not obscure the fact that differences between them and those systems we term "developed" are, in fact, more of degree than kind.

As Claude Lévi-Strauss has pointed out in his monumental and often overlooked (from a political science point of view) series of works, there are universal patterns and harmonies endemic to all societies and polities.[7] The "savage" mind, he maintains, is no different from the "cultured": it simply evaluates the physical world from another perspective. Totemism is a universal phenomenon repre-

[5] Two standard works from the United Nations Statistical Office that accent the quantifiable aspects of social and economic development are: *The United Nations Statistical Yearbook* (New York: Columbia University Press, yearly) and *The United Nations Demographic Yearbook* (New York: Columbia University Press, yearly). See also Bruce Russett (ed.), *World Handbook of Political and Social Indicators* (New Haven, Conn.: Yale University Press, 1964).

[6] Lucy P. Mair, *Primitive Government* (Baltimore, Md.: Penguin Books, 1962), pp. 7–32.

[7] Claude Lévi-Strauss, *The Savage Mind* (Chicago: University of Chicago Press, 1962); *Le Totemisme-Aujourd'hui* (Paris: Presses Universitaires de France, 1962); *Le Cru et Le Cuit* (Paris: Libraire Plon, 1964); and *Du Miel Aux Cendres* (Paris: Libraire Plon, 1966).

senting man's search for classification and order. If we accept Lévi-Strauss' basic premise, categorization of political systems and societies depends entirely upon one's criteria. For example, technological advances as one index of differentiation must be weighed against the psychological and social disorders of modern, developed, urbanized, secularized society. Although Lévi-Strauss himself distinguishes between "hot" or mobile and "cold" or static societies (depending upon what amounts to the rejuvenative and developmental capabilities of the system in question), he returns again and again to the theme of the basic humanity of all men and the related nature of their political and social creations.

Many traditional societies and political systems do in fact exhibit some traits associated with significant levels of development. This is true even of small hunting band type organizations such as the Eskimos of North America, the Bambuti pygmies of the Ituri forest, and the !Kung Bushmen of the Kalahari desert. The Bushmen, for example, number some 50,000 people divided into a great number of autonomous bands of 12–15 people. Their political process is strongly democratic and rational.[8] The headman of a particular band may or may not be the son of a headman, depending upon his competence. Collective decisions are made by the group as a whole although individuals generally initiate their own activities. In this case, there may well be a correlation between the narrow margin of survival and democratic decision making. Lacking farm crops, domestic animals, and secure water supplies and living in a hostile environment, the Bushmen cannot afford the luxury of inadequate political leadership. Because of the time-consuming nature of hunting and food gathering as opposed to cultivation or animal husbandry, there may well be a connection between formal, permanent political institutions and the agricultural revolution of 10,000 B.C.

As we shall show, however, political development as an analytic concept requires a variety of criteria, and exemplifying one characteristic of high development (in the case of the Bushmen, democratic

[8] Lorna Marshall, "The !Kung Bushmen of the Kalahari Desert," James L. Gibbs (ed.), *Peoples of Africa* (New York: Holt, Rinehart & Winston, 1965), pp. 241–278. Readers interested in sampling the wide variety of ethnic units and life styles found in Africa should consult the remainder of this work as well as Simon and Phoebe Ottenberg (eds.), *Cultures and Societies of Africa* (New York: Random House, 1960) and George P. Murdock, *Africa: Its Peoples and their Cultural History* (New York: McGraw-Hill Book Company, 1959).

decision making) does not make up for a lack of other characteristics (the Bushmen's political system clearly lacks flexibility, institutional differentiation, and explicitness as well as strong adaptive capabilities). In this study we shall consider the related attributes listed below as criteria of a developed political system.[9]

(1) *Effective linkage* A developed political system exhibits strong psychological as well as physical linkage between the central political authority and the rest of the social system. In transitional societies, for example, the central authority finds itself engaged in a long, difficult, and not always successful struggle with local authorities. This is particularly true in political systems that embrace a variety of societies. The changing relationship between the central political authority and the local power loci has not yet been studied on anything like a systematic basis, although there are signs that this is now being attempted.[10] In a developed political system, the primacy of the center is acknowledged and the different groups and regions are integrated. Effective linkage is clearly related to the development of strong regulative and symbolic capabilities, a monopoly of the legitimate use of coercion, and the existence of a set of national symbols—in short, the deep transformation of values and allegiance we refer to as nationalism.

(2) *Widened political participation* Despite the many troublesome implications of the concept of participation, it remains an intrinsic characteristic of modernity and development. Whether participation is formal or informal, meaningful or irrelevant, the very act of participation sharply increases individuals' identification with the political process. The framework of that participation, whether democratic or totalitarian, single-party or multiparty, may be of less importance than the increased role playing by the citizens of the polity. Participation usually indicates that the political elite is attached, however tenuously, to representative institutions. A new

[9] I have chosen the word "developed" rather than "modern" in order to include some of the highly efficient political systems, such as the 2nd century B.C. Roman state, which functioned in preindustrial times.

[10] A worthwhile step in this direction is represented by Harumi Befu, "The Political Relation of the Village to the State," *World Politics* (July, 1967) Vol. XIX, No. 2: 601–620.

awareness brought on by mass communications and mass politics leads to a widened sense of civic duty, as well as increased demands. Widened political participation is generally accompanied by broadening of recruitment patterns and the inclusion of a wider spectrum of socio-economic groups on the basis of achievement rather than ascription. As a result of these occurrences, the political system increases its extractive and symbolic capability.

(3) *Increased differentiation of the structural and functional aspects of political institutions*   As we indicated in our cursory examination of the Bushmen political system, decisions were made by all adult males meeting face to face. The same political actors were able to perform a variety of functions—rule making, rule enforcement, and rule adjudication. The political process could be stopped or started at will and took place only at certain times. The development of separate and autonomously functioning units with institutionalized processes and membership, combined with a centralized authority which organizes these into a coherent whole, is an indication of political development. Political institutions become permanent, on-going structures rather than intermittent stop-and-go arrangements. Institutions are created that not only outlive individuals but also have a more or less permanent existence with continually renewed membership. The increased organization represented by institutional development is an essential ingredient of an "advanced" polity for it is this "set" of institutions which enables the system to cushion challenges from the forces of change, both internal and external. They provide a kind of political insulation which permits the absorption of new individuals, groups, and pressures. Because the components of the system are differentiated and have specific tasks, they can function on a variety of levels, leaving the political center free to coordinate their activities and to set goals for the entire system.

(4) *Flexibility*   One of the most important ingredients in a developed polity is institutionalized flexibility. As used here, the term is taken to mean the ability of the political system to deal with change, to meet new situations, to formulate new goals, and to process new demands and supports. Flexibility involves both the process of structural and functional adaption and a psychological commitment

on the part of the political elite. If we think of a political system as a transformer, transmuting demands and supports into policies, goals, and achievements, flexibility represents the ability of that system to learn. It implies the ability to modify itself, to adapt to a changed environment, in short, to grow. Flexibility involves access to and use of information as well as the creation of what S. N. Eisenstadt has termed "change absorbing" institutions.[11]

Although we shall continue to stress the need for flexibility in our discussion of the African political systems, it should be pointed out that flexibility must be balanced with elements of stability and permanence. Some developing political systems at times exhibit marked flexibility in terms of decision making and goal formation, particularly when under the direction of a single charismatic leader. Highly personal rule represents one possible approach to the problem of change and may well be a desirable one in terms of initiating the modernization process. One has only to look at the roles played by the Shah of Iran, Ataturk of Turkey, or Haile Selassie of Ethiopia to become cognizant of the impact of their flexibility. Yet, the very cogency of their initial flexibility often militates against successful continuance of political development. Unless the force, vigor, and fluidity of the charismatic leader can be in some fashion institutionalized, the chances for substantial and sustained political development, even during the lifetime of the leader in question, seem highly doubtful. The recent cases of Kwame Nkrumah in Ghana and President Sukarno in Indonesia indicate the dangers of personal flexibility without institutional groundings.[12]

Institutional flexibility may take a variety of forms: the creation of an efficient and effective bureaucracy (as in India), a responsive party apparatus (as the *Partido Revolucionario Institucional* in Mexico),

[11] S. N. Eisenstadt, *Modernization: Protest and Change* (Englewood Cliffs, N.J.: Prentice-Hall, 1966), p. v.

[12] For a polemical but penetrating account of this phenomenon in Ghana, see Henry L. Bretton, *The Rise and Fall of Kwame Nkrumah* (New York: Frederick A. Praeger, 1966). A book written from a more sympathetic perspective but one which arrives at similar conclusions, is *Ghana; End of an Illusion* by B. Fitch and M. Oppenheimer (New York: Monthly Review Press, 1966). See also, John Hughes, *Indonesia Upheaval* (New York: David McKay Co., 1967), and Donald Hindley, "Political Power and the October 1965 Coup in Indonesia," *The Journal of Asian Studies* (February, 1967) Vol. XXVI, No. 2: 237–249.

or a commitment to a legal framework rather than individual leaders (as in Belgium). Perhaps one of the most exciting attempts of recent years to institutionalize flexibility while maintaining stability is represented by recent attempts at proscribed leadership turnover. In Tanzania, for example, since 1965 the powerful, mass-based single party, the Tanganyika African National Union, has provided for leadership alteration by nominating multiple candidates for most political offices. Although it is clearly too early to judge the long term validity of this approach, it does appear to represent an important step toward political development (and one which has been subsequently attempted, at least on a local level, in Yugoslavia and Poland).

(5) *Rationality*   A final value generally associated with political development is that of rationality. Applied to political systems, rationality denotes a generalized pattern of decision making based upon reasoned discussion and discourse, allocation of political roles on the basis of merit, and continuous informational assembly based upon a belief in a universe underlaid with discernible cause and effect relationships. It implies, but does not demand, a secular view of politics and society. Rationality involves the use of available information, receptivity to new information, and willingness to periodically reexamine decisions in a process of on-going evaluation. It also means that opponents of ruling political elites should be seen as part of the system and worthy of respect (regardless of the institutional format of that protection). Normatively speaking, rationality also implies a lack of illogical or absurd goal espousal and the pursuance of courses of action likely to involve the destruction of major sections of humanity. Thus, for example, since World War II rationality has had a pragmatic connotation which demands that the possible effects of a nuclear holocaust be weighed in almost every decision involving interstate activity by the great powers.

A developed political system will exhibit effective integration or linkage, widened political participation, institutional differentiation, and a rational and flexible style in its decision-making process. These attributes have a generalized, cumulative effect on the heightening of the capability of the political system. A developed political system will thus be more effective—that is, better able to function—in its international environment, and more likely to achieve a favorable pattern of problem solving, both internally and externally.

Important Variables in the Modernization Process

As we have seen, heightened capabilities and increased power are associated with economic and political development. Because of the benefits, real and imagined, accruing to a developed political system, many political leaders and other concerned elites have expressed desire to thus modernize their societies, their economies, and the political structures of their country. Political and social scientists have also accented the desirability of political development. Yet with all the writing and pronouncements, there is a good deal of confusion as to how political development may be achieved, which forces within the society are likely to help, and which are likely to inhibit its attainment. In short, we know much more about what political development *is* than *how* to achieve it.

While it is true that economic growth, social change, and political development are related, nothing like a direct, linear relationship is discernible. Much depends upon the pace of change, the time of its onset, the existing institutional framework, and the societal diversity involved. Rapid economic change may lead to political development, but it seems equally likely to lead to social disorganization and political devolution. One reason is that the process of economic change does not modernize all sectors of society, let alone all regions of the country, equally or at the same rate. Often it is not the country as a whole that develops, but specific loci or, at best, nexi within it. The resulting asynchronous and asymmetrical development may well overwhelm an underdeveloped political system by increasing demands upon it, overloading its institutions, and causing its breakdown. This is particularly likely to happen if economic change occurs simultaneously with a rapid increase in the literacy rate and expansion of the communications network. Many countries in Asia and Latin America, such as Burma and Argentina, actually show a negative correlation between high indices of literacy, per capita income, industrialization and urbanization, and discernible political development. Conversely, India and Tanzania—among the poorest and least economically developed nations in the world—currently demonstrate a high degree of political development and indicate that economic advances are by no means the crucial prerequisite for political development.

Nowhere is the confusion about political development more evident than in the conflicting assessments of the role played by various elite groups in the society. Because of the importance of political development, both as a process and as a goal, to the four African political systems under study, it is advisable that we have some rudimentary understanding of the often ambiguous roles played by a variety of groups and of the other variables intimately associated with the process; routes to modernization and political development must be determined individually—that is, in terms of the particular polity and its circumstances. As this is not primarily a work on political development, however, we shall confine ourselves to a brief examination of the possible relationship between economic and political development, relevant modes of growth and decay, and the important elite groups most often associated with development or its lack: the traditional authorities, the political elites, the bureaucratic personnel, and the military.

It is widely assumed that economic and social change, whether stimulated by exogenous forces such as a colonial authority or by internal influences, are directly related to the process of political development. The expansion of a modern economic infrastructure, the spread of a cash-economy sector, industrialization, a heavy rural to city migration, increased communications, and rising literacy rates are often thought of as leading, more or less inexorably, to new sociological patterns, increased social mobilization, and ultimately, political development.

However, the inability of this progression model to predict what actually occurs in the modernization process indicates to what extent political development is the result of a large number of complex variables—force vectors, demand pressures, informational flows, elite reactions, investment rates, and exogenous intrusions, both physical and psychological. Looking over the tremendous number of works devoted to political development, we must conclude that at the present time, we cannot say with assurance exactly which variables are likely, by themselves, to lead to political development. A particular factor may encourage development in Mexico, inhibit it in Ceylon, and play no role at all in Afghanistan. This negative assessment of the present state of our knowledge is made simply to underscore the need for additional consideration and investigation in a variety of areas. Above all, a systematic, thorough examination of political development drawn from material on Latin America, Africa, Asia, and the Middle East and extended studies of the European past is badly needed.

Nowhere is this need more critically felt than in the examination of the roles various elite groups play in the modernization process. Because elite groups are both important and readily discernible, they have been studied by psychologists, economists, sociologists, and political scientists. The salient feature of these investigations would seem to be an acknowledgment that the roles played by the members of the traditional elite, the newer political leadership, the members of the bureaucracies, and the military are various. In short, it would seem that one cannot measure modernity by overgeneralizing on the universality of its participants.

Depending upon milieu, time, circumstance, and geographical location, each of the groups may be viewed as inhibiting or encouraging political development. Often a group such as the bureaucracy may stimulate development at one point and at another, curtail it. It is hoped that our brief examination of elite groups will indicate their ambiguous and often contradictory role in the process of political development.

Because of the ramifications of modernity for their socio-economic and political positions, the traditional elite is often regarded as one of the most powerful impeding forces. Claude Welch has written in his first rate work on political development, "To weaken the hold of traditionalism is the primary problem confronting recently independent states. . . ." [13] No one familiar with the history of political development in a variety of countries would question the widespread applicability of this hypothesis. Yet, in a significant number of countries, and in widely disparate systems (such as Iran, Japan, and Buganda) the traditional elite has actually supported political development. In Africa, in particular, the traditional authorities may well be in an excellent position to encourage development if they believe they can turn modernization and political development to their own advantage. In any case, it is by no means clear that modernity is, ipso facto, destructive to traditional elites, at least in the short run. In fact, there is increasing evidence that traditional authorities, in addition to proving themselves highly resilient to the threats of

---

[13] Claude Welch, Jr. (ed.), *Political Modernization* (Belmont, Calif.: Wadsworth Publishing Co., 1967), p. 9.

change, may actually benefit from the modernization process by controlling the increased extractive and regulative capabilities of the system. Studies of political and economic development in northern Nigeria, Swaziland, and Uganda, indicate the ability of traditional authorities to flourish in the midst of the modernization process.[14]

Ethnicity, too, has been generally regarded as impeding modernization and is often viewed as a reflection of the pernicious hold of tradition. Again, it must be said that in the majority of cases this may be true—if the ethnic unit is highly organized and opposed to change. But ethnicity may encourage the process of political and social change, particularly in the initial stages of transition. Immanuel Wallerstein has pioneered work on the functional aspects of ethnicity and indicates the ways in which it may serve to increase national integration and social modernity:

> First, ethnic groups tend to assume some of the functions of the extended family and hence they diminish the importance of kinship roles; two, ethnic groups serve as a mechanism of resocialization; three, ethnic groups help keep the class structure fluid and so prevent the emergence of castes; fourth, ethnic groups serve as an outlet for political tensions.[15]

And L. I. Rudolph is highly persuasive in his arguments that parts of the traditional structure of Indian society, such as castes and caste associations, have aided and abetted both political socialization and the development of democratic political institutions and processes.[16] At the same time, we may be quite unwilling to accept the rather

[14] See especially, C. S. Whitaker, "A Dysrhythmic Process of Political Change," World Politics (January, 1967) Vol. XIX, No. 1: 190–217, and C. P. Potholm "Changing Political Configurations in Swaziland," Journal of Modern African Studies (November, 1966) Vol. 4, No. 3: 313–322. An older article and one that is now regarded as something of a classic is David E. Apter "The Role of Traditionalism in the Political Modernization of Ghana and Uganda," World Politics (October, 1960) Vol. XIII: 45–68.

[15] Immanuel M. Wallerstein, "Ethnicity and National Integration in West Africa," Cahiers d'Etudes Africaines (October, 1960) Vol. III, No. 1: 129–139.

[16] L. I. Rudolph and S. H. Rudolph, "The Political Role of India's Caste Associations," Pacific Affairs (March, 1960) Vol. XXXIII, No. 1: 5–22; L. I. Rudolph, "The Modernity of Tradition: the Democratic Incarnation of Caste in India," The American Political Science Review (December, 1965) Vol. LIX, No. 4: 975–989; L. I. Rudolph, The Modernity of Tradition: Political Development in India (Chicago: University of Chicago Press, 1967).

ingenious notion that modernization causes tribalism and ethnicity.[17] Much, of course, depends upon the relationship between the ethnic group(s) and the state in question. If the ethnic group more or less coincides with the state (even though its members may be found in other states) as do the Basotho in Lesotho, the BaHutu in Rwanda, the Somalis in the Somali Republic, and the Swazis in Swaziland, tribalism may represent a vital factor in political integration and development with minimum centrifugal strains. Conversely, if the tribal unit is well organized but subnational in scope, as the kingdoms of Ankole and Buganda in Uganda or the Ashanti in Ghana, tribalism may prove highly divisive. This is even more likely to be the case if the ethnic unit is transnational in character and desirous of autonomy as the Bakongo or Chokwe in the Congo (Kinshasa) and Angola, or the Kurds in Syria, Iraq, and Turkey. We shall be developing these arguments at some length in the chapter on the African context. The political structure and the social ethos of the ethnic group also influence their role in the modernization process. For example, the hierarchical structure and the acceptance of social innovation as a part of tradition which characterize the Ganda in Uganda may enable the tribal authority to accept the importance of development without fearing the collapse of its primacy. On the other hand, a looser pyramidal arrangement and opposition to social change, as one finds among the Ashanti of Ghana, may well impede even exogenously induced modernity. Or it may encourage it as with the Yorubas of Nigeria. Moreover, a cluster of segmented units lacking a central political authority may prove highly receptive to political modernity, as the Ibos in Nigeria or the Kikuyus in Kenya. However, when coupled with a suspicion of change and a commitment to tradition qua tradition, such organizations may prove highly resistant to political development [as in the cases of the Tiv in Nigeria, Nuer in the Sudan, Suku in Congo (Kinshasa), or the Masai in Kenya]. In short, we need far more information, comparison, and study before we can begin to generalize with precision about the role of ethnicity in political development in sub-Saharan Africa, Asia, the Middle East, Latin America, and Europe.

The role of political parties and their leaders in the modernization

[17] I am thinking here of Paul Anber's "Modernization and Political Disintegration: Nigeria and the Ibos," *Journal of Modern African Studies* (1967) Vol. V, No. 2: 163–179.

process may also be ambiguous, particularly in Africa. If the parties represent a particular ethnic group or are dominated by one, this portion of the political elite may prove highly divisive to political development. One has only to view the Ibo domination of the National Convention of Nigeria and the Cameroons, the Hausa and Fulani control of the Northern Peoples' Congress, the Ganda control of the Kabaka Yekka, or the Luo support of the Kenya People's Union to see the difficulties involved. Even if the political elite represent transtribal parties and are committed to modernization, they may succumb to the lure of patronage or display a propensity to accent the form rather than the substance of reform.

Conversely, the political elite may stress political and economic development and actively sustain these processes over a long period of time.[18] The formation of a political party represents a step towards modernity and many of the single-party regimes in Africa have provided a communications network, stimulated integration, sought to inculcate new national symbols and values, and thus widened participation in the political process. Clearly the leaders and formations of the Tanganyika African National Union, the Kenyan African National Union, the *Union Soudanaise*, the *Parti Démocratique de La Guinée*, and the United National Independence Party have all contributed to political development. Yet recent events, including a dozen coups, seem to indicate how tenuous and reversible are the gains achieved by a political elite.

In much the same fashion, the personnel of bureaucracies are often significant factors in political development.[19] Particularly in political

[18] The wide variety of political forms and the varying commitment to modernity are clearly seen in James S. Coleman and Carl G. Rosberg (eds.), *Political Parties and National Integration in Tropical Africa* (Berkeley, Calif.: University of California Press, 1964) and Aristide R. Zolberg, *Creating Political Order* (Chicago: Rand McNally & Co., 1966). Additional information is to be found in Gwendolyn M. Carter's three collections, *African One-Party States* (Ithaca, N.Y.: Cornell University Press, 1962), *Five African States* (Ithaca, N.Y.: Cornell University Press, 1963), and *National Unity and Regionalism in Eight African States* (Ithaca, N.Y.: Cornell University Press, 1966). A more theoretically oriented work is Joseph G. La Palombara and Myron Weiner (eds.), *Political Parties and Political Development* (Princeton: Princeton University Press, 1966).

[19] See especially Joseph G. La Palombara (ed.), *Bureaucracy and Political Development* (Princeton: Princeton University Press, 1963). Other works include: John D. Montgomery and William J. Siffin, *Approaches to Development Politics, Administration and Change* (New York: McGraw-Hill Book Company, 1966); Bernard S. Silberman, *Ministers of Modernization* (Tucson, Ariz.: Uni-

systems with a colonial heritage, the bureaucracy is likely to be one of the most developed institutions in the society. With its extensive administrative apparatus, it extends throughout society and is in a position to play a pivotal role in the process of social and political transformation. The bureaucracy may conduct planning on a national basis, provide an achievement-oriented nucleus for political integration, serve as a prototype for a rational decision-making hierarchy, and act as a buffer to mitigate and redirect demand pressures away from the more fragile political structures.

However, the bureaucracy may not function in this fashion. As a transitional group between the colonial authority and the indigenous society, bureaucracies often have an ambivalent attitude toward both independence and aspects of the development process associated with increasing political mobilization. Bureaucrats may view political development as a threat to their socio-economic position and act accordingly. As an organized, powerful interest group in a society where few such groups exist, the bureaucracy may itself articulate demands for salaries and authority which are impossible for the political system to satisfy. Its members may resent the intrusion of political elites. The result is often a protracted struggle between the bureaucracy and the political elite, culminating in bureaucratic involvement in politics and political involvement in the bureaucracy. This mutual intervention may prove to be highly disruptive. Many of the recent African military coups, particularly in Togo, Dahomey, the Central African Republic, and Upper Volta, have been stimulated by a bureaucratic-military alliance at the expense of the political leadership.

The military establishment is capable of playing an even wider variety of roles than the bureaucracy in the modernization process. On occasion, military personnel have intervened to replace a corrupt or inefficient oligarchy, to prevent anarchy, or to stimulate economic and political development. In short, military action can on occasion be regarded as political development. Examples of this would seem to be the intervention of the military into the political realm in

---

versity of Arizona Press, 1964); Ralph J. Braibanti (ed.), *Asian Bureaucratic Systems Emergent from the British Imperial Tradition* (Durham, N.C.: Duke University Press, 1966). Of more than passing interest is Michael Lofchie, "Representative Government, Bureaucracy, and Political Development: The African Case," *Journal of Developing Areas* (October, 1967) Vol. II: 37–56.

Brazil (1889), Turkey (1920–23), Egypt (1952), Pakistan (1958), France (1958), Congo Kinshasa (1960–64), Ecuador (1963), Ghana (1966), and Indonesia (1966).

Certainly, the army has the prerequisites to act as a force for modernity. It is well organized, efficient, often associational in character. It is one of the most modernized institutions in the society and generally draws its personnel from a nation-wide basis. The military establishment is able to insulate individuals from the shocks of moving from a traditional society to a transitional or modern one. Additionally, it may break down feudal elements, stimulate nationalism, and increase integration. From the Olympian heights of the barracks the military leadership often views with scorn the sluggish, corrupt machinations of the politicians. Because of its organization, weapons, and manpower, the military finds it easy to intervene in the political activities of the state.

Because of these factors, the praetorian impulse is widespread and not confined to the underdeveloped world for the incidence rates of military intervention in Europe, as well as in Asia, Latin America, and the Middle East, are high. In recent years, the level of involvement has reached heroic proportions in Africa. Coups have been attempted or accomplished in Algeria, Egypt, the Sudan, Mali, Kenya, Ethiopia, Uganda, Tanzania, Burundi, Congo (Kinshasa), Congo (Brazzaville), Gabon, the Central African Republic, Nigeria, Dahomey, Togo, Upper Volta, Ghana, and Sierra Leone.

Studies of these intervention patterns indicate the strengths as well as the weaknesses of the military in politics. Its input capacity is often high, and it can have a devastating impact on the political system by easily overturning the political authorities. At the same time, its propensity for the output functions is low indeed. Military personnel often have an overly sanguine view of their ability to transform society and to sustain political, social, and economic change. While capable of regulating society, the military is far less able to develop it. Society is more complex than the army and the problems of its direction far more difficult. Military leadership often becomes frustrated; coups beget countercoups. In many cases, even if it wishes to, the military is not able to satisfy enough demands or to elicit sufficient support to sustain its reforms. Additionally, the military may find it almost impossible to develop nonmilitary institutions or to successfully disengage itself from politics. One predominate pattern seems to be the replacement of existing political elites with military personnel who then attempt to take over the symbols of legitimacy and rule as presidents or prime ministers.

The phenomenon of military involvement in politics is both wide-spread and well documented with regard to Africa.[20] It will therefore be necessary for us to examine the armies in each of the African political systems we study, and to speculate upon the makeup, orientation and possible role in the delicate and Sisyphean task of nation building.

Models of Growth and Decay

Both the would-be modernizers and those who oppose political development seem to be reacting to certain "models" of development and nation building, although it is not always clear whether these models exist primarily in the minds of the elites or in those of the social scientists and economists who study them. And, as was mentioned with regard to the progression model, it would seem as if few in either category adequately or consistently distinguish between the economic and political aspects of the models.

It can be said with some assurance, however, that there exist two generalized models of nation building which exemplify a blend of economic, political, and social characteristics. There is, on one hand, a democratic, evolutionary, gradualist model distinguished by social pluralism, vibrant subgroup autonomy, a high incidence of civil liberties, and an ethos of ideological competition centered around a market economy. A second ideal type has totalitarian and revolutionary overtones. It is antipluralistic in character and accents the organic unity of society. This model exhibits strong central control over society, severely proscribes the limits of civil liberty, and is based upon

[20] The ambiguous role of the military in politics may be examined in S. E. Finer, *The Man on Horseback* (London: Pall Mall, 1962); J. J. Johnson (ed.), *The Role of the Military in Underdeveloped Countries* (Princeton: Princeton University Press, 1962); Samuel P. Huntington, *The Soldier and the State* (Cambridge: Harvard University Press, 1957) and his later *Changing Patterns of Military Politics* (Glencoe, Ill.: Free Press, 1962); Morris Janowitz, *The Military in the Political Development of New Nations* (Chicago: University of Chicago Press, 1964); and William F. Gutteridge, *Military Institutions and Power in the New States* (New York: Frederick A. Praeger, 1965).

a command economy. These two poles are represented in many minds by the United States and the Soviet Union—even though these examples are highly diluted versions of the models.

In any case, the United States and the Soviet Union seem inappropriate as models for underdeveloped nations. The size, wealth, population-resource balance, and existing political infrastructure of these two systems place their accomplishments beyond the attainment of most entities. And there are other formidable difficulties. Most political elites bent on modernization seem unwilling to accept either the slow pace and pluralistic features of the evolutionary model or the violence and oppression of revolutionary struggle. In addition, few of the elites in the underdeveloped world seem particularly anxious to achieve the alienation and dehumanization that seem to accompany modern, industrialized, urbanized society. Nor do many seem willing to pay the high costs of reaching political modernity. This reluctance is understandable for neither economic nor political development can be achieved easily or without substantial cost.[21] Because the process is largely behind us, we tend to overlook the costs in human suffering associated with economic and political modernity—irrespective of the model emulated. To take but one manifestation of the process, the American Civil War represents (among other things) a struggle between the industrial and politically centralizing elite of the North and the agricultural, decentralization-oriented elite of the South (or, in contemporary terms, the "modernizers" and the "traditionalists").[22]

This reluctance or inability to accept either of the two major models entirely has resulted in hybrid systems that borrow elements

[21] The material dealing with developmental models is extensive. Among the more widely read are, Irving L. Horowitz, *Three Worlds of Development* (New York: Oxford University Press, 1966); A. F. K. Organski, *The Stages of Political Development* (New York: Alfred A. Knopf, 1967); C. E. Black, *The Dynamics of Modernization* (New York: Harper & Row, Publishers, 1966); David E. Apter, *The Politics of Modernization* (Chicago: University of Chicago Press, 1965); John H. Kautsky (ed.), *Political Change in Underdeveloped Countries* (New York: John Wiley & Sons, 1962); Lucian W. Pye, *Aspects of Political Development* (Boston: Little, Brown and Company, 1966). See also the section on "Ideologies and Patterns of Modernization" in Claude E. Welch (ed.), *Political Modernization* (Belmont, Calif.: Wadsworth Publishing Company, 1967).

[22] Professor Peter Smith of the University of Wisconsin has indicated that this point is central to the thesis of Barrington Moore, Jr.'s "The American Civil War: The Last Capitalist Revolution," *Social Origins of Dictatorship and Democracy* (Boston: Beacon Press, 1966), pp. 111–155.

from each, as well as some original systems. Often these hybrids are authoritarian in character, involving a protracted struggle between civilian and military forces for control of the polity and displaying sporadic interference by the central authority in the society and its highly mixed economy. Edward Shils in his now classic essay, "Alternate Courses of Political Development," lists three important variations that are "outcomes of the interplay of a zealously pursued ideal and intractable necessity." [23] His tutelary democracies, modernizing oligarchies, and traditional oligarchies represent composites and variations of the more developed typologies of political democracy and totalitarian oligarchy. These mixed patterns result from the great structural variety of the existing systems, the different levels of societal and economic progress, the pace of modernization and, most importantly, what S. N. Eisenstadt has termed the "time of onset." [24]

The multifarious nature of these composites is clearly seen in the African political systems under consideration. Somalia exhibits a vibrant mix of polyarchal decision making, social cohesion, and a markedly undeveloped economy, strong local attachments, and a religious orientation. South Africa is a highly developed political system with nearly totalitarian control over politics and competing ideologies, yet it maintains one of the freest presses in Africa. Its society exhibits strong subgroup autonomy for Europeans but continual repression of African associational groups, particularly those of an economic and political nature. The economy of South Africa is based on market forces, yet the state controls hydroelectric, transportation, and steel facilities. The Ivory Coast combines rapid economic development with little discernible political development, a strong belief in economic competition, and little faith in competing political parties or ideologies. Tranzania, perhaps the most socialistically oriented of

[23] Edward A. Shils, "Alternate Courses of Political Development," *Political Development in the New States* (s'Gravenhage: Mouton and Company, 1962), reprinted in Jason L. Finkle and Richard W. Gable (eds.), *Political Development and Social Change* (New York: John Wiley & Sons, 1966), p. 460. See also Juan Linz "An Authoritarian Regime: Spain," Erik Allardt and Yrjö Littunen (eds.), *Cleavages, Ideologies and Party Systems* (Helsinki: The Academic Bookstore, 1964), pp. 291–341. Linz explores in depth the authoritarian typology that he feels is something more than either an imperfect totalitarian or an imperfect democratic form.

[24] S. N. Eisenstadt, *Modernization: Protest and Change* (Englewood Cliffs, N.J.: Prentice-Hall, 1966).

the African political systems, exhibits little in the way of totalitarian tendencies, and couples a command economy with a primarily demo-cratic decision-making process.

Concern with models of development and sporadic indications of political growth in some of the newer states have occasionally led to overly sanguine pronouncements concerning the rapidity and longevity of political development. In reality, neither the smooth progression of political development nor its irreversibility is assured. Just as eco-nomic growth can be retarded or reversed, so too political develop-ment can degenerate and the political system in question devolve. In fact, rapid economic or social progress may cause pressures to build up and create interest groups that do not accept the existing political framework. An ethos of distrust and hatred may prevent the orderly flow of information and its rational assessment and use. If there are not sufficient and properly functioning institutions of a local and regional nature—to regulate communal conflict, to mute shrill de-mand pressures at the national level, to act as baffles for dysfunctional forces—the system will be threatened. Overloading the system may cause devolution.

Now in some sense, *total* reversal of political development seldom occurs (although there are, of course, examples of this, such as the Holy Roman Empire). In a particular system, many institutions may cease to function properly or important symbols may lose their effi-cacy, but they continue to exist although the capabilities of the politi-cal system decay. The central authority may no longer be able to regulate society, let alone develop it. Many of its symbols may become outdated and unable to elicit support. Its ability to rejuvenate itself may be drastically curtailed. Its political elite may fixate upon a series of irrational goals and destroy the system in an attempt to achieve them. In short, the decline of political efficiency, decreased institutionalization, irrational decision making, reduced participation, and structural and functional rigidity are perfectly logical results of sudden changes in societal and political activity. Underdeveloped or developing political systems are not the only victims of these mal-functions. The history of France is filled with interludes of breakdown and decay. The rise of Fascism in Italy during the 1920's and Argen-tina in the 1940's, are reversals of earlier patterns of development.

What we are suggesting is that political leaders and social scientists interested in development might find it useful to concentrate upon models of decay and devolution as well as on the more ambitious models of development. Hopefully, one result of this new focus would be a more pragmatic assessment of the political system's goals and processes. Theoreticians and practitioners of political development could concentrate on spotting difficulties before they become overwhelming, correcting excesses and malfunctions, and strengthening the necessary institutions, and thus learn to preserve the often tenuous thread of political development.

Whether due to a feeling of loyalty to those studying political development or to avoid charges of academic neocolonialism, there have been few articles and books dealing with the phenomena of political decay and devolution. Two notable exceptions are Samuel Huntington's "Political Development and Political Decay," and S. N. Eisenstadt's "Breakdowns of Modernization." [25] Huntington, in particular, scores the "hopeful unreality" of those engaged in political development and argues for the need to develop strong institutions. For him, political decay results from the disequilibrating forces of interest groups and political activity and the weakness of the institutional framework (although he is less than clear in his analysis of which types of institutions are both desirable and possible). S. N. Eisenstadt sees "blockages" and "eruptions" arising from a failure to resolve conflicts within society, the all-or-nothing character of many interest groups, and a lack of symbolic capability with regard to the part of the political system's day to day functioning.

This type of observation should be amplified and the number of studies dealing with political devolution increased. With the onrush of events in the underdeveloped world, there is a critical need to examine in depth the causes of political breakdown and to generate new hypotheses capable of being tested. Political development must be viewed in the context of goal formation, that is, as one possible

[25] Samuel P. Huntington, "Political Development and Political Decay," *World Politics* (April, 1965) Vol. XVII, No. 3: 386–430; and S. N. Eisenstadt, "Breakdowns of Modernization," *Economic Development and Cultural Change* (July, 1964) Vol. XII: 345–367. As Huntington suggests, additional material lies in the area of fiction. In addition to his choice of William Golding's *Lord of the Flies* (Boston: Putnam and Company, 1963), I would add Chinua Achebe, *A Man of the People* (Garden City, N.Y.: Doubleday & Company, 1965); Jack London "The Scarlet Plague," N. D. Fabricant and H. Werner (eds.), *Treasury of Doctor's Stories* (New York: F. Fell, 1946); and Ayi Kwei Armah, *The Beautiful Ones Are Not Yet Born* (Boston: Houghton Mifflin Company, 1968).

goal among many and one that often is not a priority item for decision-makers. Despite the importance of political development for
the long-term survival of the political system and its effective functioning, many political elites seem more preoccupied with economic
development or international influence. In fact, the very elites ultimately charged with increasing political development are the decision-
makers most likely to suffer from a false perception of the existing
system's capabilities and to underestimate the inertia of the society
which supports them. By focusing upon the spectre of political devolution and decay, by accenting the temporal, regional, and institutional points where breakdowns are likely to occur, both practitioners
and theoreticians concerned with political development will be in a
better position to see the need to devote manpower, time, and treasure to the development of modern, rationally functioning political
structures and processes and to gauge their proper courses of action
accordingly.

This glance at the nature of political development was included
to give the reader some insights into the extraordinarily complex and
multidimensional character of the process. We have at best simply
touched upon aspects, factors, and theories that deserve volumes of
description and analysis. It is hoped, however, that our examination
of both the African context and specific African political systems will
be enhanced by these observations concerning the characteristics of
political development and decay.

BIBLIOGRAPHY

Almond, Gabriel A., and James S. Coleman, *The Politics of the Developing Areas* (Princeton: Princeton University Press, 1960).

Apter, David E., *The Politics of Modernization* (Chicago: University of
Chicago Press, 1965).

Black, C. E., *The Dynamics of Modernization* (New York: Harper &
Row, Publishers, 1966).

Finkle, Jason, and Richard W. Gable (eds.), *Political Development and
Social Change* (New York: John Wiley & Sons, 1966).

Holt, Robert T., and John E. Turner, *The Political Basis of Economic
Development* (Princeton: D. Van Nostrand Company, 1966).

Horowitz, Irving L., *Three Worlds of Development* (New York: Oxford University Press, 1966).

Kautsky, John H. (ed.), *Political Change in Underdeveloped Countries* (New York: John Wiley & Sons, 1962).

Kornhauser, William, *The Politics of Mass Society* (Glencoe, Ill.: The Free Press, 1959).

Levy, Marion J., *Modernization and the Structure of Societies* (Princeton: Princeton University Press, 1966).

Organski, A. F. K., *The Stages of Political Development* (New York: Alfred A. Knopf, 1967).

Pye, Lucian, *Aspects of Political Development* (Boston: Little, Brown and Company, 1966).

Shils, Edward A., *Political Development in the New States* (s'Gravenhage: Mouton and Company, 1962).

Welch, Claude (ed.), *Political Modernization* (Belmont, Calif.: Wadsworth Publishing Company, 1967).

CHAPTER III

The African Context

Africa is both large and populous. With 11,700,000 square miles and 330 million inhabitants it is the second largest and third most populous continent. Africa is also diverse. Within its borders are found a great variety of climatic, topographical, and vegetational zones and a human richness dramatically mirrored in the physical, cultural, linguistic, and political diversity of its people. The Tuareg differs from the Zulu as much as, if not more than the Norwegian differs from the Italian or the Polynesian from the Canadian. The Bergdama is as different from the Masai, the Galla from the Mbuti, the Luo from the Kru as the Englishman is distinct from the Chinese or the Brazilian from the Turk. It is the purpose of this chapter to describe the remarkably diverse anthropological and historical context of the contemporary political systems of Tanzania, the Ivory Coast, South Africa, and Somalia. We shall examine existing attempts to classify the peoples of Africa, review the legacy of European colonialism, and give an account of the great structural variety of traditional African political systems. It is hoped that this process will indicate to the reader the inadequacy of projecting the European notion of nationality onto the African continent at the present time.

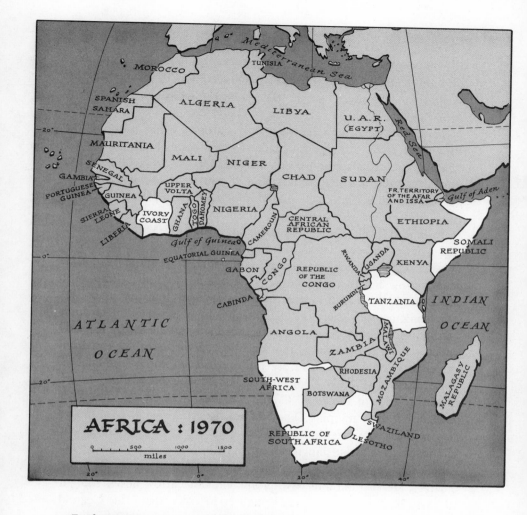

AFRICA : 1970

Early Attempts at Classification

Many of the earliest attempts to classify the peoples of Africa were based on dubious "racial" characteristics.[1] Particularly suspect were those works that attempted to correlate physical traits with cultural achievement. Although no precise classification based solely on racial characteristics is possible, and most of the attempts to do so have

[1] Perhaps the most famous attempt along these lines is C. G. Seligman, *Races of Africa* (London: Home University Library, 1930). More recent works on the subject of race include Carleton S. Coon, *The Origin of Races* (New York: Alfred A. Knopf, 1962) and Ashley Montague, *The Concept of Race* (Glencoe, Ill.: The Free Press, 1964).

largely been discredited, there are some rather persistent patterns of physical characteristics and somatological forms that seem worth mentioning, if only to accent the essential diversity of the human condition in Africa.

Simon and Phoebe Ottenberg, for example, while rejecting the validity of racial classification, talk of three distinct physical types: "Negro, Caucasoid, and Bushmen-Hottentot." [2] James Gibbs mentions Negroid, Nilotic, Bushmanoid, Pygmoid, Caucasoid-Negroid, and Caucasoid patterns.[3] George Murdock has attempted perhaps the most comprehensive classification of the African peoples and refers to Pygmoid, Bushmanoid, Negroid, Caucasoid, and Mongoloid (limited to Madagascar) types.[4] His Pygmoid groups, such as the Mbuti of central Africa, are described as being very short and having kinky hair, narrow heads, broad noses, and light yellow-brown skin. The Bushmanoid peoples of southern Africa, such as the !Kung, Xam, and Bergdama, are also short but exhibit distinctive peppercorn hair and pronounced steatopygia, thin lips, and high cheekbones. The Negroid peoples of western, eastern, and southern Africa are by far the most extensive of the groups and are represented by hundreds of ethnic groups such as the Vai, Yoruba, Kpelle, Bakongo, and Fang. Many of the peoples of the Ivory Coast, Tanzania, and South Africa fall into this general grouping. They are taller than either the Bushmanoids or the Pygmoids and have kinky hair, everted and thick lips, broad noses, and skin ranging from light brown to black. The Caucasoid pattern, exemplified by the Berbers, the Egyptians, and the Tuaregs, are also tall and have prominent but narrow noses, straight to curly hair, and are generally lighter in color than the Negroid peoples. They are found primarily in north and northeast Africa.

These broad categories based on physical traits are, of course, far too generalized to include all African groups. Many of the peoples of the Horn of Africa—the Somali, the Galla, and the Afar, for example—and some of the peoples of the Rift valley in eastern

[2] Simon and Phoebe Ottenberg (eds.), *Cultures and Societies of Africa* (New York: Random House, 1960), p. 20.

[3] James L. Gibbs, Jr. (ed.), *Peoples of Africa* (New York: Holt, Rinehart & Winston, 1965). See his comprehensive Introduction.

[4] George P. Murdock, *Africa: Its Peoples and Their Culture and History* (New York: McGraw-Hill Book Company, 1959), p. 10. His emphasis on "Cultural Codes" is seen in *Ethnographic Atlas* (Pittsburgh, Pa.: University of Pittsburgh Press, 1967), pp. 7–12.

Africa (the Masai, the Tutsi and others) do not fall easily into any of the categories mentioned above. Various attempts to label them Nilotic or Hamitic or Nilotic-Hamitic have not gained universal acceptance. In fact, attempts at physical classification are of little value beyond indicating the great diversity of Africa's peoples.

Cultural Patterns

Contemporary anthropologists have sought to avoid classifying Africans with regard to "race" and instead have attempted to separate them on the basis of cultural and linguistic characteristics. Perhaps the most comprehensive of these attempts is the culture-area concept of Melville Herskovits. Reacting to "the confusion of physical form with cultural and linguistic usage," he blends ecological and institutional factors to distinguish holistic cultural areas on the basis of political structure, aesthetic expression, lineage patterns, social stratification, modes of food production, and metaphysical views.[5] His six prominent culture areas (which existed in the 19th century) include the Khoisan, East African Cattle, Eastern Sudan, Congo, Guinea Coast, and Western Sudan. For our purposes, the East African Cattle Area, the Guinea Coast, and the Western Sudan are the most important in indicating the traditional heritage of the systems we are to examine. The Ivory Coast political system reflects both the Guinea Coast and Western Sudan areas. The Guinea Coast area was distinguished by complex market systems, a strong accent on patrilineal descent and patrilocal residence, impressive achievements in art, a highly developed cosmology, high population density, and widespread social and economic specialization. Villages were the important social units, polygamy was widely practiced, and the traditional political systems were often highly complex. The Western Sudan cultural core was distinguished by similar characteristics. Its position between the Guinea Coast to the south and the Arabic cultures to the north made it an amalgamation of these two types. It, too, displayed economic complexity within its area (agricultural societies, pastoral and herding groups were all present). Yet, in contrast to the Eastern Cattle culture area, animals were consumed and traded, not kept purely for

[5] Melville J. Herskovits, The Human Factor in Changing Africa (New York: Alfred A. Knopf, 1962), pp. 56–112.

prestige or wealth. (The Fulani, however, are a notable exception to this pattern.) Market systems were highly developed, and traditional political systems as exemplified by the empires of Ghana, Mali, and Songhay were complex and extensive. There was often social stratification along ethnic and occupational lines. The religious life of the area reflected an Islamic overlay and, in those areas where Islam was strongest, there was a decline in the artistic achievement of wood carving although not in metal working.

The contemporary political system of Tanzania is embedded within what was the East African Cattle area. This extensive nexus extended throughout most of eastern and southern Africa. Its ethos was dominated by the cattle complex "which combines elements of social and economic structure, political position and ritual, all focusing on these animals. . . ." [6] There was a dual economy. Agriculture provided subsistence, cattle, social and economic prestige. Population levels were low and settlements generally widely dispersed. Dwellings were round and usually simple in design. Descent was often matrilineal. There was minimal economic differentiation, few markets, and little use of money. Some extensive traditional political systems did develop in southern and central Africa, but few exhibited the complexity and differentiation of those found in the Western Sudan.

The East African culture area blended at its northern extremes into the East Horn area where the Somali Republic is found. Because the Somalis raise camels, sheep, and goats in addition to cattle, Herskovits does not include them in his cattle complex area: nevertheless, the Somalis exhibit a strong emphasis on pastoralism and small-unit social and political life. With the exception of the Sab clan family, who are sedentary herders and agriculturalists, most Somalis are pastoralists. Clan units and segmented political units are widespread. There are few art forms save praise poems, and little emphasis on markets and trade. There is some economic and social differentiation, but little in the political realm. Islamic religious beliefs are deeply ingrained and are perhaps as pronounced as in any of the other sub-Saharan cultural areas.

South Africa is really a blend of three major cultures. The Bantu-speaking population generally owes its heritage to the East African Cattle area, while the European section's orientation is outside of

[6] *Ibid.*, p. 62.

Africa. Smaller numbers of inhabitants, mostly in South West Africa, represent the Khoisan area of Herskovits. The Bushmen and Hottentots have a long and probably varied history which remains largely unknown. We know, however, that these groups were once in evidence throughout most of sub-Saharan Africa and were caught between the Bantu-speaking peoples moving south and the European settlers moving north from the Cape of Good Hope. They were exterminated or absorbed except for a small number of survivors who now exist in arid areas of the Kalahari Desert. Their economic and political organizations are almost undifferentiated. Hunting and food gathering form the basis of life. Religion and cosmology are approached pragmatically, although art forms, particularly their famous rock paintings, are highly developed.

Although, for our purposes, the Herskovits scheme provides a general background for the traditional African political systems, its inclusive and abstract nature tends to ignore widespread diversity within these areas. It fails, for example, to explain the existence of pastoralists and agriculturalists, both of whom exist within the East African Cattle area, and it does little to explain the development of similar political forms irrespective of the cultural area. Thus other anthropologists attempt to select more limited and specific components. Gibbs, for example, suggests grouping African societies on the basis of food production, or what he calls the "major forms of subsistence." [7] There are four primary modes: food gatherers or foragers (Bushmen of southern Africa), hoe agriculture based on small family plots (Baulé, Anyi, Bakwe, Assini, and other groups in the Ivory Coast), pastoralism or herding (Masai of Tanzania, Somalis of the Somali Republic), and a blend of pastoralism and agriculture called mixed farming in which livestock is present and prized but generally not viewed as a source of food (Swazi, Zulu, Xhosa of South Africa). While this approach has the virtue of simplicity, it represents hardly more than a rudimentary starting point for classification.

Linguistic Groups

The multidimensional nature of culture, the inadequacy of single-factor classification, and the unreliability of physical traits have in-

[7] Gibbs, *op. cit.*, Introduction.

spired attempts to classify the African peoples on the basis of linguistic groups. Although linguistic classification predates the present era and existing works have built upon the accumulation of data over a long period of time, perhaps the single most impressive achievement in this area was Joseph Greenberg's "complete generic reclassification" in 1955 based on similarities of form and substance.[8] He classified over 1000 languages into six major stocks (Niger-Congo, Songhai, Macro Sudanic, Central Saharan, Afroasiatic, and Click) and six minor stocks (Maban, Fur, Temainian, Kordofanian, Koman, and Nyangiya). In the decade following this important accomplishment, Greenberg and others have engaged in mass comparisons and correlated hundreds of additional languages. Underlying similarities became apparent and he was able to substantially reduce the number of categories.[9] The major linguistic stocks, their primary subdivisions, and some prominent examples are summarized below. Following this outline, we shall distinguish the major linguistic units found in each of the African political systems that will concern us in Chapters IV through VII.

I. Congo-Kordofanian
   A. Niger-Congo (six major categories including such tribal languages as Wolof, Fulani, Ibo, Tiv, and the Bantu Group)
   B. Niger-Kordofanian (Laro, Moro, Tima)
II. Nilo-Saharan
   A. Sònghai (Songhai)
   B. Saharan (Baz, Daza)
   C. Maban (Mine, Mimi, Runga)
   D. Fur (Fur)
   E. Chari-Nile (Masai, Luo, Nuer, Suk, Nandi)
   F. Koman (Koma, Gube, Uduk)
III. Afroasiatic
   A. Semitic (Amharic, Arabic, Tigren)
   B. Egyptian (Egyptian)
   C. Berber (Tuareg)
   D. Cushite (Galla, Somali, Afar, Beja)
   E. Chad (Hausa, Tur, Diryawa)

[8] Joseph H. Greenberg, *Studies in African Linguistic Classification* (Branford, Conn.: Compass Publishing Co., 1955).
[9] Joseph H. Greenberg, *International Journal of African Linguistics* (January, 1963) Vol. XXIX, No. 1: 1–171.

IV. Khosian
    A. South African Khosian (!Kung, Xa
       Hottentot)
    B. Sandawe (Sandawe)
    C. Hatsa (Hatsa)

There has been some criticism of this classification and it seems likely that the present ordering will be modified as more data is processed.[10] Nevertheless, the Greenberg arrangement points up the extensive linguistic diversity found in Africa and illustrates the resulting fragmentation of African peoples. While there are some languages that are spoken by more than 1 million persons (Amhara, Tigrinya, Bakongo, Ganda, Yoruba, Sotho, Swahili, Ibo, Somali, Hausa, Zulu, Xhosa, Kikuyu), this is generally not the case. The Ivory Coast, for example, exhibits over sixty languages primarily drawn from the Niger-Congo subgroup of the Congo-Kordofanian stock. Tanzania has over a hundred linguistic patterns, including Chari-Nile speakers of Nilo-Saharan stock, Sandawe and Hatsa speakers of Khosian stock, and various groups of Congo-Kordofanian stock. Tanzania also exhibits a lingua franca, Swahili, which is an amalgamation of the Bantu subfamily of the Congo-Kordofanian stock and Arabic. South Africa has substantial numbers of persons who speak English and Afrikaans, two European orientated languages, and many Bantu-speaking Africans of the Congo-Kordofanian stock, as well as smaller numbers of people who use forms of the Khosian stock. Only Somalia exhibits anything like uniformity, with most linguistic groups within its borders belonging to the Cushite Family of the Afroasiatic stock. The political implications of such diversity are considerable. The existence of so many indigenous African languages has undoubtedly curtailed the formation of national entities and hindered the process of indigenous politics and communication.

In addition to the multitude of languages developed within Africa, additional linguistic factors were introduced in the form of Arabic (north and north central Africa), Swahili (east Africa), and the host

[10] See especially Harold K. Schneider, "Confusion in African Linguistic Classification" and replies by Greenberg and Murdock in *Current Anthropology* (February, 1964) Vol. V, No. 1: 56–57. Most of the discussion centers around the terms chosen for the basic linguistic groups rather than the divisions themselves.

, Nama,

g the colonial period of the late 19th
ed into Spanish Sahara, Rio Muni, and
Iorocco. German came to Togo, the
l South West Africa. Afrikaans, an off-
n South Africa. Portuguese was brought
Portuguese Guinea, Angola and Mozam-
Eritrea, Somalia, and Ethiopia. French
es of North Africa, French West Africa,
a, the Congo, and Ruanda-Urundi, while
English was used in Gambia, Sierra Leone, Ghana, Nigeria, South
Africa, Tanzania, Kenya, Uganda, British Somalia, Ethiopia, and the
Sudan.

Colonial Experiences

In addition to introducing new linguistic patterns, the colonial
partition of Africa in the latter decades of the 19th century cut across
existing physical, cultural, and linguistic units as well as economic,
political, and ethnic groupings. At this time it is difficult to assess
objectively all the ramifications of the European occupation. Certainly, the European powers came for a variety of economic, strategic, social reasons; for prestige, wealth, living space and, on occasion,
philanthropy. The colonial countries created new administrative entities, superimposed a grid of rather artificial order across most of
Africa, and introduced medical and technological advances. On one
level, the colonial experience served to unify areas by providing a
focal authority (often an enemy) and, at least briefly, a common
historical experience. In addition, for the 5–10% of the indigenous
population who became literate, the language of the colonial authority provided a medium of communication.

Yet, the European penetrations also reinforced and, in some cases,
created tribal, linguistic, and ethnic divisiveness. At the very least, the
colonial experience set up new lines of division (such as Anglophone
vs. Francophone Africa) which may prove difficult to obliterate, and
established an international economic relationship with the metropole
which will have a pejorative impact on the creation of inter-African
economic units. Although this is not an historical work, a brief
analysis of colonial styles and an assessment of their impact on

African political systems are not irrelevant here.[11]

The onset and style of British colonial rule differed from area to area.[12] It has generally been characterized as "indirect," referring to the widespread practice of allowing the traditional tribal authorities to remain in place and of ruling the Africans through these leaders. British rule in Northern Nigeria, Buganda, and Barotseland are classical examples of this style. In other areas, particularly those with large numbers of European settlers, a type of dual rule developed, whereby Europeans and Africans were administered as separate, albeit connected entities. Irrespective of the context, however, the African authorities suffered a loss of power and, in many cases, of legitimacy.

Generally speaking, British colonial policy was designed to provide a stable framework for commerce, industry, and some settlement. There was no attempt to transform all aspects of African life. Colonies were expected to pay for their administration, and education was largely entrusted to church groups and philanthropic organizations. The British did permit some freedom of association in the form of cultural societies, labor unions, and, ultimately, political parties. At the same time, there existed firm social segregation or color bar, and most Africans were denied direct participation in the governmental process until the 1950's. The British pattern existed in Somalia (1941–50), Tanzania (1918–62), and South Africa (1795–1909).

The French colonial system, at least in theory, was based on the concept that the colonies were a part of France and that, as such, they should be integrated economically and politically into a larger

[11] Several general introductions to the colonial styles may be found in Dorothy Dodge, *African Politics in Perspective* (Princeton: D. Van Nostrand and Company, 1966), pp. 23–50; Thomas Hodgkin, *Nationalism in Colonial Africa* (New York: New York University Press, 1956); and D. K. Fieldhouse, *The Colonial Empires* (New York: The Delacorte Press, 1967). Walter R. Crocker, *On Governing Colonies* (London: G. Allen and Unwin, 1947), provides an interesting description on the operational aspects of colonialism.

[12] There is a vast literature on the British Colonial impulse. Among the most useful are Ronald Robinson and John Gallagher, *Africa and the Victorians* (London: Macmillan and Company, 1965); Robert Huttenback, *The British Imperial Experience* (New York: Harper & Row, Publishers, 1966); Lord Hailey, *Native Administration in the British African Territories* (London: His Majesty's Stationary Office, 1953); and Robin W. Winks (ed.), *British Imperialism* (New York: Holt, Rinehart & Winston, 1963).

framework, with a small number of elite Africans being gradually absorbed into French life. Thus, there was strong emphasis on a central administration and control over the educational, economic, and political life of the territories. In reality, the policy was applied differently from place to place and time to time. On occasion, the French used a type of indirect rule (*politique des races*).[13] The Berbers of Morocco, the Agni of the Ivory Coast, and the Tuaregs of Mauritania, Mali, and Niger were treated in this way, although the French attempted to rule most of sub-Saharan Africa more directly. The French government drew a pronounced line between its citizens (the literate, assimilated Africans) and its subjects. Individuals could attain equal status with Frenchmen, but, generally, this trend was not permitted to interfere with a view of the colonies as a source of manpower for France, an outlet for the goods of the metropole, and a source of raw materials. Forced labor (*corvée*) was widely practiced until 1947; the precise degree of segregation varied from area to area, often depending upon the number of European settlers. Yet Africans participated in politics on all levels, and, particularly during the Fourth Republic, African members of the French National Assembly played important roles in metropolitan politics. There were many direct cultural, economic, and political links between the metropole and her colonies. Even after independence, these ties have remained exceptionally strong. The Ivory Coast, long under French control, fits this pattern very closely.

We mention the Belgian and Portuguese colonial styles despite their lack of relevance for the political systems under consideration, because they offer some interesting contrasts and similarities. The Belgian colonial operation began in 1885 when the Congo Free State became the personal fief of Leopold II.[14] Even after the territory

[13] Stephen Roberts, *History of French Colonial Policy* (London: P. S. King and Company, 1929); Michael Crowder, *Senegal: A Study in French Assimilation Policy* (Oxford: Oxford University Press, 1962); R. Betts, *Assimilation and Association in French Colonial Theory* (New York: Columbia University Press, 1961); François Luchaire, *Les Institutions Politiques et Administratives des Territoires d'outremer après La Loi-Cadre* (Paris: Librairie Generale de Droit et de Jurisprudence, 1958).

[14] For the early period see John de Courcy MacDonnell, *King Leopold II, His Rule in Belgium and the Congo* (London: Cassell and Company Ltd., 1905). The span of Belgian rule is well covered in Paul Bouvier, *L'Allession du Congo Belge à L'Independence* (Bruxelles: L'Institut de Socologie de L'Université Libre de Bruxelles, 1965); Belgian Ministers des Colonies, *La Reorganisation Politique*

became a Belgian colony in 1908 and Ruanda-Urundi was added as a mandate in 1924, the style remained overwhelmingly paternalistic. Control was centralized and there was a strong accent on economic development. Assimilation was not a major goal, and the distinction between European and *évolué* African was nearly as great as that between *évolué* and the mass of *indigènes*. The Roman Catholic Church offered one of the few avenues for upward social mobility and even here, results were highly mixed. The Belgians introduced widespread medical facilities and primary and technical education, but drastically limited the number of Africans attending secondary and university facilities.[15] Investment, both public and private, was extensive, and the Congo evolved a highly developed economic infrastructure. However, neither political parties nor independent African trade unions were allowed until just prior to independence, and ethnic and regional fragmentation was encouraged. Preparation for independence was minimal.

The Portuguese came to Africa in the 16th century and have remained ever since. For centuries, they administrated their colonial areas in a haphazard and sporadic fashion.[16] The ravages of slaving and the importation of the feudal *prazo* system did much to insure that the writ of the colonial governors seldom extended much beyond the coast. A tiny fraction of the Africans became assimilated into the

---

Indigène de Ruanda-Urundi (Bruxelles: Belgian Ministere des Colonies, 1952); Roger Anstey, *King Leopold's Legacy* (London: Oxford University Press, 1966); and Ruth Slade, *King Leopold's Congo* (London: Oxford University Press, 1962).

[15] Dodge estimates, for example, that prior to independence 60% of school age children in the Congo were in primary school, 2.2% in secondary education (Dodge, *op. cit.*, p. 51). The Belgian case is given in J. Vanhove, *L'Oeuvre d'Education au Congo Belge et au Ruanda-Urundi* (Bruxelles: Encyclopedie du Congo Belge, 1953).

[16] James Duffy, *Portugal in Africa* (Cambridge: Harvard University Press, 1962) and *Portuguese Africa* (Cambridge: Harvard University Press, 1959), and Ronald H. Chilcote, *Portuguese Africa* (Englewood Cliffs, N.J.: Prentice-Hall, 1967) present a stern indictment of Portugal. Antonio de Figueiredo, *Portugal and its Empire: The Truth* (London: Victor Gollancz, 1961); Adriano Moreira, *A Policy of Integration* (Lisbon: Secretariado Nacional da Informaqao, 1961) and *Portugal's Stand in Africa* (New York: University Publishers, 1962) provide a somewhat different perspective as does Alberto Franco Nogueira, *The United Nations and Portugal* (London: Sedgwick and Jackson, 1963) and *The Third World* (London: Johnson Publications, 1967). Gilberto Freyre, although speaking about Brazil in his *New World in the Tropics* (New York: Alfred A. Knopf, 1959), indicates what might have been.

neo-indigena class (assimilados and Europeans), but, generally speaking, scant opportunity for education, a high incidence of forced labor, and strict enforcement of the caderneta or passbook system, as well as generally harsh treatment, insured that few Africans ever crossed the cultural barrier. Although the colonial system was one of direct control, the Portuguese often encouraged tribal separatism and ethnocentricity. Color bar was less severe than in the English, Belgian, or even French territories, but was largely outweighed by a lack of civil liberties, few opportunities for African associations and low levels of economic activity. Even after the colonies themselves became overseas provinces of Portugal (1951) and all persons in the colonies became citizens (1961), free political and economic associations were not permitted. (It should perhaps be borne in mind that the Portuguese government has never been famous for extending these rights to its population in the metropole.) Since 1961, economic development has been stressed and settlement by Europeans encouraged. But the Portuguese government is not planning to grant independence to Guinea, Angola, or Mozambique in the near future.

The Italians were among the last of the European powers to acquire colonies in Africa, arriving in the 1880's, and although of only minor consequence to most of the continent, they did play an important role in the Horn of Africa.[17] Libya, Ethiopia, Eritrea, and Somalia, at one time or another, were under Italian control. For the most part, Italian colonial rule was direct, although in the remote areas of Ethiopia and Somalia it was seldom much in evidence. The economic sphere was characterized by monopolies and parastatal organizations. In exchange for the development of a physical infrastructure and exposure to Italian culture, the colonies provided living space for Italian immigrants, some raw materials, and prestige. Particularly after the Fascists came to power, there was a good deal of official color bar, and the Africans were denied political participation. Nevertheless, on the local level, many Italian settlers enjoyed more or less amicable relations with the peoples of the Horn, and many stayed on after

17 See M. H. Macartney, *Italy's Foreign and Colonial Policy* (London: Oxford University Press, 1938); Tommaso Tittoni, *Italy's Foreign and Colonial Policy* (London: Smith, Elder and Company, 1914); Luigi Villari, *The Expansion of Italy* (London: Faber and Faber, 1930); F. Quaranta Di San Severino, *Development of Italian East Africa* (New York: Italian Library of Information, 1940); and R. R. DeMarco, *The Italianization of African Natives* (New York: Columbia University Press, 1943).

Eritrea was merged with an independent Ethiopia and Somalia became independent. Interestingly enough, although the British conquered Somalia during 1941, the area was handed back to the Italians for administrative purposes under United Nations auspices from 1950 until 1960. Most importantly for the future of the Somali political system, Italian administration of the Horn during the initial stages of World War II gave the Pan-Somali leaders a firm precedence for the idea of a Greater Somalia encompassing portions of Ethiopia and Kenya.

German colonial rule extended over Togo, the Cameroons, South West Africa, Ruanda-Urundi, and German East Africa (which later became Tanganyika).[18] From 1884 to 1906 German rule was strongly militaristic and repressive. There were major revolts in South West Africa (Hereros) and German East Africa (Maji-Maji). Exploitive German companies vied with each other for economic spoils and made little attempt to ameliorate the plight of the Africans. After the German elections of 1906, however, the style of German rule changed dramatically and a strong, vigorous policy aimed at long-range economic and political development was implemented. After military pacification, each of the colonial areas came under the direction of a governor and large numbers of developmental schemes were inaugurated. In the expectation that the colonies would provide the raw materials for an industrial Germany, physical infrastructure and plantation agriculture were developed. European settlers, however, were never numerous and totaled only 25,000 in 1914. German colonial authorities, while strict and harsh, generally enjoyed a reputation for fairness and relied on a modified form of indirect rule with some local self-government and native treasuries. The German government established government schools and subsidized mission work in the area of education. It was the official policy of the government to restrict both forced labor and corporal punishment, although these undoubtedly occurred as late as World War I. With the defeat of Germany during World War I, the German colonial areas were

[18] Perhaps the best works on Germany's colonial history are Mary E. Townsend, *The Rise and Fall of Germany's Colonial Empire 1884–1918* (New York: Howard Fertig, Publisher, 1966), and Harry R. Rudin, *Germans in the Cameroons 1884–1914* (London: Jonathan Cape, 1938). Two more political works are Henrich Schnee, *German Colonization Past and Future* (New York: Alfred A. Knopf, 1926), and G. L. Steer, *Judgement on German Africa* (London: Hudder and Stoughton Ltd., 1939).

divided among Britain, France, Belgium, and South Africa. German East Africa became Tanganyika under British control and a League of Nations mandate. Partially because of this dual authority and the small numbers of European settlers, Tanganyika developed a rather unique political system and emerged in 1961 as the first independent state in East Africa.

When one reads of the differing colonial policies of the European powers, the Afrikaner style is often overlooked. To be sure, the 60% of the European population of South Africa whose native language is Afrikaans is indigenous to Africa, at least to the extent that they have no European homeland to which they can return. Nevertheless, it is important to see that the blend of Dutch and French Huguenot cultures which merged to form the Afrikaner national group represents a colonial system in its own right. The Afrikaans-speaking settlers, arriving in South Africa in the 17th century, moved quickly and resolutely to establish hegemony over the indigenous peoples, the Bushmen and the Hottentots. In their migrations north, they eventually ran into another surging people, the Bantu-speaking tribes who were moving south. Both were modified pastoral cultures; both were aggressive, hardy, and, to a certain extent, ethnocentric, for their world views encouraged a belief in their own primacy. The Boers, as the Afrikaans-speakers became known, had a colonial style all their own. Intensely paternalistic and committed to direct rule of individual Africans, they demanded obedience and observance of European law. Only recently has there been an attempt to move toward a more indirect type of rule with regard to the Africans, and even that seems spurious in its application.

Whether Europeans have been in Africa for three centuries as the Portuguese and the Afrikaners or for three decades as the Germans, they have had an impact on Africa and have influenced the formation of contemporary political systems. Yet, one should not, as so many observers of the African scene have done, overestimate the lasting impact of the colonial experience. It may have had profound influence on individuals and even societies, but, as African political systems emerge over time, the colonial overlay seems to be less of a factor in shaping the course of politics within a given system. It will be one of the fundamental theses of this book that it is traditional African political systems and styles that shape most directly the present course of politics in Africa. Of the African political systems we are about to study in detail, only the South African system, with its 3.5 million Europeans, is clearly of European origins and even here, the present course of politics seems to be shaped more by African phenomena, or at least phenomena in Africa, than by European heritage or political values. In short, it is indigenous, not exogenous, forces that are likely to endure over time as African styles and values reassert themselves.

In order to understand the present political context, therefore, we must examine in some detail the types of African political systems found in traditional, i.e. pre-European, African societies and, in the following chapters, relate them to the present systems.

Structural Variety of Traditional African Political Systems

The ethnic, cultural, linguistic, and historical diversity of Africa— in short, its societal environment—is amply reflected in the great structural variety of traditional African political systems. There are systems based on kinship, territory or both. Some political systems have appointed leaders, some have inherited positions, some have leadership posts that must be earned. Some African political systems reflect classless societies, others have extensive class orientation to political roles, some are even based on castes. Decision making is polyarchal in some, hierarchical in others, and still others have strong elements of bargaining among religious and political elites. There are small-scale political systems involving a few families, middle-range systems involving thousands of families and hundreds of thousands of persons, and large-scale political systems that involve millions of people. All exhibit marked structural and functional diversity. Peter Lloyd has rightly concluded:

> . . . there is a wider range in traditional African political systems than exists today among the industrialized nations in spite of the oft proclaimed communist-democratic dichotomy.[19]

It is important for our examination of contemporary African political systems that we appreciate the basic plurality of politics in Africa,

[19] Peter C. Lloyd, "The Political Structure of African Kingdoms," *Political Systems and the Distribution of Power*, American Sociology Association Monographs No. 2 (New York: Frederick A. Praeger, 1965), p. 107.

that we analyze the strains and tensions concomitant with this wide range of political forms, and that we see this diversity as one of the "givens" of contemporary African political systems. Many writers on contemporary Africa have, for example, fixated on the pejorative aspects of one such "given," tribalism. Yet tribalism may be functional or dysfunctional depending upon circumstances. Tribalism or ethnicity is certainly a factor to examine in explaining political phenomena, but it is but one factor in many. Political life styles of various groups may well be more significant in shaping the future of African political systems than the more popular, but less precise, concept of tribalism.[20] As will be seen, there is a cogent need to study in detail relationships between subnational political units and national political systems and thus relegate "tribalism" to its proper place as a subsidiary causative factor.

The pioneering attempt to classify in some organized fashion the multitude of African systems on the basis of political organization appeared in 1940. M. Fortes and E. E. Evans-Pritchard, in their introduction to *African Political Systems*, developed a classificatory scheme based on those aspects of the system "concerned with the control and regulation of the use of force" and the relationship between political authority and kinship.[21] They concluded that there are three major categories of political systems: hunting bands, segmentary lineage societies, and primitive states. Hunting and foodgathering bands, such as one finds among the Bushmen, the Bergdama, and the Mbuti, are entities where "political relations are coterminous with kinship relations, and the political structure and kinship organization are completely fused." [22]

Segmentary lineage societies, however, exhibit political activities that exceed kinship relations and are, in effect, "stateless" political systems where political authority is dispersed throughout clan-group segments which are "spatially juxtaposed and structurally equiva-

---

[20] Herskovits, *op. cit.*, pp. 69–70; I. Schapera, *Government and Politics in Tribal Societies* (London: C. A. Watts, 1956), p. 7; Jan Vansina, *Kingdoms of the Savanna* (Madison, Wisc.: University of Wisconsin Press, 1966), p. 15; and Richard Sklar, "Political Science and National Integration," *The Journal of Modern African Studies* (1967) Vol. 1: 1–13.

[21] M. Fortes and E. E. Evans-Pritchard (eds.), *African Political Systems* (London: Oxford University Press, 1940). See especially the Introduction, pp. 1–23, in the 1962 edition.

[22] *Ibid.*, p. 7.

lent." [23] Many African political units are variations of this type—the Nuer, the Logoli, the Tallensi, Ibo, Luo, Nandi, and Masai. Primitive states, on the other hand, are characterized by centralized authority, well-defined legal and administrative institutions, and a hierarchical decision-making pattern. The Baganda, Zulu, Bemba, and Ashanti groups all belong to this general category.

African Political Systems stimulated anthropologists to examine the basic assumptions concerning political communities. I. Schapera, for example, in his important work *Government and Politics in Tribal Societies,* departed somewhat from the Fortes–Evans-Pritchard formula and challenged the view that political aggregates were essentially kin groups.[24] He developed the notion of a "political community" which is "a group of people organized into a single unit managing its affairs independently of external control." [25] Schapera indicated how membership in such communities developed through conquest, immigration, acceptance of refugees, or the formation of new units. Dealing primarily with the Khosian and Bantu-speaking peoples of southern Africa, he encountered hunting bands and primitive states; the latter he distinguished according to the nature of political authority, the rights and obligations of that authority, and the way in which it was attained.

Whereas Schapera concentrated on centralized political communities, Lucy Mair attempted to expand the category of segmented systems and to distinguish several discrete types.[26] Evans-Pritchard had stressed the attributes of those segmented systems, such as the Nuer, which represented a "pure" type of this form. Mair found that some segmented systems, primarily those of the Masai, Nandi, Kipsigis, and Meru, are based on age-sets which cut across many segments and act as political cement. Quasimilitary in character, these age-sets involve a 3–4 year process of socialization during which time all men of the same age live together. These sets are formed every 10 or 15 years and divide the tribe into age-groups: boys, warriors, and elders. After the training period, warriors return to their segments, but when

[23] *Ibid.,* p. 13.
[24] I. Schapera, *op. cit.,* pp. 1–37.
[25] *Ibid.,* p. 8.
[26] L. P. Mair, *Primitive Government* (Baltimore, Md.: Penguin Books, 1962). Her classification includes "Minimal Government," pp. 61–78, "Diffused Government," pp. 28–107, and "African States," pp. 125–251.

group action is needed, the age-sets come together again. Political authority is diffused among the segments and decision making is polyarchal and generally open to all males. There is a slight bias toward a gerontocracy, but much emphasis is also placed on achievement, especially in warfare. There is some political specialization in the form of a war prophet, who acts as a unifying link between the elders and the warriors. The Nyakyusa, a Bantu-speaking group in Tanzania, offer an interesting amendment to the age-set pattern. In the case of the Nyakyusa, the age-sets themselves are never dispersed; instead, generational villages are set up and members of the particular age-set live together, bringing their wives and relatives to live with them.

As other anthropologists recognized the need for a "dynamic" analysis of the "process of decision making and conflict resolution," [27] political anthropology became a subfield. Max Gluckman, Jan van Velsen, Victor Turner, Marc Swartz, and Edgar Winans have all made important contributions to our understanding of politics in traditional African settings.[28] However, anthropologists have often confused structure with process, overestimated the ritual aspects of political offices, and failed to distinguish between the form and substance of power.[29] These difficulties have been compounded by the

[27] Marc J. Swartz, Victor W. Turner, and Arthur Tuden (eds.), *Political Anthropology* (Chicago: Aldine Publishing Company, 1966), p. 2. See also Lloyd, *op. cit.*, and R. G. Abrahams, *The Political Organization of Unyamwezi* (Cambridge: Cambridge University Press, 1967). Stanley Diamond has also indicated the directions in which political anthropology should move: "Introduction: Africa in the Perspective of Political Anthropology," Stanley Diamond and Fred G. Burke (eds.), *The Transformation of East Africa: Studies in Political Anthropology* (New York: Basic Books, 1966).

[28] Max Gluckman, *Politics, Law and Ritual in Tribal Society* (Chicago: Aldine Publishing Company, 1965); Jan van Velsen, *The Politics of Kinship* (London: Manchester University Press, 1964); V. Turner, *Schism and Continuity in an African Village* (Manchester: University of Manchester Press, 1957); and Edgar V. Winans, *Shambala: The Constitution of a Traditional State* (Los Angeles, Calif.: University of California Press, 1962). An earlier work which is, among other things, an in depth study of the political process is J. Herskovits, *Dahomey* (New York: J. J. Augustin—Publisher, 1938).

[29] After this chapter was written but before it was published, an article by Carl J. Friedrich, "Some Thoughts on the Relation of Political Theory to Anthropology," *American Political Science Review* (June, 1968) Vol. LXII, No. 2: 536–545 appeared. While differing somewhat in emphasis, Friedrich underscores the difficulties in making valid political pronouncements on the basis of existing material, and documents the confusion between power and authority found in

activities of political scientists dealing with the African context. By and large, political scientists (particularly Americans) ignored Africa until the late 1950's and then often concentrated on the largest ethnic units or the emerging "national" politics. Generally speaking, they were less concerned with traditional African political systems than with the new states and their institutional framework.[30] Thus there have been few attempts to classify African political systems in any comprehensive fashion or to incorporate the new data that has accumulated during the past decades.

Hopefully future research will evidence a more comprehensive type of cooperation between anthropologists and political scientists. Both groups seem to be turning toward microstudies of individual units or expanded single-factor descriptions of several units which may provide sufficient material for a second general analysis of traditional African political systems. It is hoped that the conceptual framework developed in Chapter I will serve as a guide to indicate what variables must be examined and will also prove to be a convenient way of organizing the material thus accumulated. In terms of African political communities, who are the principal decision makers? What are the levels of participation in the decision-making process? What are the criteria for membership in the body politic? Are there fixed units with proportional representation? Is there a ruling class? If so, is it based on ethnicity (Fulani, Tutsi) or upon family (Swazi)? If there are central political authorities, how are they chosen—by what criteria and by what process? Even if the ruling authorities are drawn from a single family, kin group, or clan, the political process may be examined in terms of elites and counterelites. How are politics conducted? We know, for example, far more about the political structure than about the political process. Perhaps much of the information we seek about traditional African systems in history will never be obtained, but we

---

many anthropological works such as J. Daryll Forde (ed.), *Ethnographic Survey of Africa* [50+ volumes] (London: International African Institute, various dates); *Human Relations Area Files* (New Haven, Conn.: Yale University Press, ongoing); and George P. Murdock, *Ethnographic Atlas* (Pittsburgh, Pa.: University of Pittsburgh Press, 1967).

[30] The work of David E. Apter is an exception to this observation. His *Gold Coast in Transition* (Princeton: Princeton University Press, 1955) and *The Political Kingdom in Uganda* (Princeton: Princeton University Press, 1961) attempt to deal with both traditional political systems and their development in a modern setting.

must make the attempt before the living links with those systems disappear.

Decision making has probably been more extensively covered than either of the other two major categories suggested for a comparative approach to politics, capabilities analysis, and goal orientation. Yet, all are needed if we are to understand how traditional African political systems function. If there is a central political authority, for example, what are its areas of competence, what is its functional relationship to subunits? Even if there is no central authority, what are the regulative capabilities of the system? How are laws enforced? Who administers the use of physical force? To what extent are the political authorities limited in their actions by custom and metaphysical views? What are the rights of individuals within the system? What is the extractive capability? Are taxes, labor, and allegiance readily obtained and, in turn, what are the distributive capabilities of the political authorities? Land, slaves, war booty, cattle and positions of authority—all of these are dispersed in a process of demand satisfaction. Whose demands?

The rejuvenative capability of the political systems is of particular importance and yet has received very little attention and study (the symbolic capability and the process of political and religious legitimacy, on the other hand, perhaps have been overstressed). We know very little about the actual process by which political systems expand or contract. In fact, we have a depressing lack of information on the origins, growth, and decay of even the most important, largest, and most studied systems. We seldom know, for example, how information was obtained—let alone know how it was utilized by the political authorities. Jan Vansina has done intensive work on the Lunda political community and indicates what can be accomplished with proper focus. The Lunda group, unlike the very similar Luba community, was able to expand over a period of decades due to the process of positional succession and perpetual kinship whereby a "successor inherited, not only an office but also the personal status of the deceased including his name and kinship relations." [31]

In much the same fashion, we know almost nothing about the goals held by most traditional African systems: survival, freedom, stability, political development, welfare, international objectives and the like.

[31] Vansina, *op. cit.*, p. 82.

On occasion we know what ruler X or headman Y wished for his immediate objective, but we know precious little as to what prompted the expansion of the empire of Mali, the kingdom of Bakongo, or, on a less grand scale, what goals were sought by smaller, more recent, political communities. We have assumed that survival and stability, particularly in the realm of tradition, were widely held goals, almost universal in their appeal—but were they? The endless migrations across Africa, the trading impulse, the developed market systems in the Sudanic area and on the coast of the Indian Ocean, the architectural creations at Zimbabwe and elsewhere, these speak of more than stability and survival. It is hoped that we may someday be able to answer these questions, at least about recent traditional systems and that the information thus accumulated will be arranged and ordered by means of a conceptual framework.

One of the few attempts to compare traditional political systems—and one which represents an important step forward—is S. N. Eisenstadt's "Primitive Political Systems: A Preliminary Comparative Analysis." [32] While maintaining the original distinction between segmented and centralized societal types originated by Evans-Pritchard, Eisenstadt attempted to subdivide these into more workable categories that would reflect the substantial differences existing within the broad groupings. In presenting the Eisenstadt scheme, we shall attempt to include examples germane to our areas of concern—South Africa, Tanzania, the Ivory Coast and Somalia—even though these were not part of the Eisenstadt material.

SEGMENTARY TYPES

(1) *Band organizations* Eisenstadt does not group these relatively undifferentiated political systems into a separate category. He agrees with earlier works that stress the kinship base and small-scale character of these communities, but feels that they are more properly classified under segmentary types due to the diffusion of political power among a variety of units having the same cultural background. There are few political positions, and decision making is democratic. We have already referred to the Bushmen, Bergdama,

---

[32] S. N. Eisenstadt, "Primitive Political Systems: A Preliminary Comparative Analysis," *American Anthropologist* (1959) Vol. LXI: 200–220.

and Hottentot groups of South Africa as being typical examples of this type. The Bahi in Tanzania are similar in organization.

(2) *"Classical" segmentary systems* These rely on lineage groups as the basis for political and social interaction. There is a good deal of interaction among the segments and a strong sense of corporate allegiance, although there is often competition among lineages. Eisenstadt uses the Tallensi, Kavirondo and Nuer as examples, but the pastoral Somalis of the Horn of Africa are also close to this pattern, and more important for our purposes. The Somali "nation" of nearly 4 million is divided into large clan families (such as the Dir and the Hawiye), clans, primary lineages, and "dia-paying" groups. The dia-paying group represents the smallest segment of Somali society and is based on "the payment and receipt of blood compensation." [33] There are few normal political structures, and there are no age-sets. Decision making is egalitarian and done on an ad hoc basis. Groups, lineages, and clans may combine for common action, but this is only on an individual and specific basis. There is some social and economic specialization (warriors, ritual specialists, and occupational groups), but little political specialization. The democratic nature of this pattern and the culture commonality of the Somali peoples account for much of the success of the contemporary Somali political system.

(3) *Universalistic segmentary groups* In these systems, the territorial units are not composed of homogeneous kin groups. Main political roles are "allocated according to universalistic criteria of membership." [34] Achievement in warfare and cattle raising is important; membership in age-sets is universal. Politics is generally informal and the decision-making process is again quite egalitarian in character, although there is competition among various individuals and clan groups for leadership. The Masai of Tanzania and Kenya and a variety of groups in Kenya, such as the Nandi and Meru, are examples of this type. Variations are also found among the Sandawe, Iraqw, and Nyakusa of Tanzania (although the Iraqw have hereditary

---

[33] I. M. Lewis, "The Northern Pastoral Somali of the Horn," in J. L. Gibbs (ed.), *Peoples of Africa*, pp. 321–360.
[34] Eisenstadt, *op. cit.*, p. 207.

leaders) and the Ajukru of the Ivory Coast.

(4) *Associational groups* Eisenstadt's fourth category of segmented groups is based on hereditary political positions and widespread associational organizations. It is generally limited to the Plains and Pueblo Indians of North America and need not concern us.

(5) *Ritually stratified systems* "Among them we find some degree of differentiation and stratification in the ritual-symbolic field, but very little in any other major field of social life." [35] Kin groups are more or less self-sufficient in economic and political terms, but "interact" for ritual concerns. There is much competition for ritual positions, and there is a strong class orientation. The Shilluk of the Sudan and especially the Ankole of Uganda are variations of this model. The separation of the east African Ankole into two classes, the Bahima and the Bairu, parallels political and social development among the Hutu and Tutsi of central Africa and offers a substantial amendment to the widely held belief that traditional African society is classless. In the Ankole system, there is competition among "nobles," primarily for ritual positions even though little political authority accrues to a holder of such positions.

(6) *Acephalous, autonomous village systems* These systems, found primarily in west Africa, are based on associations which may be joined by individuals whose positions of importance are based not primarily on kinship but on achievement. The affairs of the village are supervised by elected officers and village councils. Communal economic activities are widespread. The Ibos, Yorubas, and Ibibios of Nigeria are prominent examples of this type, as are the Anyi, Bete, Baoulé, Didia, and Bakwe of the Ivory Coast. Also, many of the Swahili-speaking and the Zaramo and Keveri groups of the Tanzanian coast in former times exhibited this loose, achievement-oriented type of system including a republican form of town meeting (although conversely, many of these city-states also exhibited patterns of hierarchy and ascription). Political positions are often determined by the associations.

[35] *Ibid.*, p. 209.

CENTRALIZED POLITICAL SYSTEMS

(1) *Centralized monarchies* Distinguished by a strong central political administration, heterogeneous membership, and territorial basis, the centralized monarchy is a prevalent pattern of African politics. It is found among the Fipa of Tanzania and the Zulu, Nguni, Swazi, and Tswana of South Africa. Membership in this type of community is not based solely upon kinship, but also upon direct allegiance to the central political authority, the king or paramount chief (although the king is usually chosen from one hereditary kin group). There are age-sets loyal to the king. The king's administration is made up of *indunas* who may be commoners or nobles, and he has the power to call for communal work and to lead the country to war. Subgroup autonomy is limited, although participation in the king's council and tribal assemblies is open to all. There are subordinate chiefs but these are often appointed at the will of the king. All tribal land is vested in his person and he is the religious as well as the political center of the group. The Zulus, numbering perhaps 500,000 in the 19th century and over 3 million today, are an important example of this type.

(2) *Federative monarchies* While these systems exhibit a strong central tendency, at least in comparison to segmentary groups, extensive self-regulation is left to the subgroups. Political participation is through the medium of one's existing leaders. The king's councils are usually made up of the leaders of subgroups. Communal activities are determined and regulated by the heads of specific lineage groups. There are generally no age regiments. Perhaps the most famous of these federative monarchies is the Ashanti of Ghana but, with minor variations, this prototype is also found in southern and central Africa among the Pondo, Bemba, and Xhosa, and among some of the Akan people of the Ivory Coast. In Tanzania the Lungu, Haya, and Hehe (until 1894) also exhibit most of the characteristics of a federated monarchy while the Vidunda, Zigula, and Shambala have paramount chiefs.

(3) *Federative monarchy with associated bases* These are found primarily in west Africa in the countries of Sierre Leone, Liberia, and the Ivory Coast. There is a central political authority

whose position is inherited, but there is also a series of associational groups which cut across clan and kin lines. These are not simple age regiments, but are rather societies which form a link between the subgroup of clan or village and the central political authority. The Poro and Sande societies that originated among the Mende are perhaps among the best known.

The Eisenstadt scheme, then, offers an important step toward an eventual classification of African political systems on the basis of political structure and process. Nevertheless, as Eisenstadt himself recognized, it is only a preliminary step, for it omits some political types and fails to incorporate all traditional systems known to exist, particularly those in Francophone Africa. For example, where does one put the Chagga or the Sukuma of Tanzania? Both are "segmented" into many chieftanships but each "segment" has a strong central political authority. Are they "developing" centralized systems or "devolving" segmented systems? There remains a pressing need not only to correlate existing material but to accumulate new material in such a way that it will lend itself to political analysis.

Despite the difficulties presently associated with cataloguing traditional African political systems, we can discern two major strands of African political behavior.[36] One strain can quite properly be labelled autocratic. Hierarchical decision making was prevalent and where this was coupled with strong central control and weak countervailing influences, individual freedom and political participation were limited. There is a theme of divine kingship and many instances of authoritarian rule. Empires were often developed and destroyed on the strength of arbitrary rule. Yet, the evidence, however incomplete, suggests that we can no longer cavalierly state that "It is almost as though all of Africa south of the Sahara were permeated, as it were, by a mental blueprint of a despotic political structure. . . ."[37]

[36] For those interested in the history of Africa, Roland Oliver and J. D. Fage provide an excellent introduction, A Short History of Africa (Baltimore, Md.: Penguin Books, 1962). Other works include Basil Davidson, A History of West Africa to the 19th Century (London: Longmans, Green and Company, 1965); A. J. Wills, The History of Central Africa (Oxford: Oxford University Press, 1964); Kenneth Ingham, A History of East Africa (New York: Frederick A. Praeger, 1962); C. W. deKiewiet, A History of South Africa (Oxford: The Clarendon Press, 1958); E. A. Walker, A History of Southern Africa (London: Longmans, 1957); Donald L. Wiedner, A History of Africa South of the Sahara (New York: Random House, 1962); and Robert I. Rotberg, A Political History of Tropical Africa (New York: Harcourt, Brace & World, 1965).

[37] Murdock, op. cit., p. 37.

In fact, the reverse may be true. Although there were, from time to time, African political systems that were ruled by personnel who could be termed despotic and whose rule was largely unchecked, an equally pronounced, if not more prevalent strand would be one of diffused power and egalitarian participation. Diffused political authority, widespread participation in the decision-making process and the selection of leaders, the African tradition of "talking until they agree," all seem more widespread than the "despotic" pattern. Many hunting bands and a variety of segmented political systems are based on at least a modified version of the polyarchal model. Age-sets and associations, to name but two institutions often encountered in such a setting, seem to have played an important role in adding an achievement orientation to politics.

Even where the central political authority had considerable power of a hierarchical nature, there existed a series of checks and balances of a social, political, and religious nature to the arbitrary use of that power.[38] Most rulers in African traditional systems, even if they were paramount chiefs or kings, were felt to rule by consent and could be dealt with in a variety of formal and informal ways if they abused their office or its powers. One of the most well known and amply documented institutionalized methods was the "destoolment" process practiced among the Ashanti. Chiefs who behaved arbitrarily or unfairly toward their subjects could be removed from office.[39] Another would be the council of commoners among the Shambala who nominated the king's successor. Further, most African communities exhibited a strong accent on the sharing of wealth, communal ownership or, at least, access to land, and a marked thrust toward social welfare concepts. This ethos undoubtedly conditioned the political process. The political authority, for example, was expected to be generous to his subjects (or, in present terminology, to exhibit a strong distributive capability) and to "watch over them." There were other political curbs: leaders were expected to accept advice from their councils and advisors and to permit and encourage the appointment of commoners

[38] John Beattie, "Checks on the Abuse of Political Power in some African States: A Preliminary Framework for Analysis," *Sociologus* (1959) Vol. IX, No. 2: 97–115.

[39] See especially K. A. Busia, *The Position of the Chief in the Modern Political System of Ashanti* (Oxford: Oxford University Press, 1951); also E. W. Smith, *The Golden Stool* (London: Halloran Publishing House, 1927).

and nonkinsmen. Dynastic rivalry, sorcery, and migration all were checks on the despotic use of political authority. Even more importantly, the threat of assassination was a significant curb on any leaders with an inclination to ignore the wishes of their followers.

The existence of these two patterns of African (although by no means exclusively African) political behaviors, which are often found within a single modern state, have collided to influence the form as well as the substance of politics in Africa. The single-party apparatus with professed internal democracy may be viewed as an attempt to reconcile these two distinct patterns. Post-independence Africa, and the political forms that have evolved within it, now seem to reflect the tensions and processes in existence in traditional African political systems as well as the superimposed colonial models. As will be demonstrated in the following chapters, moreover, it seems likely that it will be the traditional African techniques and forms that assert themselves over time against the colonial overlay and exogenous extensions.

The existence, then, of a large and dynamic population, distinguished by cultural, ethnic, historical, and political diversity and currently divided into over forty independent entities, provides the background for contemporary African political systems. This most complex of contexts has produced a great variety of political patterns. It is to four important types of patterns that we now turn.

BIBLIOGRAPHY

Baumann, H., and D. Westermann, *Les Peuples et Les Civilisations de l'Afrique* (Paris: Payot, 1962).

Forde, C. Daryll (ed.), *Ethnographic Survey of Africa* (London: International African Institute, 50+ volumes, various dates).

Fortes, M., and E. E. Evans-Pritchard (eds.), *African Political Systems* (London: Oxford University Press, 1962 edition).

Gibbs, James L. (ed.), *Peoples of Africa* (New York: Holt, Rinehart & Winston, 1965).

Gluckman, Max, *Politics, Law and Ritual in Tribal Society* (Chicago: Aldine Publishing Company, 1966).

———, *Seven Tribes of British Central Africa* (Oxford: Oxford University Press, 1951).

Herskovits, Melville J., *The Human Factor in Changing Africa* (New York: Random House, 1958).

Mair, Lucy P., *Primitive Government* (Baltimore, Md.: Penguin Books, 1962).

Murdock, George P., *Africa: Its Peoples and their Culture History* (New York: McGraw-Hill Book Company, 1959).

Ottenberg, Simon and Phoebe (eds.), *Cultures and Societies of Africa* (New York: Random House, 1960).

Schapera, I., *Government and Politics in Tribal Societies* (London: A. Watts, 1956).

CHAPTER IV

The South African Political System

The South African political system encompasses 790,000 square miles (including South West Africa) and 18.8 million people. It is embedded within a group of distinct and pluralistic societies. There are 13 million people of African descent, who are subdivided into numerous linguistic, cultural and historical entities such as the Zulu, Xhosa, and Sotho. There are 3.5 million Europeans, primarily of British and Afrikaner heritage, but also of diverse linguistic and religious backgrounds. In addition, there are 1.9 million Coloreds, persons of mixed ethnic backgrounds but primarily Afrikaans-speaking, and 550,000 Asians, mostly Indians but with some Chinese and Pakistanis. The Asians are divided into two major religious and five major linguistic groups. There are smaller numbers of Bushmen and the descendants of Hottentots.

The history of the interaction of these groups spans five centuries and is of enormous complexity. British and Dutch colonial authorities, independent African groups, and large numbers of European settlers formed and reformed political communities as they vied for control of southern Africa. After centuries of turmoil and conquest, the Union of South Africa was accomplished in 1910 by the merger of two former British colonial areas (Natal and the Cape Province), two defeated Afrikaner republics (the Transvaal and the Orange Free State), and many traditional African political systems which had already been absorbed by the European units. Each of the entities as well as South West Africa, which came under the effective control of the Union in 1919, has had a long and convoluted history in its own right.[1]

The present political framework is modeled after the British Westminster model, although since South Africa became a Republic on May 31, 1961, the State President, not the Queen, is the formal head of government. Executive power is vested in the office of State President. He calls and dissolves Parliament, receives ambassadors, enters into, and ratifies treaties, is commander-in-chief of the military, and stands at the apex of European and non-European government.[2] An electoral college, consisting of the members of Parliament, the House of Assembly and the Senate, elects the State President for a term of 7 years.

Legislative power is centered in Parliament, the Prime Minister, and his Cabinet. "Parliament shall be the sovereign legislative authority in and over the Republic and shall have full power to make laws for the peace, order and good government of the Republic."[3] The lower house of Parliament, the House of Assembly, is composed of 166 European members elected from single member constituencies by Europeans over the age of 18. The Transvaal elects 73 representatives, Cape Province 54, Natal 18, the Orange Free State 15, and South West Africa 6. In addition, there are 4 Europeans chosen by the Colored voters of the Cape Province, but this representation is in

[1] See especially C. W. deKiewiet, A History of South Africa (Oxford: Oxford University Press, 1957); Eric A. Walker, A History of South Africa (London: Longmans, Green and Company, 1957); Sheila Patterson, The Last Trek: A Study of the Boer People and the Afrikaner Nation (London: Routledge and Kegan Paul, 1957); and F. A. Van Jaarsveld's two works, The Awakening of Afrikaner Nationalism 1868–1881 (Capetown: Human and Rousseau, 1961) and The Afrikaner's Interpretation of South African History (Capetown: S. Mondium Publishers, 1964).

[2] Republic of South Africa, Act to Constitute the Republic of South Africa and to Provide for Matters Incidental Thereto: Act No. 32, 1961 (Capetown: Government Printer, 1961), Section 16. The difficulties inherent in studying a political system by analyzing its constitution are well illustrated here. In point of fact, the President is primarily ceremonial. Executive power is actually exercised by the Prime Minister.

[3] Ibid., Section 59.

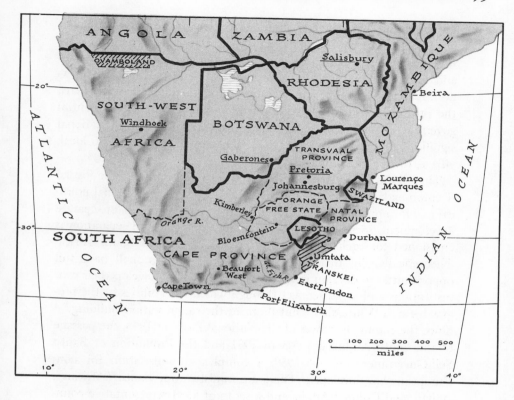

the process of being eliminated. The Senate has 54 members: 43 elected by adult European suffrage and 11 nominated by the State President in consultation with the Provincial Councils. Two senators are supposed to be familiar with the interests of the Colored community. Although both chambers may introduce bills, the House of Assembly has the right of fiscal initiation and the power to pass bills twice to override a rejection by the Senate (the exceptions to this are bills relating to the status of English and Afrikaans as the official languages and the representation of non-Europeans, Sections 108 and 118). The Prime Minister is chosen by majority vote of Parliament and presides over the Cabinet. All members of the government are Europeans.

Each of the provinces, plus South West Africa, has some local jurisdiction, although most powers are vested in the central government. There is an Administrator appointed for 5 years by the State

President and a Provincial Council elected by adult Europeans. The provincial councils are empowered to pass on matters of local taxation, hospitals, roads and bridges, fish and game matters, and primary and secondary education for Europeans. The State President, however, retains a veto over any decision by the Council. In recent years, the provincial councils have declined in importance as the central government has extended its control over local matters of national significance (such as non-European education). There are also local, village, town, and municipal councils.

These local, provincial, and national assemblies provide the formal decision-making apparatus for Europeans. There is no national political role for non-Europeans. Under the theory of apartheid, or separate development, social, residential, economic, and political separation is envisioned for each of the major "racial" groups in South Africa. Theoretically, "in their own areas the non-Whites shall have full opportunities to develop in every sphere, they shall develop their own institutions and social services through which the abilities of the progressive non-White shall contribute to their own nation building." [4] Since the coming to power of the National Party in 1948, the passage of the Bantu Authorities Act of 1951 and the Promotion of Bantu Self-Government Act of 1959, a complex administration for non-Europeans has developed. There are ministries for Bantu (African), Indian, and Colored Affairs and a series of local representative councils. Particularly in the cases of the Indians and Coloreds, these councils are of little import. Some attempt has been made to evolve a more elaborate administration for Africans who have been divided into tribal units, with local, district, and regional councils and, in the case of the only functioning Bantustan (or homeland), the Transkei, a territorial council. [5] By 1968, however, there were only four urban Bantu councils. The limited nature of the prerogatives of these councils, the veto power retained by the central European government, the powerful status of the European Bantu Affairs Commissioner, and

[4] National Party Manifesto, *Die Transvaler*, March 29, 1948.
[5] Because of the lack of relevance and import of Bantustan politics for the national politics of South Africa, I have avoided going into detail on this subject. Those interested should examine G. M. Carter, Thomas Karis, and Newell Stultz, *South Africa's Transkei: The Politics of Domestic Colonialism* (Evanston, Ill.: Northwestern University Press, 1967) and Christopher R. Hill, *Bantustans: The Fragmentation of South Africa* (London: Oxford University Press, 1964).

the use of chiefs appointed and paid by the government severely curtail their political importance, but the structure does exist.

The political framework of South Africa also includes an independent judiciary with a Supreme Court consisting of a Chief Justice, eleven Judges of Appeal, and both provincial and local divisions. Judges are appointed by the State President upon the recommendation of the Minister of Justice and the Cabinet. They hold office until age 70. The law is basically Roman-Dutch in character with some infusion of English common and commercial law. There is no bill of rights, however, and the courts generally lack the prerogative of legislative review except:

> No court of law shall be competent to inquire into or to pronounce upon the validity of any Act passed by Parliament other than an Act which repeals or purports to repeal or amend the provisions of section one hundred and eight or one hundred and eighteen.[6]

Most trials are conducted by judges without juries.

There is a concurrent set of courts for Africans (except in instances when they are parties of Supreme Court cases) under the direction of magistrates and Bantu Affairs Commissioners. There is also a Bantu Appeals Court which may allow an appeal to the Supreme Court. The South African judiciary has enjoyed something of a reputation for independence, although recently the increasing number of political appointees to the courts, the lack of training and impartiality exhibited by the authorities in the Bantu courts, and the poor quality of most lower courts have diminished its stature.[7]

The political frame of South Africa, then, with its functional separation of power and different political "tracks" for various groups, would seem to allow for political participation on the part of the various cultural, ethnic, and linguistic communities, in spite of the constitutional domination by Europeans. This appearance is deceptive. The existence of a plural society, a variety of interest groups, a half dozen national political parties, and two territorial parties (African), and even the presence of a vibrant opposition press and con-

6 Republic of South Africa, Act No. 32, 1961, Section 59.
7 Leonard M. Thompson, *Politics in the Republic of South Africa* (Boston: Little, Brown and Company, 1966), p. 70.

siderable latitude in interest articulation, should not obscure the fact that the South African political system is controlled by a small number of European decision-makers.

This chapter is not designed to be a description of all aspects of the political history of South Africa: this has already been done.[8] What we shall attempt to do, through the use of the conceptual framework outlined in Chapter I, is to distill the essence of South African political life and to specify those crystals of political reality that are likely to determine the future course of politics in South Africa.

Participation in the Political System

Of far more significance than the elaborate framework of the South African constitution is the fact that politics in South Africa is based on the primacy of an aristocracy of color—a rigid hierarchy of racial castes—with a direct correlation between one's skin color and the efficacy of one's political participation. The principal decision-makers in South Africa are all European and, generally, Afrikaans-speaking. For all intents and purposes, no other groups count politically.

Three broad patterns of political life categorize politics in South Africa. We have already alluded to the first, the politically irrelevant pluralism. In addition, there is a widespread and increasing value-consensus as to the goals of the system among the principal decision-makers, and a discernible narrowing of the political area with a corresponding limitation of participation.

The South African political system could not always be so categorized. There were times in its history when it was thought that the structure of political life might permit some upward mobility for non-Europeans both as individuals and as groups. On occasion it

---

[8] See Gwendolyn M. Carter, *The Politics of Inequality: South Africa since 1948* (New York: Frederick A. Praeger, 1958); Leo Marquard, *The Peoples and Policies of South Africa* 3rd edition (Capetown: Oxford University Press, 1962); Thompson, *op. cit.*; Alex Hepple, *South Africa: A Political and Economic History* (New York: Frederick A. Praeger, 1966); John Cope, *South Africa* (New York: Frederick A. Praeger, 1965). Other works of note are Pierre Van den Berghe, *South Africa, A Study in Conflict* (Berkeley and Los Angeles, Calif.: University of California Press, 1967) and Thomas Karis, "South Africa," in Gwendolyn M. Carter (ed.), *Five African States* (Ithaca, N.Y: Cornell University Press, 1963), pp. 471–616.

could even be imagined that political life would eventually be opened up to all qualified persons, regardless of race. Africans and Coloreds were once on the common rolls in the Cape and Natal, and there were strong African interest groups, such as the African National Congress, dedicated to the political advancement of non-Europeans.[9]

However, these phenomena, never very efficacious, have always been overshadowed by a countervailing push to restrict non-European participation in national politics and to limit the influence of those Europeans bent on a liberalization of the political culture. After the 1909 Act of Union, one sees a gradual shutting-off of access to the decision-making process, a closure of the channels to political authority, a narrowing of the political arena. The South African Act itself was predicated on the notion that the common roll of the Cape (and, to a lesser extent, of Natal) would not be exported to the other provinces.

In 1930 European women were given the vote, but non-European women, regardless of qualification, were excluded. By 1931 qualifications for European voters in the Cape Province had been abolished, while those for the Africans and Coloreds were raised so that the number of non-European voters declined both proportionally and absolutely. In 1936 Africans were taken off the Cape common rolls and given a separate roll by which to elect three Europeans to the House and four to the Senate. In 1945, compulsory registration was introduced for Europeans. In 1946, African representation on local councils was eliminated, the limited franchise for Indians in Natal was repealed, and reregistration for Indians and Coloreds was made mandatory. Not only were non-Europeans deterred from participation, but also, in 1950, the multiracial Communist Party was outlawed, "communism" being broadly defined. During 1956, after years of struggle, the Colored voters were taken off the Cape common roll and placed on a separate roll. The separate roll for Africans was abolished in 1960, and their political life relegated to tribal "homelands." During the early 1960's most important non-European political interest

[9] Although the Common Roll has always been an explosive subject in South Africa, the numbers of non-Europeans involved were always insignificant. In 1935, for example, in Natal, there were 91,726 Europeans, 343 Coloreds, 1 African, and 10 Asians, while on the Cape Roll there were 382,103 Europeans, 21,596 Coloreds, 10,628 Africans, and 1,401 Asians [Elizabeth Landis, "South African Apartheid Legislation II: Extension, Enforcement and Perpetuation," *Yale Law Journal* (January, 1962) Vol. LXXI, No. 3: 466–467.

groups, including the African National Congress and the Pan African Congress, were outlawed. On February 16, 1968, a government commission examining "Improper Political Influence and Political Representation of Various Population Groups" recommended the abolition of Colored representation in Parliament and the prohibition of multiracial parties (such as the Liberal Party). These recommendations were subsequently voted into law.

The leaders of the South African political system, in addition to narrowing the formal political arena, have also drastically curtailed attempts of individuals and groups to move outside the framework. During the 1950's and early 1960's various non-European, multiracial, and European groups attempted to achieve decision-making status through a series of boycotts, stay-at-homes, strikes, and mass protests. Ranging in size from the 200 members of the Congress of Democrats to the 100,000-person African National Congress (and including the South African Colored People's Organization, the South African Indian Congress, the South African Council of Trade Unions, and the banned Communist Party), these groups attempted to protest against the pass laws, which demanded that non-Europeans carry a set of identification papers with them at all times, the Group Areas Act, and the Suppression of Communism Act. On June 26 and 27, 1955, 3000 delegates of these organizations met at Kliptown outside Johannesburg and issued a Freedom Charter which stated:

> We, the people of South Africa, declare for all our country and the world to know:
>
> that South Africa belongs to all who live in it, black and white, and that no Government can justly claim authority unless it is based on the will of all the people;
>
> that our people have been robbed of their birthright to land, liberty and peace by a form of Government founded on injustice and inequality;
>
> that our country will never be prosperous or free until all our people live in brotherhood, enjoying equal rights and opportunities.[10]

Although the participants in the Congress of The People were able to marshal large numbers of persons to march, to turn in passes, and to participate in civil disobedience campaigns, and, although

[10] Thompson, *op. cit.*, p. 177.

the African National Congress (ANC) and its post-1959 offshoot, the Pan African Congress (PAC), mobilized significant sections of the African community, they were not successful in acquiring any decision-making authority. Faced with intensified government harassment, wracked by personal and ideological differences within their leadership, lacking sufficient funds, and hobbled by a lack of organization and fluctuating membership, the movement lost force.[11] Its culmination (or denouement, depending upon one's perspective), occurred on March 21, 1960, at Sharpeville, outside of Vereeniging, when the police opened fire on an orderly crowd of 5000 led by the Pan African Congress. Sixty-nine Africans were killed and 178 wounded.[12]

Using post-Sharpeville marches and riots as a pretext, the government declared a State of Emergency, banned the African National Congress and the Pan African Congress, imprisoned or banned most of the African leadership, and detained some 20,000 persons.[13] Driven underground, denied any formal access to the national political arena, and despairing over the causal efficacy of nonviolence as a political tactic, some non-Europeans and Europeans turned to terroristic activities in an attempt to influence the political process. *Umkonto we Sizwe* (Spear of the Nation) grew out of the ANC and concentrated on the destruction of rail and communication facilities and government buildings, while the *Poqo* (Pure) of the PAC attempted more generalized terror, often against Europeans or progovernment chiefs.

[11] This exciting and frustrating subject is covered in a variety of sources. Edward Feit seems to overestimate the importance of European Communists, but generally presents a dispassionate account of African movements in his *South Africa: The Dynamics of the African National Congress* (London: Oxford University Press, 1962) and *African Opposition in South Africa: The Failure of Passive Resistance* (Stanford, Calif.: The Hoover Institution, 1967). See also Leo Kuper, *Passive Resistance in South Africa* (London: Jonathan Cape, 1956); Edward Roux, *Time Longer than Rope: A History of the Black Man's Struggle for Freedom in South Africa* (Madison, Wisc.: University of Wisconsin Press, 1964); and Mary Benson, *The African Patriots* (London: Faber and Faber, 1963), which cover a wider frame. On the other hand, Govan Mbeki, *The Peasants' Revolt* (Baltimore, Md.: Penguin Books, 1964); James Kantor, *A Healthy Grave* (London: Hamish Hamilton, 1967); and Albert Luthuli, *Let My People Go* (New York: McGraw-Hill Book Company, 1962) concentrate on the 1950's and 1960's.

[12] Hepple, *op. cit.*, 165. For an in-depth analysis with excellent photographic evidence of the event, see Ambrose Reeves, *Shooting at Sharpeville* (Cambridge: Houghton Mifflin Company, 1961).

[13] *Africa Report* (June, 1960): 8.

In South West Africa, the South West Africa People's Organization (SWAPO) likewise undertook a modest policy of selective sabotage. European-led, multiracial organizations, such as the African Resistance Movement, also attempted to use force to influence the decision-making process.

On balance, the thrust for non-European participation in the decision-making process served primarily to legitimize counterterror on the part of the government and to solidify most Europeans behind the existing regime. The government acted swiftly and decisively to counteract these movements. As will be seen in the section on regulative capacity, new laws such as the General Law Amendment Act of 1962 (Sabotage Law), the General Law Amendment Act of May 1963 (No Trial Act), the implementation of the 90- and 180-day detention acts, mass arrests, widespread bannings, and systematic use of force cut deeply into the forces of the counterelites. July 1963, for example, saw the arrest of the principal leadership of the ANC and the Congress Alliance (including Nelson Mandela, Walter Sisulu, Govan Mbeki, and Denis Goldberg) at Rivonia, outside Johannesburg. Subsequent arrests virtually dismantled both *Poqo* and *Umkonto we Sizwe*, as well as other, smaller groups such as the *Yui Chui Chan* Club, the Non-European Unity Movement, and the National Liberation Committee. Potlako Leballo remains acting president of PAC, and Oliver Tambo leads the ANC. Both are in exile.

The demonstrated ability of the central political authority to control the opposition, and the growth of European support for the government prompted by the turmoil of the late 1950's and early 1960's currently hamper any group seeking to alter the status quo. Dissatisfaction, even hatred, is very widespread among the African population, and causes for internal revolt are clearly not lacking. But in the face of the government's exceptionally powerful regulative capability and willingness to utilize whatever force necessary to maintain itself, and hampered by a lack of political organization and leadership, African enthusiasm for revolt is lacking. In essence, an almost totalitarian atomization of the opposition has already taken place. Most associational groups dedicated to the violent overthrow of the government have been decimated and their leadership imprisoned or exiled.

European domination has always been the central belief of most white South Africans. Jan Christian Smuts put it simply:

> There are certain things about which all South Africans
> agree, all parties and all sections, except those who are
> quite mad. The first is that it is a fixed policy to maintain
> white supremacy in South Africa.[14]

White supremacy, whether called segregation, apartheid, or separate
development, is the basic core value upon which most Europeans
agree. Most of the struggle between the two political elites, the
English- and the Afrikaans-speaking communities, has centered around
Afrikaner nationalism, the establishment of a republic, and connections with Great Britain. From 1912 until 1949 South Africa was
generally ruled by a coalition of those favoring ties wi+h Great Britain
and a merger of Afrikaans and British culture. Thi; coalition was
initially headed by Louis Botha and Jan Christian Smuts under the
banner of the South African Party. J. B. Hertzog's Afrikaner Nationalist Party, which provided the opposition from 1912 to 1924,
called for "two streams" for South Africa, British and Afrikaner.
Following labor strikes, bitterness concerning Smuts' and South
Africa's role in World War I, and severe inflation, Hertzog formed a
Pact Government with the small Labor Party, but the coalition
dissolved in 1933 over the question of the gold standard.

In 1933 Smuts and Hertzog joined forces and formed the United
Party which ran South Africa until 1948 with Hertzog as Prime
Minister until 1939. Hertzog finally left the United Party over the
question of South African involvement in World War II, taking
perhaps a third of the party with him. Dr. D. F. Malan and the
"purified" Nationalist Party provided the major opposition until
1948 when he formed a coalition with the Afrikaner Party of N. C.
Havenga (the heir to the Hertzog forces). The coming to power of
the Nationalists, primarily on the issue of *swart gevaar*, or black peril,
represented more than the triumph of an ordinary party: the Nationalist Party, first under Malan (1948–54), then under J. G. Strijdom
(1954–58), Dr. Hendrick Verwoerd (1958–66), and now B. J. Vorster
(1966–present), is the political incarnation of Afrikaner nationalism.
It has, in the eyes of its proponents, struggled long and hard against
domination by British imperialism, faced cultural destruction by the

---

[14] Jan Christian Smuts remains the quintessence of European South Africa.
Here was a man who could support self-determination in the League of Nations
and write the preamble to the United Nations Charter without applying either
one to non-Europeans in South Africa.

English-speaking Europeans, fought against being overwhelmed by African nationalism, and now confronts isolation by the United Nations and the Afro-Asian countries. With each successive election since 1948, a greater and greater percentage of the European electorate has accepted its vision for South Africa and recognized its ability to maintain European control. The Nationalist Party now controls 126 of 170 seats in the House of Assembly, 41 of the 54 seats in the Senate, 4 out of 5 provincial councils, and a majority of the local councils.

It is likely to stay in command. In the first place, it enjoys some mechanical advantages. (1) 60% of the European population is Afrikaans-speaking so that, barring any major shift of Afrikaner votes to the English-oriented United Party, it can count on a majority of the popular vote. (2) Although the House of Assembly is based on proportional representation, delineation commissions must review the district sizes every 5 to 10 years and are empowered to vary the size of the constituencies up to 15%. These commissioners, nominated by the Prime Minister, have tended to make the rural (and since the English-speakers are 97% urbanized, this means, in effect, Afrikaner) constituencies smaller, thus giving the Nationalists 5 to 6 more seats than they would ordinarily have. (3) South West Africa, which is primarily Nationalist in sentiment, is overrepresented in Parliament, its constituencies being one half the size of those in South Africa. (4) The constituencies for the House of Assembly are gerrymandered so that the United Party (UP) strongholds (Durban, Cape Town, Johannesburg, Port Elizabeth) are isolated. The UP wins there by a wide margin and thus wastes total votes, while the Nationalists control the swing, peri-urban districts by including large numbers of rural voters.

In addition to these advantages (which in themselves make it difficult to imagine the Nationalists being defeated in national elections), the Nationalists have the support of many English-speaking persons, and this support has grown markedly since 1961. The decolonizing experience in Africa and Great Britain's apparent willingness to sacrifice the political hegemony of the white settlers to African majority rule have diminished the ties that once bound English-speaking South Africans to Great Britain.

The United Party remains the major party of opposition, heir to some "moderate" Afrikaner and British traditions. Led by Sir D. P.

deVilliers-Graaff since 1956, it controls 39 seats in the House, 11 in the Senate, and the Provincial Council in Natal, and in the elections of March 1966 polled some 480,000 votes. It opposes, as unnecessary, "petty" apartheid and suggests a "race federation" rather than separate development, but it is firmly committed to a policy of segregation and during the last election ran on a platform of "white supremacy at all costs." Style, not goals, distinguishes it from the National Party; and, since it cannot compete with the National Party in terms of organization, population support, or ideology, many of its earlier supporters are content to vote National. Taken together, the support among Europeans for the National and United Parties represents a clear mandate for policies of European domination and indicates a basic value-consensus.

The Progressive Party, headed by Dr. Jan Steytler and represented by Mrs. Helen Suzman in the House of Assembly, does offer an alternative to the policies of the Nationalists and the United Party. It stands for a multiracial society and a qualified franchise, and it opposes most aspects of the present apartheid policy. Formed in 1959 by eleven United Party members of Parliament and the beneficiary of substantial financial support from Sir Harry Oppenheimer, its base of support has steadily diminished and few South Africans (32,000 in March 1966) accept either its goals or its means. It is indeed a reflection on the political ethos of white South Africa that a party advocating qualified franchise should be regarded as revolutionary rather than simply quaintly conservative.

The Liberal Party, which originated in 1953 and had expressed an acceptance of eventual African majority rule through a one-man, one-vote formula, officially disbanded in 1968 under the terms of the Prohibition of Political Interference Bill. A majority of its 3000 members were African.

The parties of the far right, the Republican Party and Conservative Nationalists, enjoy only a bit more support—which reinforces the basic premise that the majority of Europeans support the present goals of the regime. Both are heirs to a radical strain in Afrikaner politics, extending far back into history, that erupted as rebellion during World War I and reappeared in the phenomena of the *Ossewa Brandwag* and New Order Party of the World War II era, whose pro-Nazi leaders accused Dr. Malan of the Nationalists of being "liberal." In much the same fashion Professor C. F. van der Merwe, head of the Republican Party, labelled Verwoerd an "ultra-liberal" during 1966. Both the Republicans and the Conservative Nationalists contend that the present government has done too much for the non-Europeans, particularly the Africans. Since most South Africans find this difficult to believe, less than 1% of the electorate supported the parties in the last election.

Given the narrowness of the political arena, the suppression of opposition groups, the levels of value-consensus, and the demographic, cultural, and mechanical advantages of the Nationalists it seems extremely unlikely that it will be displaced by parliamentary means, and its impressive capabilities would seem to rule out its violent overthrow. In short, the National Party represents a political system within a system. It is certainly not a "national" party in the accepted meaning of the term, although it probably speaks for a substantial majority of the Europeans in South Africa. Its organization reflects the two basic strands of Afrikaner political life. It is federally organized but maintains a tight, well-disciplined decision-making apparatus and demands complete loyalty from its members. Within its parliamentary caucus, and more specifically, within the party directorate and the Cabinet, all crucial decisions on national policy are made. Although the national leadership is linked to the provincial branches by cross membership in the executive committee of the provincial branches, there is a good deal of local autonomy. One hesitates to apply the term "democratic" to such a narrow frame of internal decision making, but its traditions are strongly egalitarian and extend back to the frontier ethos of the Voortrekkers and the radical democracy of their Volksraads or legislative assemblies. These traditions do not, of course apply to non-Afrikaners, and there is a firm demand for party discipline and solidarity once decisions have been made.

The National Party, although the most important personification of Afrikaner nationalism, is not the only one, and a variety of Afrikaner interest groups act as mutually reinforcing agents of political socialization. There are various youth groups—the *Voortrekkers* (Boy Scouts), the *Nasionale Jeugbond* (Youth League), and the *Afrikaanse Studentebond* (university students). The political world-view of the Afrikaner people is also reinforced by the major Dutch Reform Churches (the *Gefedereerde Nederduitse Gereformeerde Kerk*, the

Gereformeerde Kerk van Afrika, the *Nederduits Hervormde Kerk*),
and such voluntary associations as the *Federasie van Afrikaanse Kul-
tuurvereniginge* (cultural societies) and the *Reddingsdaadbond* (savings groups). In fact, the whole notion of Afrikaner communal
solidarity and National Party support is aided and abetted by a great
variety of economic, social, and educational institutions.[15] The inter-
locking membership of these various groups and the control. of the
communications media used by most Afrikaners, including the South
African Bureau for Racial Affairs, give the system a good deal of internal cohesion. Nationalist leaders are influential members of the
Die Afrikaanse Pers and *Die Nasionale Pers* which publish the six
Afrikaans dailies.

There is also the Broederbond.[16] Founded after World War I to
advance Afrikaner interests in all sectors of public life, it remained a
secret and powerful organization, almost a government in exile during
the regimes of Botha, Hertzog, and Smuts. It served as a powerful
socializing agent to promote Afrikaner solidarity. Its present status
is unclear, but it is thought to have had a major role in the selection
of the present Prime Minister, B. J. Vorster, after the assassination
of Prime Minister Verwoerd on September 4, 1966. Additional Afrikaners control the military, the national police, and the various
bureaucracies which give the Nationalists a good deal of leverage
against would-be defectors as well as a tremendous source of patronage.

[15] S. Trapido, "Political Institutions and Afrikaner Social Structures in the
Republic of South Africa," *American Political Science Review* (March, 1963)
Vol. LVII, No. 1: 75–87. Recently a good deal has been written about the
divergence between the *verligte* ("enlightened") and *verkrampe* ("narrow")
wings of the National Party. See for example Patrick O'Meara, "Tensions in the
Nationalist Party," *Africa Report* (February, 1969): 24, 41–45. This bifurcation
should not be exaggerated for their differences are of degree rather than kind and
in no way reflect substantial disagreement over the core values of European
supremacy and Afrikaner hegemony, although it seems likely that the more extreme of the *verkrampe* faction may break off to form another splinter party of
the right.

[16] Cope, *op. cit.*, p. 124. The role of the Broederbond is still in question.
Carter provides a good deal of insight into its history and internal dynamics
during the 1950's (Carter, *op. cit.*, pp. 221–236), but opinions on its present
size and importance clearly differ. Edward Munger, *Afrikaner and African Nationalism* (London: Oxford University Press, 1967), says it is "moribund," p. 65,
but Thompson estimates its present strength at 3–5,000, *op. cit.*, p. 134.

In short, from the point of view of the average Afrikaner, the National Party is a reflection of his cultural, economic, social, and political values. Its methods are his methods, its goals, his goals. It has proven itself capable of preserving white dominance and of keeping anti-Afrikaner groups of all ethnic communities in check. Its regime represents the final triumph of Afrikaner nationalism over a hostile world.

The dominance of the Afrikaner form of nationalism and the National Party's seemingly unassailable political position should not obscure the fact that there is opposition to both. There are some weak African working associations, a few religious opponents (especially from the Anglican, Methodist, and Catholic Churches), and even an occasional predicant from one of the Dutch Reformed churches. There are the Black Sash, the Institute of Race Relations, the Christian Institute, and the diverse National Union of South African Students. Tribal parties exist in the Transkei and the English-language press is reasonably free. It is important to remember that these exist, but one should not overestimate either their general influence or their capacity to alter political events. South African society is not yet entirely totalitarian, but the circle of safety for political activity seems to grow smaller every year.

Given all these factors, how can we classify the decision-making process in South Africa? Carter refers to the "politics of inequality." [17] Thompson feels that it is a "caste system" [18] while others have termed it a police state or a Fascist system.[19] van den Berghe has stated that ". . . the South African brand of tyranny is that of an obsolete, nineteenth century colonial state." [20] And he is most persuasive in his argument that South Africa cannot be characterized as a true Fascist system, lacking as it does a single mobilizing party, significant levels of social mobility, a charismatic leader, and a substantial decision-making role for the military elite.[21] At the same time, there remain similarities between South Africa and the model of syncretic politics outlined by A. F. K. Organski—at least in the narrower sense of the

[17] Carter, *op. cit.*, title.

[18] Thompson, *op. cit.*, 165.

[19] Brian Bunting, *Rise of the South African Reich* (Baltimore, Md.: Penguin Books, 1964).

[20] Pierre L. van den Berghe, *South Africa, A Study in Conflict* (Berkeley and Los Angeles, Calif.: University of California Press, 1967), p. 96.

[21] van den Berghe, *op. cit.*, pp. 78–86.

kinds of elites who have decision-making authority in the South African context.[22]

Organski feels that the syncretic pattern is an alliance between the industrial and agricultural elite to stave off the political aspirations of the lower classes and to mitigate the turmoil caused by modernization. Modernization and industrialization encourage rural-to-city migration, destroy the traditional value system which has kept the lower classes in their place for centuries, and ultimately cause the political eclipse of the agrarian elite. In the face of lower-class revolution, both elites recognize the need to resolve their differencs (which are considerable) in order to preserve the status quo.

Clearly race is a critical variable in South Africa, one which distinguishes it from the Organski pattern, but the type of socio-economic alliance outlined above is evident. Now that Afrikaner nationalism has triumphed, it is possible to see the political system of South Africa as a firm alliance between these two elites: the rural, agriculturally oriented Afrikaners and the urbanized, industrialized elite of British origin. Although the European population is 84% urbanized, the rural orientation of the Afrikaner community, in terms of both mythology and ideology, should not be overlooked, for many continue to view the platteland as home. Of the twenty-one men in the present cabinet, all but two are Afrikaans-speakers, all but three are from rural backgrounds, and ten are still farmers and ranchers; the present State President, Jacobus Fouche, was formerly Minister of Agricultural Technical Services and Water.[23] Since 1961, moreover, there have been discernible signs of a *toenadering* or "getting together." The Afrikaners have given up their earlier cry for nationalization of industry. Prime Minister Verwoerd appointed two English-speaking cabinet members, A. E. Trollip of Labor and Immigration and F. W. Waring of Information and Tourism, and the

---

[22] A. F. K. Organski, *The Stages of Political Development* (New York: Alfred A. Knopf, 1965), pp. 122–158.

[23] Thompson (*op. cit.*, pp. 116–120) provides a striking portrait of the cabinet. In September, 1966, P. C. Pelser became Minister of Justice when B. J. Vorster became Prime Minister, and on January 9, 1967, Nicholas Diederick became Minister of Finance while Jan Haak switched from Planning and Mines to Economic Affairs and Dr. Carel de Wet became Minister of Mines. Thompson's observations, however, remain incisive. It is true, of course, that a majority of Afrikaans—speakers are themselves urbanized, but their symbolic referents remain overwhelmingly rural.

Nationalist government now consults regularly with major industrialists. Problems of labor recruitment and regulations concerning mining and farm subsidies have all been worked out. In exchange, the industrial elite have insured a continuous inflow of the foreign investment so important to the economic development of South Africa —investment which recently approached $4.8 billion, including $2.8 billion from Great Britain. And the English-speakers, who once shunned Afrikaners, now openly recruit them for positions on company boards.

However, the future of the South African system appears to be substantially different from that of the syncretic systems. First, Organski feels that the agricultural elite are eventually overwhelmed by the industrial elite and that, by the time the bargain is struck, they have already lost the struggle. This is clearly not the case in South Africa where the rurally oriented Afrikaners appear to be solidifying their political control against all opponents and enlarging their share of the industrial sector. Second, in his analysis of Spain, Italy, and Argentina, Organski remained convinced that syncretic systems are essentially short-lived, because the agricultural and industrial elites cannot, over time, prevent the lower classes from moving, first as individuals, then as groups, into the arena of political power. South Africa does not appear to fit this pattern, because there is clearly more agreement among the decision-making elites in South Africa that this must be prevented than there was in the other cases, and, more importantly, because the line between the elites and the lower classes, between the political power and political serfdom, is far more easily demarcated along racial lines. Black men, even brown men, simply do not cross the political lines or enter the decision-making realm in South Africa. Given the basic unity of the political elite, their regulatory and extractive capabilities, and their determination to maintain their own position regardless of cost, it seems likely that South Africa will offer a substantial amendment to the longevity of the syncretic model.

Capabilities Analysis

South Africa offers an excellent example of the importance of examining in detail the various capabilities of a political system. Only through such an examination is it possible to explain the ease with which the small, ethnocentric, racial minority of South Africa is able to maintain its privileged position.

REGULATIVE CAPABILITY

The regulative capability of the South African political system is impressive. Whether one looks at the legal structure and its enforcement, information regulation, or political and economic controls, one is led to the conclusion that the central political authority is extremely powerful.

The legal framework of apartheid is both extensive and complicated.[24] It should be remembered that racial segregation, European domination, and strict law enforcement did not originate with the coming to power of the Nationalists in 1948. Their roots run deeply throughout the history of southern Africa, and the post-1948 laws often merely legalized existing custom. "Native reserves" were set up in the 1840's, codified and expanded in the Native Land Act of 1913 and in the Native Trust and Land Act of 1936. Acts and regulations regarding urban migration and political activities for non-Europeans existed prior to World War II.

Systematic application of apartheid, however, awaited the Population Registration Act of 1950 and the complete classification of all persons in South Africa in a National Register on the basis of appearance, general acceptance, and repute or association. Thus, a European or white is "a person who in appearance obviously is, or who is generally accepted as, a white person, but does not include a person who, although in appearance obviously a white person, is generally accepted as a coloured person." A Bantu or native is "a person who in fact is, or is generally accepted as, a member of any aboriginal race or tribe in Africa," while a colored is "a person who is not a white person or a native." In 1951 a separate category was created for Asians. Because of the ascriptive nature of South African society, the penalties attached to the non-European classification, and the mixed character of most groups, the process of population registration turned out to be difficult and often heart-breaking.

Following the division of South Africa into "racial" groups and the

[24] Elizabeth Landis, "South African Apartheid Legislation I: Fundamental Structure," *The Yale Law Journal* (November, 1961) Vol. LXXI, No. 1: 1–52 and "South African Apartheid Legislation II: Extension, Enforcement and Perpetuation," *The Yale Law Journal* (January, 1961) Vol. LXXI, No. 3: 437–500.

setting-up of group areas, the process of regulation was further enhanced by the euphemistically entitled Natives (Abolition of Passes
and Coordination of Documents) Act of 1952, which actually instituted a new process of internal control. All African males over age
16 now had to carry reference books which included identity cards,
employment information, proof of ethnic origin, photographs, population registration number, tax information, and a permit to be in
European areas. In January 1956, the reference book system was extended to African women, and by August 1, 1966, all South Africans
over age 16 were required to carry identification cards. While Europeans are seldom asked to produce their cards, unless they are
suspected of some crime (usually "political"), the existence of passes
provides a convenient means for controlling political and economic
activity and enables the police to stop anyone at anytime. Due to the
magnitude of the problems of population control, the South African
authorities have been unable to totally eliminate "improper" African
presence in European areas. But with nearly 400,000 arrests yearly
since 1955 and by dramatically increasing their regulation of non-
European movement, the authorities have checked the precipitous
rush of African rural-to-city migration which threatened to inundate
the white population centers (even though that migration continues).

The police have gained considerable power since World War II,
and their enforcement of existing laws has taken on new dimensions.
The Public Safety Act of 1953 increased the ease with which police
could be granted emergency powers. By the Criminal Procedure and
Evidence Amendment Act (1955) police gained the right the dispense
with search warrants if their procurement would result in the escape
of the suspect. By far the most significant regulatory statutes are those
contained in the General Law Amendment Acts of 1962, 1963, and
1964. Often referred to as the "Sabotage" and "No-Trial" Acts, they
enable the government to declare a state of emergency almost at will,
provide for arrest without a warrant, indefinite detention without
charge (the acts call for 90 and 180 day detention, but detainees are
simply redetained at the end of the period), and imprisonment without trial for individuals who have served a jail sentence for political
crimes. Most importantly, they drastically expanded the definition of
"sabotage." A person is guilty of sabotage:

> if he commits any wrongful and wilful act, whereby he
> obstructs, injures, tampers with or destroys (a) the health

or safety of the public; the maintenance of law and order; (b) the supply of water, light, power, fuel or foodstuffs; sanitary, medical or fire extinguishing services; postal, telephone, telegraph or radio services; or the free movement of traffic; (c) any property; or if he attempts to commit such offence, or conspires with or encourages any other person to do so; or, if in contravention of any law, he possesses any explosives, firearms or weapon, or enters or is upon any land or building.[25]

Sabotage has been further categorized as any attempt to encourage social or political change and provides for a variety of punishments ranging from banishment and banning, house-arrest, confiscation of property, and imprisonment to capital punishment.

Taken together with the provisions of the Suppression of Communism Act and Riotous Assembly Act, the General Law Amendment Acts give the Minister of Justice formidable latitude in controlling individuals and groups bent on any substantial alteration of the status quo. Persons suspected of such desires may be deported, confined to particular locations, placed under house-arrest without charge, forbidden to appear at public gatherings, or denied a public forum for their views. Over 750 are currently banned in South Africa.[26] Mrs. Helen Joseph, the first European to be so punished, is on her 10th year of house-arrest. Albert Luthuli, the Nobel Prize winner and leader of the ANC, was arrested in 1956, never brought to trial, and restricted from 1959 until his death in 1967. Added to the considerable numbers of banned persons are those arrested and jailed for "political" crimes. In an interview with a seemingly sympathetic reporter, Prime Minister Vorster admitted to the incarceration of 1439 persons, including 24 Europeans, but the figure is probably far larger.[27]

[25] Hepple, *op. cit.*, 168. It seems likely that even more Draconian elements will be added to the South African security apparatus in the future as the government sees a need for them.

[26] Muriel Horrell, *A Survey of Race Relations in South Africa* (Johannesburg: South African Institute of Race Relations, 1967).

[27] Alan Drury, *A Very Strange Society* (New York: Trident Press, 1968), p. 416. It is illuminating, for example, that Major General R. J. van den Berghe, Inspector-General of Police, stated that in 1965 alone 787 persons were convicted of sabotage and treason, 44 for communist activities, 1,244 for supporting the PAC and 805, the ANC, *Africa Report* (October, 1966), 46. Also, according to a statement given in *The House of Assembly Debates,* January 28, 1966, cols. 261–2, the number of prisoners doubled from 1956 to 1965.

We have mentioned but a few of the most prominent laws that give the South African political system wide latitude in insuring conformity of behavior and in regulating most political activities of its citizens. Of equal significance is the ability of the internal security forces to enforce those laws. Both the police and the military have extensive internal capabilities. Since 1947, when the South African Special Branch was established to combat "subversive" organizations, the police force has been substantially improved, in terms of training, quality of manpower, and numbers. The police in South Africa now number 29,600 (including nearly 15,200 Africans who serve without firearms), and are well equipped for most paramilitary activities with helicopters, armored cars, and heavy weaponry.[28] There are also 6000 reservists. As will be seen in the section on goals, the South African police have a tradition of determination and the proven international capability to capture refugees in Swaziland, Lesotho, and Botswana. South African police and military personnel are currently serving in Rhodesia and Mozambique. It should also be pointed out that the South African police have an extensive informer network among non-Europeans, and this has severely hampered growth of antigovernment organizations.

The army, too, has been expanded and upgraded with a shift in emphasis from international (dating from World War I and II) to internal concerns. From 2,000 men in 1960 it has grown to a sizable establishment with 26,500 men on active duty, including 5,500 regulars, the rest trainees, and a reserve force of 50,000. In addition, there are 210 part-time, highly mobile, commando units, involving 51,500 men with 250 light aircraft in support. The air force (4000 men) and the navy (3500) add mobility and firepower. With the exception of some service and labor units, the armed forces are entirely European.

Since the United States (1963) and Great Britain (1964) instituted arms embargoes, South Africa has developed self-sufficiency in the manufacture of small arms and ammunition and has turned to France

---

[28] For these and other figures on the South African Defense Establishment, see David Wood, *The Armed Forces of the New States*, Adelphi Papers No. 27 (London Institute of Strategic Studies, 1966) and Neville Brown and W. F. Gutteridge, *The African Military Balance*, Adelphi Papers No. 12 (London: Institute of Strategic Studies, 1964). For a detailed and depressing assessment of South Africa's ability to crush internal unrest, see J. E. Spence and Elizabeth Thomas, *South Africa's Defense*, Security Studies Paper No. 8 (Los Angeles, Calif.: University of California Press, 1966).

for extensive hardware, including jet fighter-bombers, submarines, helicopters, and a countrywide radar net. Since the topography and semiarid climate are not conducive to guerrilla movements and since residential segregation has been planned on the basis of military containment, it seems likely that the internal security forces of South Africa will have the capacity for control in the foreseeable future. There is some evidence, for example, to suggest that, despite the legal sanctions for the death penalty, it is seldom used, and one could argue that this reflects the relative security of the regime.[29] Perhaps most importantly for a continued, strong regulative capability, the South African ruling elite exhibits the will to use the means at their disposal to maintain their position.

The control of information is also an important aspect of the regulative capacity of a political system and may be examined under two overlapping headings, positive and negative dissemination.

There are 1.1 million radio sets in South Africa, and the South African government controls the South African Broadcasting Company and its Radio South Africa, Radio Bantu, and Springbok Radio (the commercial station). It broadcasts in English and Afrikaans, as well as in Zulu, South Sotho, Tswana, Xhosa, and Venda-Tsonga. There is also a South African Press Association which draws upon Agence France Press, *Deutsche Press*, Associated Press, and United Press International as well as Reuters, but it edits a good deal of the material. Both organizations give full play to unpleasant developments in the rest of Africa, race relations in the United States, and the threat of the black African states to the north.[30] Prominent members of the National Party are on the controlling boards of these corporations as well as those of the influential Afrikaans dailies, such as *Die Burger, Die Transvaler*, and *Die Vaderland*. B. J. Vorster, for example, is on the board of directors of two of the three Afrikaans newspaper concerns. These outlets, coupled with the extensive publications of the Department of Information, insure that the government's position on most matters is well known and championed. There are, of course,

[29] Munger, *op. cit.*, p. 11.

[30] The pseudoenvironment of myth and stereotype and the political implications resulting from such a lack of information are discussed at some length in C. P. Potholm, "South Africa and the Future: Illusion and Necessity," *Africa Today* (October, 1967) Vol. XIV, No. 5: 18–23, and Allistair Sparks, "South Africa: A View from Within," *Africa Report* (March, 1967), 40–45.

some differences within the Afrikaner press. *Die Burger*, for example, is generally less wedded to the government's position than the other two.

Much of the propaganda rests on the rather fragile notion that black Africa stands poised north of the Zambezi ever ready to overwhelm the sturdy white encampments to the south. This is the Africa of violence, hatred, anarchy, and reverse racialism. It is also, of course, an Africa that exists primarily in the minds of the whites, an Africa taken out of context, a fragmentary and half-real world, tailored to suit the demands of the moment, a world view in which the African past replaces the future and the present in terms of causal efficacy.

The Congo "savagery" and Mau Mau "terror" are remembered, expanded, and vocalized, although the actual casualty figures in both of these instances are seldom known and never mentioned. The fact that tens of thousands of Africans were killed in these uprisings, and in their suppression, is forgotten. What is remembered is the manner in which a particular white settler or missionary was killed or how much cruelty the Africans showed toward livestock. Because these incidents and pseudo-incidents reinforce justification for apartheid they are allowed to overshadow the peaceful transition to statehood of the former French colonies, the general acceptance of black government by the whites who remained after independence all over Africa, and the emergence of moderate racial elements in most of the African nations.

Very little information on how the Africa of 1969 operates ever filters into the thought patterns of the white South African. To a certain extent, the Nationalist government has been very clever in portraying the options open to the white community in very harsh terms: *baasskap* or chaos. At the same time, the government could not have been so enormously successful in perpetuating this thesis if it had not struck a resonant chord in most of the white community. Few white South Africans care to know that the white settler population has greatly expanded in the Ivory Coast since independence, or that the remaining whites in Kenya were satisfied enough with their lot in multiracial Kenya to send a delegation to Rhodesia prior to the Unilateral Declaration of Independence (UDI) to plead against it. These facts are not important to most South Africans—in fact, they are disregarded. What is important, even crucial, is the publication of incidents that seem to justify the continuance of apartheid.

It is a curious fact that most white South Africans who pride them-selves on being such perspicacious realists where the African is con-cerned, should so cavalierly ignore any empirical evidence from the north.

On the negative side, the government created a Publications Con-trol Board in 1963 under the Publication and Entertainment Act of 1963 to oversee the various provisions of the Suppression of Com-munism Act, the Public Safety Act, the Criminal Law Amendment Act, and the Extension of University Education Act which pertain to publications. It currently consists of eleven men, a majority of whom are Afrikaners, who appraise books and films on both moral and political grounds. Their primary concern is with foreign works, since domestic publishers are likely to avoid publishing anything suspect. Perhaps 100 foreign works are banned a year. With films, morality is often of greater concern than politics. In addition, the government has refused to establish a television network. Although the reasons given are inflation and/or multiracial programs, it seems more likely to be due to the fact that television would cut into the Afrikaans newspapers, particularly in the area of advertising. Since most foreign features would be in English, the cost of creating parallel Afrikaner programs would be exorbitant. Fear of English cultural domination is probably also a factor. The government is increasing its already sophisticated capability to jam foreign broadcasting and is encourag-ing the use of FM rather than AM radios, although at the present time little attempt is made to interfere with foreign programs.

The English press is another matter. It remains reasonably free, although the major concerns (such as the Argus Printing and Publish-ing Company and the South African Associated Newspaper Group) do engage in extensive self-censorship or "voluntary censorship." Most of the eleven English dailies formerly published statements by such groups as the ANC and PAC and even took ads for proposed meetings and strikes, but this is no longer done. In addition, the Government has imposed indirect censorship by forbidding the publication of statements by banned persons and by requiring a $30,000 deposit to be forfeited by papers that are banned under the Suppression of Communism Act. If these means do not suffice, the government takes more decisive action. During June and July of 1965, for example, the *Rand Daily Mail* and the *Sunday Times* published a series of articles highly critical of prison conditions. Police raided the editorial offices on numerous occasions, jailed the informants, and took successful legal action against the editors. Newspapers and periodicals (such as *Drum, Post,* and *World*) intended for African, Indian, and Colored audiences, are also closely watched and subject to harassment.

Thus, although the government has not fully utilized its massive regulatory power in the case of the English-language press, the threat of its power has curbed the freedom of the press. While the government does not currently enjoy a communications monopoly, the trends in that direction are discernible.

In terms of the economy, the political system of South Africa exhibits a strong regulative capacity. Europeans outnumber non-Europeans in organized labor three to one, and African labor unions are not recognized.[31] Job reservation for Europeans dates back to the early part of the twentieth century and is very much in existence today. The Promotion of Industrial Conciliation Act of 1956 and the Native Labour (Settlement of Disputes) Act of 1953 and (amended in) 1955 make strikes or other collective action by Africans illegal and subject to criminal penalties and warn against admitting Africans as members of any union. These acts set up "optional" work committees in various industries and provide for regional committees and a Central Bantu Labor Board whose membership is all European. Thus, non-European participation in economic decision making approximates their position in political decision making, for they are forced to accept the agreements made "on their behalf" by the European unions. These restrictions, coupled with the threat of being "endorsed out" of European areas and sent back to the tribal reserves (where employment possibilities are meager at best) do much to enervate any agitation for better pay, improved working conditions, or some decision-making authority.

EXTRACTIVE CAPABILITY

Much of South Africa's ability to pursue her major internal and external goals is directly related to her considerable national wealth. South Africa is the most highly developed, industrialized nation in Africa. It maintains a balanced economy with an

---

[31] Republic of South Africa, *State of South Africa: Economic, Financial and Statistical Year Book for the Republic of South Africa 1966* (Johannesburg: DaGama Publication, 1967), p. 268.

extensive physical infrastructure and has ample capital for investment.[32] Only in the area of human resources are there indications of
diminished capability and this lack is perhaps more relative than
absolute.

South Africa's agricultural base, however, is not impressive. One-
half of its total area is near-desert, and 86% of it is semiarid. A mere
6% is under cultivation, and that portion is characterized by poor
soil (a persistent lack of phosphates) and low yields. Soil erosion and
a lack of dependable rainfall likewise contribute to low yields:

> Agriculture in South Africa is poor and precarious. Much
> of it is beyond the reach of modern science and technical
> progress. The expenditure and effort required to overcome
> many of its handicaps are too great to be profitable. Indeed,
> South Africa is not an agricultural country. It has no nat-
> ural advantages which, by the help of science and organi-
> zation, could win for its agricultural products a truly
> commanding position in the markets of the world.[33]

Irrigation, extensive use of fertilizer, and the economies of scale have
altered conditions somewhat, and South Africa is now self-sufficient
in corn, wheat, sugar, citrus fruits, potatoes, and tobacco, and a major
exporter of wool, wine, and cattle products.

But it is clearly mineral wealth that gives South Africa a strong
economy. It has vast, untapped reserves as well as booming, current
production. Fifty million tons of coal, for example, were produced in
1964, while there remain 75 billion tons in reserve. In the same year,
South Africa produced over a million tons of iron (reserves of 130
million tons), 1 million tons of manganese (reserves of 1 billion tons),
800,000 tons of chrome, 200,000 tons of asbestos, 64,000 tons of
copper, and 3,000 tons of uranium, as well as smaller amounts of tin,
nickel, and lead.[34]

[32] W. H. Hutt, *The Economics of the Color Bar* (London: Andre Deutsch,
1964); D. Hobart Houghton, *The South African Economy* (London: Oxford
University Press, 1964); H. I. Andrews *et al.* (eds.), *South Africa in the Sixties*
(Cape Town: South African Foundation, 1965); William Hance, *The Geography
of Modern Africa* (New York: Columbia University Press, 1964), pp. 515–582;
and Ralph Horwitz, *The Political Economy of South Africa* (New York: Frederick A. Praeger, 1967).

[33] deKiewiet, *op. cit.*, p. 259.

[34] Republic of South Africa, *Year Book 1966*, p. 114ff., and *International
Financial Statistics* (November, 1968) Vol. XXI, No. 11: 274–275.

The heart of the South African economy is gold. In 1965, $1.1 billion was produced, and this amounted to nearly 10% of the South African gross national product. As deKiewiet has remarked:

> Here was an industry which feared neither locusts nor cattle diseases, neither drought nor summer floods. Its product always commanded a ready sale in the financial centres of the world. . . . The number of fine ounces won, the expenditures in wages and salaries, foodstuffs and stores, taxes and repairs moved between exceptionally narrow limits. Like a great flywheel, the mining industry gave stability to a country that otherwise would have been singularly sensitive to movements in world economy.[35]

Additionally, it is gold that has, over the years, attracted foreign investment in large enough amounts to develop a physical infrastructure, stimulate subsidiary manufacturing, and provide for a favorable balance of trade. At the present time there is $4.8 billion worth of foreign investment in South Africa including $2.8 billion from Great Britain, $600 million from the United States, and smaller, but rapidly increasing, amounts from France (nearly $300 million), Japan, Switzerland, and Belgium.

This capital, initially attracted by the gold and what has characteristically been a stable economy, has enabled South Africa to develop an extensive infrastructure including 234,000 miles of roads, 15,000 miles of rails, a hydroelectric capacity of 20 billion units of electricity yearly, and first-rate port facilities at Cape Town, Durban, Port Elizabeth, and East London.[36]

Manufacturing, too, has grown precipitously until it now ranks as the major factor in the economy. There are subsidiary plants from major American and British firms which earn a return of approximately 20% a year. The South African government has aided investment by allowing for a free-market system in some sectors while insuring control by substantial investment and participation in the commanding heights of the economy: railroad, airline, fuel, fertilizer, telecommunications, hydroelectric, and iron and steel industries. The

---

[35] deKiewiet, *op. cit.*, p. 156.
[36] Republic of South Africa, *Year Book 1966*, pp. 205 and 216.

political system of South Africa, thus, rests upon a strong, balanced economy, with an impressive gross national product of $11.2 billion (30% of Africa's total) spread out among agriculture (9%), mining (13%), manufacturing (28%), and commerce (13%), and distinguished by a growth rate of over 5% a year.

The national wealth of South Africa, as will be demonstrated, is distributed unevenly and inequitably, but it should be remembered that enough of it seeps down to the average non-European worker that 1 million non-South African migrant workers are present yearly in the republic. On balance, the extractive capability is strong and powerful, and reasonably secure. It gives the present regime wide latitude in the area of rewards, pays the costs of internal security, and together with South Africa's strategic position astride the world's trade routes, gives it a good deal of leverage in the international community.

Not that the South African extractive capacity is without flaws. It is estimated that the gold reserves in the republic may run out in 50 years or less.[37] South Africa lacks indigenous oil deposits and for a nation which uses over 700 million gallons of oil per year, this is a major weakness. Or was. Since the early 1960's, South Africa has taken steps to reduce her reliance on sources that could be eliminated through boycotts and sanctions. First, she has begun a program to extract oil from coal, an expensive process, but one which already yields 80 million gallons a year. Second, the South African government has established five oil refineries and a series of storage facilities for a year's supply of oil, and these are to be expanded to hold a 2 year supply. Finally, the government has obtained, with French aid, its own fleet of oil tankers and crude oil concessions in Iran.

South Africa does share with many other African countries the difficulties stemming from the lack of a national language. Already bilingual, South African insistence on African education being conducted in the African languages is clearly a wasteful process, as is her reliance on migrant labor for the mines and the corresponding need for Fanakalo, a lingua franca for these temporary workers.

More serious is the waste of human resources. Because three-quarters of the population is poorly nourished, inadequately educated, and

[37] Hance, op. cit., p. 524.

denied social, economic, or political advancement beyond certain rudimentary levels, there is an enormous waste of talent.[38] Just as it is impossible to compute the human suffering caused by apartheid, so it is extremely difficult to even estimate the loss of talent, time, and treasure, both in terms of maintaining apartheid and in terms of its effects. Certainly job reservation, a lack of educational opportunity, and the ascriptive nature of placement in the economic sphere detract from the maximum utilization of the population. In many ways, of course, this is the supreme irony and tragedy of South Africa. The land is rich enough, the population dynamic enough, and the industrial base already extensive enough to support the entire population at a level that would warrant the envy of most of the world. That such a level of attainment has not already been achieved seems less the fault of economics, ethnicity, or culture, than that of an inequitable and pernicious political system and its concomitant atrophied social system.

DISTRIBUTIVE CAPACITY

In analyzing the South African distributive capability, the frame of reference of southern Africa must be taken into account. Rewards in South Africa, both quantitatively and qualitatively, are distributed largely on the basis of race. Lower wages, smaller and fewer good pieces of land, inferior education, and far less status are generally disbursed to non-Europeans than to Europeans. It should be borne in mind, however, that by comparison to the surrounding areas of southern Africa—the former High Commission Territories of Swaziland, Lesotho, and Botswana, Mozambique, Malawi, Rhodesia, and Madagascar—the Africans, Indians, and Coloreds in South Africa are generally better off, in every category, save those of status and land. This explains in part why there are more than 1 million "foreign" Africans in South Africa at the present time, and why keeping Africans out of South Africa is probably a more pressing concern than restraining those who wish to flee.

As has been indicated, there are strands of economic interdepen-

---

[38] United Nations Economic Commission for Africa, *Economic and Social Consequences of Racial Discriminatory Practices* (New York: United Nations Publication, 1963); and United Nations Economic, Social, and Cultural Organization, *Apartheid: Its Effects on Education, Science, Culture and Information* (Paris: UNESCO Publications, 1967).

dence which link all of South Africa's population groups together (Africans, for example, provide a majority of the personnel in each industry). Allocation of rewards, however, is not one of them. The 1966 per capita income figures tell the story: Europeans $3651, Coloreds $605, and Africans $220.[39] Even if one adds to the African income the cheap housing and more or less free medical care available to most urban Africans, wage differentials, even in comparable positions, remain five or six to one or even higher. European domination of the skilled professions and control of managerial positions remain secure through the provisions of the Industrial Conciliation Act of 1956, the Wage Act of 1957, and the Amendment Act of 1959. It is true that in some areas, particularly in the Cape Province, jobs reserved for Europeans are being filled by non-Europeans, particularly Coloreds. Some have argued that the booming economy is causing a breakdown of the color bar and, hence, aiding integration. In point of fact, it simply means that there are not enough Europeans to fill the positions. Should Europeans object to non-European participation in certain jobs, as they have in the mining industry, the process is readily reversed.

Still, even with an inequitable distribution of wealth, non-Europeans have at least a billion dollars of purchasing power a year and 100,000 of the 1 million motor vehicles registered in South Africa are owned by non-Europeans (this represents a higher percentage of privately owned cars than exists in the Soviet Union).[40] A higher standard of living and a good deal of consumer buying power is not universal, however. Because of inflation and the increased cost of commuting to work, 68% of African families in Johannesburg fall short of minimum living standards despite a 14% increase in wages in the last 5 years.[41] Irrespective of why the material lot of the non-European has been improved or even that his medical and economic status has improved, a crucial question remains. At what point does a class, a people, or an ethnic group cease to accept a few material benefits in place of respect, health in place of political prominence, safety in place of dignity?

From the European point of view, however, the distributive capability of the system is first rate. Their per capita income is among

[39] Cope, op. cit., p. 31.
[40] Ibid., p. 33.
[41] Africa Report (April, 1968), p. 31.

the highest in the world, and 62% of European families have one or more servants.[42] They are accorded the status of being addressed as *baas* or master, and their political, social, and economic positions are secure. It seems safe to say that nowhere in the world do so many white people live so well, so cheaply. For the South African of today, the long sought-after *lekke lewe*, or sweet life, has at last been achieved.

In terms of land, the South African system has also rewarded the European well, albeit at the expense of the non-European. The Native Trust and Land Act of 1936 added 7% of the area of South Africa to that portion reserved for Africans, but this merely brought the total area set aside to 13%. The other 87% was reserved for the 20% of the population that was white. Somewhat less inequitable ratios exist for South West Africa and the former High Commission Territories. Were the African areas of Lesotho, Botswana, and Swaziland incorporated in the Republic, the non-European share would rise to nearly 45%. In addition, most of the African land is fragmented into 230 tiny, uneconomical plots, and, despite all that has been claimed to the contrary, is generally of poor quality. The Transkei (with 16,000 square miles) and Zululand are exceptions in that they are substantial in size and generally of better quality than the African land in the Transvaal and Orange Free State, but the crowding of 30% of the African population into the reserves, the lack of supporting industry, and the corresponding need to farm and graze reduces the viability of even that land. The so-called Tomlinson Report of 1955 indicated the magnitude of the problem at that time and the costs of rehabilitating the African areas.[43] Virtually nothing has been done to alleviate the problem, since in the "African" urban townships Africans are not permitted to own land, but can merely lease it. Other non-Europeans are even less well off in the area of territorial allocation. Various acts of Parliament (notably the Natal Pegging Act of 1943) eliminated the prospect of additional Asian freehold land in Natal (they had already been forbidden to own land in the Orange Free State and Transvaal) and made the prospects of

[42] E. J. Kahn, Jr., *The Separated People* (New York: W. W. Norton & Company, 1968), p. 40.
[43] Union of South Africa, *Summary of the Report of the Commission for the Socio-Economic Development of the Bantu Areas Within the Union of South Africa* (Pretoria: Government Printer, 1955), Parts II and III.

additional land ownership by the Coloreds equally unpromising. The Colored section of Cape Town, District Six, was recently taken over by the city government and the Coloreds moved en masse to a new, sterile "homeland." Land tenure is thus extremely inequitable and a major source of non-European irritation.

In the area of education, distribution is likewise quantitatively and qualitatively uneven. We shall be talking about the qualitative side of the educational process in the section on the rejuvenative capacity, but the quantitative side merits our attention here. Whereas European education is compulsory and free, for Africans it is neither. Whereas the government spends $240 per year on European children, the figure for Africans was $20.[44] No comparable figures are available for Colored or Asian children since they are financed out of the general consolidated Revenue Fund.[45] According to a United Nations' survey, 99% of the Europeans in the 7–15 age groups are in school, only 37% of Africans are.[46] Thus, proportionally and absolutely, there are more Europeans being educated than Africans at every stage in the educational process. The African in-school population falls away rapidly after the first few grades, for example, from 221,234 in standard 1 to 948 in standard 10.[47] Fifty-five thousand Europeans attend universities vs. 956 Africans.[48]

Thus, the distributive process, whether of land, wealth, or education, is inequitable. Ascription is the overwhelming criterion for the levels of attainment. Few ever exceed the boundaries established by birth. The distributive capability is far more uneven and less impressive than either the regulative or extractive capability (at least for non-Europeans), although the economic rewards of the system probably, in the context of southern Africa, constitute a support for the political system.

REJUVENATIVE CAPABILITY

The rejuvenative capacity of the South African political system is the least impressive of its capabilities. The inordinately large role played by ascription in the process of role allocation

[44] Andrews, *op. cit.*, p. 24.
[45] Republic of South Africa, *Year Book 1966*, pp. 99–106.
[46] U. N. Economic Commission for Africa, *op. cit.*, p. 63.
[47] *Ibid.*, p. 70.
[48] Republic of South Africa, *Year Book 1966*, pp. 99–106.

definitely sets limits on the search for talent. It is ironic, but true, that "ethnicity" and "tribalism," particularly white tribalism, are more pronounced in this political system than in most other African systems. Generally speaking, political, economic, and social recruitment is based upon one's "racial" group. Even within the European community, there is a definite bifracation, with the English-speakers gravitating toward business and commerce and the Afrikaners more likely to be absorbed into the bureaucracies, army police, and politics, as well as farming.

On the positive side, the lengthy and comprehensive process of socialization which the Afrikaner elite undergoes provides for a basic loyalty to the political system and gives the decision-making group a kind of toughness and solidarity that is not found in many other political systems. The *laager* mentality, the feeling of being against the world, has many objective flaws, but over the short term at least, it provides a cohesion to the internal center of the political system. Some have suggested, however, that the very historical forces that caused this cohesion are the same pressures that will ultimately cause it maximum difficulty:

> Despite the freshness of their own struggle, few Afrikaners recognize that the deep human emotions—the desire for self-determination and for equality of treatment and the pride which burned deep into the Afrikaner soul and sparked the anti-colonial fight—are the same fundamental emotions producing similar determination in African hearts.[49]

But particularly in the area of African education, the South African political system is working very hard to prevent the buildup of those forces. We have already alluded to the process by which Europeans are civically educated and to the pressures on them to accept the mores of the system. We have also stressed the regulative aspects of the system which reinforce the non-Europeans' lack of faith in their ability to change the political structure. Since the Bantu Education Act of 1953, the central government has taken over African education by supervising the Bantu Community schools, the Government Bantu Schools, and those Missionary Schools still in existence. The entire purpose of this comprehensive program seems clear. H. Verwoerd put it quite simply:

[49] Munger, *op. cit.*, p. 64.

> Education must train and teach people in accordance with the opportunities in life, according to the sphere in which they live. Good racial relations cannot exist where education is given under the control of people who create wrong expectations on the part of the native himself.[50]

As the recent UNESCO report on apartheid outlined, the South African education system is designed to perpetuate African occupations at the "menial" levels of society and to maintain and reinforce the present political system.[51]

The government has eliminated the multiracial character of university education (which was generally confined to the University of Cape Town and Witwatersrand) and substituted separate colleges for Coloreds and Indians. It has further attempted to divide Africans by providing separate colleges for Tsonga and Venda, Zulu and Swazi, Sotho and Xhosa. On the lower levels, schools are separated on the basis of "tribes" and the medium of instruction up to standard 6 is the tribal language. The new curriculum is designed "to arouse the pride of the Bantu in all that was good in their past" and accents religious instruction, hygiene, handicraft, gardening, and, at the upper levels, Afrikaans and English. There seems little question that this policy, coupled with inadequate schools, undertrained and underpaid teachers, and the accent on neotribalism, does much to keep the African masses fragmented and unable to achieve a suitable frame of reference within which to organize successfully. Considering the system as a whole, the weak aspects of the rejuvenative capability are probably more than balanced by the substantial regulative, distributive, and extractive capabilities. These alone should assure the European minority of the strength to maintain itself for the foreseeable future.

SYMBOLIC CAPABILITY

The apparent strength of the South African political system and the willingness of its principal decision makers to use that power to insure the maintenance of their primary goals, accounts for the system's symbolic capability. Most observers of South Africa have commented on the lack of national symbols and the low levels of loyalty to the nation state (as opposed to the loyalty to one's

---

[50] U. N. Economic Commission for Africa, *op. cit.*, p. 62.
[51] UNESCO, *op. cit.*, pp. 25–95.

particular ethnic group or caste). There are, for example, three de facto "national" anthems ("*Nkosi Sikilel'i Afrika*," "God Save the Queen," and "*Die Stem van Sud Afrika*") and we have already mentioned the social, ethnic, and historical fragmentation that would militate against a common, mutual experience. Moreover, the entire, theoretical structure of apartheid is based on the existence of contiguous "nations." Yet, against this subnational fragmentation, there are two powerful sources of identification which, taken together, provide South Africa with a strong symbolic capability. For the non-Europeans, the levels of governmental repression, the elimination of non-European leaders, the anomie and isolation of individual Africans and the hopelessness most feel at the prospects of removing the present system, all provide a powerful conditioning force. The pervasive fear and the kind of hopelessness that enervates revolutions are part of the negative legitimacy outlined in Chapter I.[52] The maintenance of the system by fear, terror, and repression helps to explain the present tranquility which seems to exist in contemporary South Africa.

For the Europeans, there is another type of legitimacy that elicits their support for the present system. It is one based upon legality and a curious type of "merit." [53] South Africans are deeply concerned with legalism and it pervades the entire political system. The seemingly endless laws and acts which cover the land three and four tiers deep, and the need for a legal cloak to justify disenfranchisement, repression, and inequitable allocation of rewards all point to a strong European belief in the need to legitimize political action. This belief comes close to being an obsession. During 1967, for example, thirty-seven Ovambo Africans were captured in South West Africa. It was claimed they were bent on sabotage. Since there was no law in force for South West Africa comparable to the General Law Amendment Act of 1962 at the time, they were kept in a South African jail for almost a year until Parliament passed such a law for South West Africa and made it retroactive to 1962. Of the defendants, one was

[52] This aspect is often overlooked in revolutionary theory. The Africans in South Africa must think that they have the power to overthrow the system if they are to do so.

[53] There are also strands of charismatic legitimacy in the careers of "Oom" Paul Kruger, Dr. D. Malan, and even Dr. H. Verwoerd, but these seem overshadowed by "legality" and "merit" (for Europeans).

acquitted, one died during the trial, three pleaded guilty to violation of the Suppression of Commission Act, and the rest were found guilty under the new Terrorist Act Extension. This incident and others, such as the vast legal charade that was undertaken to remove Coloreds from the common roll in 1956, illustrate to what extent a belief in the law supports the system.

But the South African symbolic capability is further enhanced by the "merit" of the regulative, extractive, distributive, and rejuvenative capacities—*the power*—of the system. From the European point of view, it simply works: it delivers the goods. It gives most Europeans wealth, job security, safety, deference, and status; it gives them the right to command, and promises to maintain these payoffs far into the future. This, coupled with the European belief in the fundamental legality of the system, provides the major source of support that the regime enjoys. This is of enormous import for the future, for as long as South Africans of every group continue to believe that the present system will endure and will achieve its goals, there will be no change in South Africa.

Goals of the Political System

We have, in effect, already alluded to the two primary goals of the South African political system: survival and the continuation of the present form and style of command decision making. These are the basic core values of South Africa, and both are non-negotiable, either domestically or internationally.

As we mentioned in Chapter I, survival is a paramount goal for most political systems, although there is often a discrete difference between the survival of the regime and that of the political system as a whole. In South Africa, however, because there is such a close correlation between the present regime and the de facto political system, the goal of survival takes on new dimensions. Both Europeans and non-Europeans feel that the survival of the political system depends upon the survival of the Nationalist regime. Since both the present regime and the political system are so irrevocably wedded to a policy of racial segregation, to a denial of basic human rights for non-Europeans, and to perpetual European domination, the survival of South Africa in its present form takes on an ominous meaning. It seems to threaten racial harmony and peaceful interaction among various ethnic groups, in both South Africa and southern Africa generally. Thus, the primacy of the goal of survival for the South African political system cannot be viewed with the same objectivity as the survival of Denmark or of the Philippines.

Closely related and of paramount importance for the principal decision-makers of South Africa is the goal of command decision making. As analyzed in the section on decision making, a fundamental premise of the South African political system is that political power *ought* to remain in the hands of an elite and, more specifically, an Afrikaans-speaking, European elite. This command decision-making ethos is most holistic in character, for it is widely and deeply felt among Europeans that social and economic control, as well as political control, ought to rest with that elite. There are even indications that, on occasion, command decision making is held to be of as great importance as the matter of survival.

There is, for example, the South African government position on immigration. One would assume that the more Europeans there were in South Africa, the fewer the chances that a non-European revolution would succeed. Yet the Afrikaner elite has consistently restrained and limited immigration, even while professing to encourage it.[54] The ability to be assimilated into the Afrikaner culture has been generally held as a more critical criterion than support for European hegemony or apartheid. After World War II, the Nationalist government dampened the flow of immigration by passing the Citizenship Act of 1949, which increased the difficulty of becoming a South African. More recently, although European immigration has been running at an average yearly rate of nearly 40,000 since 1963, there seems little doubt that the flow would be much higher were the Nationalists less particular about the cultural background of the immigrants, and less concerned that the new arrivals might "blot out" Afrikaner culture. Religion, in particular, seems to be of concern to the present political elite (recent immigrants from southern Europe have been 23% Roman Catholic vs. 7% in the present South African population).

Just as the present political elite has been unwilling to compromise on the matter of culture, so too, it has made no attempt to co-opt

---

[54] This xenophobia probably dates back to the middle of the 19th century when the Boer Republics were under constant pressure from Great Britain and *Uitlanders* or foreigners.

the non-African groups into the political elite and thereby reduce from 5–1 to 4–1 the majorities opposed to the regime, particularly in the case of the Coloreds who feel estranged from the African community. The cost of turning their opposition into supports would seem to be low indeed. Only modestly preferential treatment would probably insure a lack of opposition, if not outright support. Moreover, the Colored community is culturally and linguistically European in orientation. But because it is generally held that the Coloreds would be more likely to support the United Party or the Progressive Party than the Nationalists and because of the Afrikaners' compulsion to draw racial lines more strictly, this pragmatic strategy is not even considered. The reluctance to even entertain such a course of political action does seem to reverse the goal order of survival and Afrikaner hegemony, although the survival of the political system, the retention of command decision making, and the continued existence of the present Afrikaner regime are probably viewed as being inextricably bound together.

A third primary goal of South Africa, one which is not characterized by such extreme rigidity as survival and command decision making, is the maintenance of stability and the status quo, not only in South Africa proper but in southern Africa in general. In addition to supporting conservative African leadership in Swaziland, Lesotho, and Botswana, and Malawi, South Africa has in recent years moved to cooperate directly with the European regimes in Rhodesia and Mozambique. South Africa was initially opposed to the Unilateral Declaration of Independence (UDI) by Rhodesia during November 1965, for the South African leadership feared that the Rhodesian regime would be defeated. Nevertheless, once it became clear that Great Britain would not intervene directly and that the United Nations sanctions were not likely to be effective, South Africa cooperated with the Smith regime by allowing Rhodesia to export many of her products through South African firms, by sending them oil, and by having the South African reserve bank recognize the Rhodesian pound.

In addition, South African military involvement forms a critical part of the new "forward strategy." South African police and army detachments are now operating in both Rhodesia and Mozambique against the African resistance movements there. B. J. Vorster matter-of-factly confirmed their presence early this year when he stated: "We shall fight terrorists wherever we are allowed to fight them." [55] South Africa has long demonstrated an international security capability. As far back as 1963, her police moved into Lesotho to capture refugees (Ganyile case), and during 1964 and 1965 rounded up a number of South African exiles in Swaziland. Since the departure of the last British troops from southern Africa during November of 1966, South Africa's military presence in southern Africa is now unchecked. The removal of the Royal Irish Fusiliers from their base at Matsapa, Swaziland, has generally been overlooked in the Western press, but it was a matter of great import for southern Africa. The troops had long been regarded as an indication of the British commitment to the area and offered the remote hope that exogenous force might be utilized to support "moderate" forces in the area. When these troops were not used against Rhodesia following UDI and were subsequently withdrawn, that hope faded.

Some have suggested that South Africa could live with—and in fact, might favor—African regimes in Rhodesia and Mozambique if they were not overwhelmingly hostile to the existence of South Africa. A ring of black buffer states similar to the Malawi of Dr. Kamuza Banda might indeed prove to be better political insulation for the South African political system than the present European minority governments which attract so much international opprobrium and guerrilla activity. While it is interesting to speculate about the possibility of such an arrangement, it does not seem to be a current goal of South Africa. Despite a good deal of talk about a "détente" with black Africa, South Africa, for purely domestic reasons, could not stand by and watch these European regimes fall, and would, in any case, be most unwilling to gamble on the long term good will of those black states which she did not control rather directly. The central purpose of South African military, diplomatic, and economic involvement in the surrounding areas of southern Africa would seem to be the prevention of revolutionary alteration of the status quo.

At various points in our discussion of South Africa we have referred to the ingredients in the South African situation—and, by extension,

[55] Stanley Uys, "White Africa vs. Black," *The New Republic* (January 27, 1968), 12.

in southern African—that hinder the achievement of such revolution. It is now time to draw together these strands.

We have stressed the lack of African political organization, a result of continual and severe harassment by South Africa. That lack is of enormous import. As the failure of the guerrilla uprising in the Congo during 1964 indicates, such organization is critical to any would-be revolutionary movement. Regardless of external support, strong motivation, and modern equipment, a mass revolution without trained, organized, political cadres seems doomed to failure, particularly against a regime as powerful and as dedicated to its own survival as South Africa. There are also some numerical handicaps to internal revolution. The ratio of non-European to European in South Africa is on the order of 5–1 and, even assuming majority support for the revolution, this is probably not enough to offset the tremendous regulative capabilities of the South African regime. Certainly, it seems small in comparison with the ratios of 200–1 (Kenya) or 3000–1 (Nigeria) which proved to be so irresistible historically elsewhere.

But even more critical than the lack of overwhelming numbers of trained cadres within South Africa is the absence of a dichotomy between the white settlers in South Africa and a metropolitan government in Europe. By and large, the French and English settlers lost their political hold in Africa because the mother country came to the point where, for economic, political, or moral reasons, it was willing to place Europeans under African majority rule. This element, so crucial to the decolonization of Algeria and Kenya, is not present in South Africa. The white settler in South Africa is perhaps not significantly more ruthless than was his counterpart in Algeria or Kenya, but he has no powerful overseas group to curtail the implementation of that ruthlessness.

Lacking sufficient organizational strength to promote economic or passive resistance, without a focal point for what international pressure exists, and unable to count on massive military support from other African countries, those who would alter the status quo often advocate a guerrilla campaign to wear down the present regime. But even in this regard, the geography and topography are not conducive to guerrilla warfare and militate against a successful uprising. Those exiles who would pin their hopes on a guerrilla campaign would be well advised to consider the lack of a contiguous sanctuary and suitable terrain. The Kalahari, the Karoo, and the barren areas of the northern Transvaal act as formidable barriers to a successful campaign. There are no rain forests, no impenetrable areas, no common boundaries with governments friendly to an African-led uprising. In addition, the well developed infrastructure of South Africa aids the defense. Road, rail, and air mobility give the South African armed forces a substantial advantage in choking off and isolating any incipient uprising before it becomes widespread (as in the so-called "Peasants Revolt" of 1960 in Pondoland).

Thus, without proper organization, under increasing surveillance, lacking adequate logistic support from the countries north of the Zambezi River and without the kind of topography necessary to sustain a guerrilla uprising, the non-European in South Africa seems clearly on the defensive. It seems extremely unlikely that any African uprising could succeed in the foreseeable future.

As committed as South Africa is to the goals of survival, continued command decision making, and maintenance of the status quo, her leadership is apparently willing to experiment with new methods for preserving the primacy of her position. Since 1966, South Africa has accented a new goal, that of international influence. The new directions of foriegn policy under the leadership of Foreign Minister Hilgard Müller have reversed an earlier trend toward retrenchment and isolation which characterized South Africa's diplomatic stance from 1948 onward and which culminated in the withdrawal of South Africa from the British Commonwealth in 1961.

While these new diplomatic and economic moves do not have global, or even a continental, emphasis, they are concerned with developing "openings to the north." South Africa has offered economic aid, technical assistance, and diplomatic recognition to "any state willing to ask for it." Given South Africa's preeminent economic and military position in southern Africa this policy makes sense, for it is the presence of South Africa which makes of southern Africa a coherent, well-defined international subsystem.[56] South Africa

[56] For an analysis of South Africa's importance to the subsystem of southern Africa, see Larry Bowman, "The Subordinate State System of Southern Africa," paper delivered at the African Studies Association meeting (November, 1967); C. Potholm, "After the Rhodesian Unilateral Declaration of Independence: An Assessment of Southern Africa," *Journal of Asian and African Studies* (October, 1967) Vol. II, No. 4: 245–251; Peter Robson, "Economic Integration in

looms large in this arena and overshadows the smaller, less rich, and far weaker African states of Lesotho, Botswana, Swaziland, and Malawi. The levels of their dependence vary, but in all cases are considerable. Lesotho and Botswana send over 300,000, Mozambique 200,000, and Malawi 80,000 migrant workers to South Africa yearly, and their earnings represent a major source of revenue for those countries. In Lesotho, for example, 50% of adult males are away at any given moment, and migrant workers are the single largest source of national income. Swaziland, Lesotho, and Botswana are also bound up in a customs union with South Africa and share a common currency and banking facilities. South Africa provides the major share of their imports, and, with the exception of Swaziland, takes most of their exports. South African capital has been instrumental in the development of Swaziland, and there are plans for South Africa to build the new capital of Malawi at Lilong we, to harness the waters of the Orange river in Lesotho, and to develop the $380 million hydroelectric plant on the lower Zambezi at Cahora Bassa in Mozambique. There is even talk of a common market for southern Africa involving 44 million persons and eight countries. In light of the substantial extractive and distributive capabilities of South Africa and the already advanced state of her manufacturing facilities, she should continue to dominate the area. Even Zambia, for example, which is attempting to withdraw from the southern African nexus and reverse the patterns of her trade, has had to substitute South Africa for Rhodesia as her foremost African trading partner.

In return for economic largesse and a reduced amount of South African interference in the internal affairs, the African territories of southern Africa have muted their public criticism of apartheid, curbed the activities of South African refugees in their countries, hindered the return of would-be revolutionaries, and provided diplomatic support at the United Nations and the Organization of African Unity. They seem to have accepted the economic and military realities of their situation. Bound up in the context of southern Africa, they are cognizant of South African power and have therefore sought a politi-

Southern Africa," *Journal of Modern African Studies* (December, 1967) Vol. V, No. 4: 469–490; and Ernest A. Gross, "The Coalescing Problem of Southern Africa," *Foreign Affairs* (July, 1968) 743–757. The South African view of the subsystem is clearly seen in Eschel Rhoodie, *The Third Africa* (New York and Cape Town: Twin Circle Publishing and the *Nasionale Bockhandel*, 1968).

cal accommodation with that power.[57] Lesotho and Malawi have diplomatic relations with the Republic, and it seems likely that Botswana and Swaziland will follow soon. Even Mauritius, perched far away in the Indian Ocean, seems likely, for economic reasons, to eventually recognize South Africa.

One should not overestimate the internal ramifications of these developments. Some have argued that this new shift in international diplomacy signals a fundamental change in South African, particularly Afrikaner, attitudes. This is not the case, for the South African leadership takes a most instrumental view of the new diplomacy. It is to be used to enhance, not reduce, the chances of maintaining European supremacy in South Africa. In their own inimical way, for example, the South Africans are now building "self-contained" quarters near Cape Town for the black diplomats to avoid any meaningful relaxation of social apartheid.

The goals of survival, command decision making, and the maintenance of the status quo, as well as the ancillary goals of freedom from external pressures and the desire for international influence, provide the major thrust for the South African political system. Other goals seem of little concern.

Political development, for example, has been ignored as a goal of the regime. The extension of the apartheid formula to Ovamboland in South West Africa and the other proposals of the Odendaal plan mean that there will be further geographical fragmentation, not integration, of the system.[58] The rhetoric surrounding the theory of separate development and the implementation of "positive" apartheid should not obscure the lack of participation at the national level. The coercive character of the linkage between the political center and the various ethnic groups, the narrowed rather than widened process of decision making, and the rigidity of national goals

---

[57] See R. P. Stevens, *Lesotho, Botswana and Swaziland* (New York: Frederick A. Praeger, 1967); and C. P. Potholm, "The Protectorates, the Organization of African Unity and South Africa," *International Journal* (Winter, 1966–1967) Vol. XXII, No. 1: 68–72.

[58] We have not dwelt on the question of South West Africa except to point out that it is an integral part of the South African political system. The United Nations General Assembly Resolution voting to end South Africa's mandate and the International Court of Justice's rather strange decision that Liberia and Ethiopia had no right to bring their cases to the court (after hearing that case for six years) both underscore the irrelevancy of such decisions.

indicate a substantial lack of political development. One could even argue that although the means taken to insure European hegemony are rational enough, the basic goal—racial domination and European hegemony—is, in 1969 Africa, irrational.

In much the same fashion, democratic decision making—despite all the pronouncements to the contrary—is hardly a pursued goal of South Africa. Except within the narrow arena of Afrikaans politics, nonleaders simply do not choose their leaders. At the national level, there is virtually no participation in the decision-making process by non-Europeans. Nor is it likely that there will be soon. It is difficult to imagine the South African political system reversing the century-old pattern of political behavior which runs counter to democratic, nonracial decision making.

Another goal which is often stated, but seldom followed, is that of welfare. As we noted in the section on the distributive capacity of South Africa, there has been some improvement in the living conditions for non-Europeans in urban areas and that most of the shanty-town slums that were such an integral part of *Cry, the Beloved Country* and *Come Back Africa* are no longer in existence. At the same time, the improvements and the increased health benefits are available primarily to those urban non-Europeans whose health and general conditions impinge most directly upon Europeans. In the rural areas, African infant mortality statistics are not even kept and the average life expectancy for Africans is not computed (whereas Europeans can expect to live 64 years, Asians 55, and Coloreds 44).[59] Medical facilities, health and accident benefits, even old age pensions ($170 yearly for Europeans, $30 for Africans), are so grossly inequitable and the educational systems so uneven that one may well question the ultimate South African commitment to the goal of welfare qua welfare.[60]

The goals of the South African political system, when taken with an analysis of its decision-making process and its capabilities, lead to the following conclusion: that the South African political system is a syncretic alliance between the agricultural and industrial elite of the country, both groups being European. Its political system is oligarchial in scope and racial in tone. Yet, because of its strong

[59] Muriel Horrell, A *Survey of Race Relations in South Africa* (Johannesburg: South African Institute of Race Relations, 1967), p. 296.
[60] *Ibid.*

extractive, regulative, distributive, and symbolic capabilities, it is a system that is likely to endure despite internal opposition and pervasive international hostility to its ideology, and it is likely to achieve its major goals. In light of this, one wishes one could agree with the brave and optimistic words of Thomas Karis:

> At some time between 1963, the PAC's proclaimed year of liberation, and the year 2000, which is a good round number and only thirty-seven years hence, existing trends suggest that white domination will come to an end.[61]

But South Africa's determination to maintain European hegemony, coupled with her power to do so, makes these words seem more hope than prophecy.

The real tragedy of the South African situation is thus not only the denial of basic human rights for three-quarters of the nation, but the needlessness of that denial. At the very time when white South Africa is most firmly entrenched and in the best position to liberalize some of their more odious social and political policies, the government is moving inexorably toward tighter control over the non-European population and a more retractable position with regard to the opinions of the rest of the world. The South African ruling elite, both English- and Afrikaans-speaking, could change the structure and substance of apartheid far more easily and far more peacefully than either the non-Europeans from within or international pressure from without. These ruling groups will not, and therein lies the real tragedy of this beautiful and rich land and its tough, resilient, inequitable political system.

BIBLIOGRAPHY

Carter, G. M., *The Politics of Inequality: South Africa Since 1948* (New York: Frederick A. Praeger, 1958).

deKiewiet, C. W., *A History of South Africa* (Oxford: Oxford University Press, 1957).

Horrell, Muriel, *A Survey of Race Relations in South Africa* (Johannesburg: South African Institute of Race Relations, yearly).

[61] Karis, *op. cit.*, p. 605.

Horwitz, R., *The Political Economy of South Africa* (New York: Frederick A. Praeger, 1967).

Luthuli, Albert, *Let My People Go* (New York: McGraw-Hill Book Company, 1962).

Marquard, Leo, *The Peoples and Policies of South Africa*, 3rd edition (Cape Town: Oxford University Press, 1962).

Roux, Edward, *Time Longer than Rope: A History of the Black Man's Struggle for Freedom in South Africa*, 2nd edition (Madison, Wisc.: University of Wisconsin Press, 1964).

Thompson, L. M., *Politics in the Republic of South Africa* (Boston: Little, Brown and Company, 1966).

van den Berghe, P. L., *South Africa, A Study in Conflict* (Berkeley and Los Angeles, Calif.: University of California Press, 1967).

van Jaarsveld, F. A., *The Awakening of Afrikaner Nationalism 1868–1881* (Cape Town: Human and Rousseau, 1961).

CHAPTER V

The Tanzanian
Political System

/ The political system of Tanzania encompasses over 363,000 square miles, including the islands of Pemba and Zanzibar, and is hence the size of Germany and France combined. There are some 12 million persons under its jurisdiction, the vast majority of whom are of African descent. There are also 125,000 Asians, 30,000 Arabs, and 17,000 Europeans. Inhabitation of what is now Tanzania has been of long duration, and anthropological investigations indicate that it may have been the original home of man.[1] /

Much of the early history of this area remains to be reconstructed, although the evidence now suggests that there was extensive African settlement from 200 B.C. onwards. Migrations of Nilo-Saharan peoples from the north and Bantu groups from the west overwhelmed the Khosian peoples already in residence. Arabs and Persians arrived by

---

[1] Findings in the Olduvai Gorge indicate that man and his immediate ancestors may be 6–10 million years old. See L. Leakey, *Adam's Ancestors* (New York: Longmans, Green and Company, 1934) and *The Progress and Evolution of Man in Africa* (London: Oxford University Press, 1961). Especially interesting is Sonia Cole, *The Prehistory of East Africa* (New York: The Macmillan Company, 1963).

138

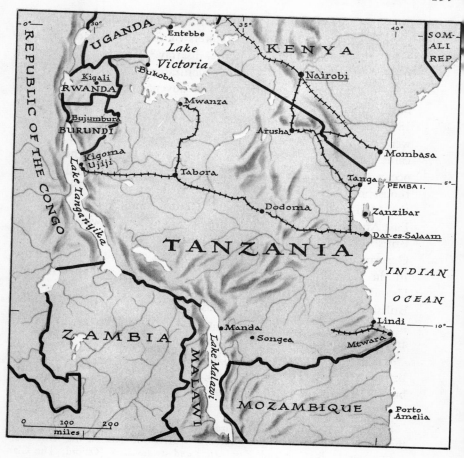

the 7th century, and, by the 12th, there was a widespread trading culture involving the urbanized, Islamic city states on the coast and the African political communities such as the Azanians in the interior. The resulting blend of these groups, termed Swahili, ushered in a golden era of trade and commerce and extensive contact with Arabia, India, and China. The arrival of the Portuguese during the 16th century, disrupted and, in many areas, terminated the flourishing trade, even though the Arabs reasserted their sway over the coast and new African empires arose in the interior.

In 1832 the Sultan of Oman moved to Zanzibar and sent his slave and ivory gathering expeditions far inland, devastating large portions of the interior. Subsequent African penetrations from the south, primarily the Ngoni peoples, further disrupted the indigenous societies, so that when the European explorers of the 1850's and 1860's arrived, the situation was in some disarray.[2] German involvement, through the Society for German Colonization and the German East African Company, grew after 1884 as adventurers, missionaries, and businessmen signed treaties with various African political figures. In 1890 the German government established a protectorate over what were to become Ruanda-Urundi and Tanganyika, while Zanzibar came under British "protection." African resistance to the German occupation was both widespread and bloody, with several hundred thousand Africans being killed in the Hehe uprising of 1891–94 and the Maji-Maji revolt of 1905–07. German military pacification of East Africa continued until the eve of World War 1, when a series of British, South African, and Belgian armies fought the resourceful German General Paul von Lettow-Vorbeck and his African troops. In the European peace settlement, the Belgians acquired Ruanda-Urundi, the Portuguese some minor territory in the south, and the British a League of Nations mandate over the rest of the country, soon renamed Tanganyika. African deaths due to the war, influenza, and a subsequent famine were catastrophically high.[3]

Under the direction of Sir Donald Cameroon (1925–31), Great Britain attempted to govern Tanganyika by means of indirect rule, but was hampered by the lack of political infrastructure and ethnic

[2] Many histories have overemphasized the Arab and European contributions to the history of this area, partially because of a lack of data on the African accomplishments. R. Coupland, *East Africa and its Invaders* (Oxford: The Clarendon Press, 1938) and *The Exploitation of East Africa 1856–1890* (London: Faber, 1939); Kenneth Ingham, *A History of East Africa* (New York: Frederick A. Praeger, 1962); and J. P. Moffett (ed.), *Hnadbook of Tanganyika* (Dar es Salaam: Government Printer, 1959) are works in this tradition. More balanced accounts are contained in Roland Oliver and Gervase Matthew (eds.), *History of East Africa* (Oxford: The Clarendon Press, 1963); Z. Marsh and G. W. Kingsnorth, *An Introduction to the History of East Africa* (Cambridge: Cambridge University Press, 1965); and two works by Basil Davidson, *The African Past* (New York: Grosset & Dunlap, 1964), pp. 101–171, and *The Lost Cities of Africa* (Boston: Little, Brown and Company, 1959), chapters 5–11. Other interesting accounts include two works by G. S. P. Freeman-Grenville, *Medieval History of the Coast of Tanganyika* (London: Oxford University Press, 1962) and *East African Coast, Select Documents* (London: Oxford University Press, 1962).

[3] Moffet, for example, puts the death toll from influenza alone at between 50 and 80 thousand (*op. cit.*, p. 91).

fragmentation of the African population into over 120 units. The small numbers of European settlers, the paucity of mineral wealth, and the global economic depression likewise encouraged imperial neglect. Until after World War II, there were few national institutions and taxes were not collected on a country-wide basis until 1950. Africans were not elected to the territorial legislative council until 1949 and did not serve on the executive council before 1951. Nevertheless, once begun, African political participation expanded rapidly, greatly aided by the role of the United Nations Trusteeship Council.

/There had been an African political organization, the Tanganyika African Association, as early as 1929, but it played a minor political role until Julius K. Nyerere, a teacher educated at Makerere College and Edinburgh University, transformed it into a political party in 1954. Renamed the Tanganyika African National Union, TANU was from its inception a nontribal, African party dedicated to an evolutionary attainment of African majority rule (although it did support European and Asian candidates in the multiracial elections of 1958). It was opposed by the conservative, multiracial United Tanganyika Party which sprung up in 1956 as a British-supported counterweight. Both the United Tanganyika Party and the regionally orientated Tanganyika Federal Independence Party proved to be ephemeral and faded away by 1958. From the first, TANU demonstrated wide-spread popular support and won the elections of 1958 and 1959, despite a restricted franchise, a ban on civil servant participation in politics, and colonial harassment. The new administration of Sir Richard Turnbull recognized the primacy of TANU and when the party ran unopposed in 58 of 71 constituencies in 1960 and won 12 of the remaining 13, Nyerere was asked to form the first African government.[4] Independence followed in December of 1961.

/Tanganyika, like so many other former British territories, inherited a political framework based on the Westminster model. However, early in 1962 Nyerere resigned as Prime Minister in order to revitalize

[4] For a variety of documents describing the British administration of Tanganyika, the reader should consult (in addition to Moffett) D. C. Cameron, *My Tanganyika Service and Some Nigeria* (London: Allen and Unwin, 1939); Lord Hailey, *Native Administration in the British African Territories* 5 vols. (London: H. M. Stationary Office, 1950–1953); Margaret L. Bates, "Tanganyika," in Gwendolyn M. Carter (ed.), *African One-Party States* (Ithaca, N.Y.: Cornell University Press, 1962), pp. 395–485; and B. T. G. Chidzero, *Tanganyika and International Trusteeship* (London: Oxford University Press, 1961).

the party, to draw the rural population into political participation, and to work for the establishment of a republic. A new constitution was drawn up which retained the ministerial system but which also included a strong presidential chief executive and a vice-president who acted as a prime minister.[5] Tanganyika became a republic in December 1962, and Nyerere, as the TANU candidate, was overwhelmingly elected as President. Rashidi Kawawa, who had served as Prime Minister in Nyerere's absence, became Vice-President.

Yet the Tanganyikan political system did not function as its leaders had hoped. The merger of the miniscule African National Congress into TANU and the disbanding of the last splinter party, the People's Democratic Party in 1963, created a de facto single-party state. Because of a lack of opposition, it was felt that TANU, as an effective institution, might well wither away, and that the heretofore representative function of the government would be undercut by meaningless elections. Therefore, the President appointed a commission to examine the ways in which a blend of direction and democratic participation might be achieved within the framework of a single-party system.[6] The formation of the commission and the subsequent implementation of its unusual proposals were acts of great import and political courage, particularly in the context of an army mutiny, labor unrest, and a hasty merger with the islands of Zanzibar and Pemba which had recently undergone a bloody revolution.[7]

Participation in the Political System

The recommendations of the President's Commission became the basis of the Interim Constitution of July 1965, and the de jure forma-

[5] Government of Tanganyika, *Proposals of the Tanganyika Government for a Republic* (Dar es Salaam: Government Printer, 1962). In the presidential elections of that year, Nyerere received 1,127,978 votes while the candidate of the splinter African National Congress, Zuberi Mtemvu, received 21,276.

[6] Government of Tanganyika, *Report of the Presidential Commission on the Establishment of a Democratic One-Party State* (Dar es Salaam: Government Printer, 1965).

[7] The convoluted story of the events leading up to the African Revolution on Zanzibar is most extensively covered in Michael Lofchie's *Zanzibar: Background to Revolution* (Princeton: Princeton University Press, 1965). John Okello, who led the revolution, has written a very interesting account of it in *Revolution in Zanzibar* (Nairobi: East African Publishing House, 1967). Another version is to be found in the *Nationalist* of January 12, 1965. A detailed and scholarly description of the merger of Tanganyika and Zanzibar during March 1964, as well as subsequent developments on Zanzibar has yet to be written.

tion of a single-party state, the United Republic of Tanganyika and Zanzibar, later called Tanzania. We shall examine in turn the political framework which resulted, the process of decision making that occurs within it, and the environmental factors that encourage its operation.

By way of introduction, it is necessary to qualify the description of the Tanzanian political system. It is not, strictly speaking, a single-party regime. The Afro-Shirazi Party on Zanzibar and TANU on the mainland retain their individual identities, although they participate jointly in major political decsions affecting both areas. In addition, Tanzania is not actually a "united" republic. Although the Zanzibaris were initially overrepresented in the national government (7 of 22 ministries and 40 seats in the National Assembly), the system remains a federation, for the Revolutionary Council on Zanzibar retains de facto control over its own defense, internal security, public service, and immigration operations. For these reasons, and because the poly-archal decision-making features found within the mainland system have not yet been duplicated on the offshore islands, our analysis will deal essentially with the mainland portion of the political system of Tanzania.

The President of the United Republic stands at the head of the political structure. He is both head of state and commander-in-chief of the armed forces.[8] Elected by universal adult suffrage after being nominated by an electoral conference of TANU and the Afro-Shirazi Party, the President is the repository of all executive power, appointing the Cabinet and the important regional commissioners.[9] He serves for a period of 5 years or until Parliament is dissolved (he may dissolve it, but must then stand for reelection along with its members). There are two Vice-Presidents. The first is the chief executive for Zanzibar and the head of the Afro-Shirazi Party. The second is the leader of the National Assembly. Julius Nyerere is currently the President, while Abeid Karume is the First Vice-President and Rashidi Kawawa is the Second Vice-President.

The National Assembly is the chief legislative organ.[10] Its membership reflects a blend of direct and indirect representation. In 1968, there were 107 elected members from single-member con-

[8] Government of Tanganyika, *The Interim Constitution of Tanzania and the Constitution of the Tanganyika African National Union* (Dar es Salaam: Government Printer, 1965), Section 6 (1).
[9] *Ibid.*, Section 12 (1).
[10] *Ibid.*, Section 24 (1).

stituencies (which average 30,000 persons in size, but which range from a 5,000-member district on Mafia Island to a 60,000-member district in Dar es Salaam, the capital). An additional 15 members are selected by the executive committee of TANU to represent the "national institutions," such as the National Union of Tanganyikan Workers (NUTA), the Union of Women of Tanzania, and the Cooperative Union of Tanganyika (CUT). The 17 regional commissioners of Tanganyika and the 3 from Zanzibar are also members, as are up to 32 persons from the Revolutionary Council of Zanzibar. In addition, the President may appoint up to 10 members from Tanganyika and up to 20 from Zanzibar. Thus, the total membership of the Assembly may legally reach 204, but has generally fluctuated between 180 and 190. The Assembly is charged with making laws of the land, and may override a Presidential veto by a two-thirds vote (although the President may then dissolve the Assembly and take the issue to the people).

The judiciary consists of a Chief Justice and a High Court appointed by the President "after consultation with the Chief Justice," as well as subordinate and local courts. Judges serve until age 62 (65 with Presidential approval) and can be removed "only for inability to perform the functions of his office . . . or for misbehavior," as stipulated by a tribunal of fellow judges.[11] There is no bill of rights, although the Preamble to the TANU constitution embodies most of the basic individual freedoms normally found in a bill of rights. There is also a Permanent Commission of Inquiry to investigate any abuse of authority by state officials. The legal fabric of present day Tanzania has been woven from a variety of threads—African customary law, British common law, and Islamic law—and is in the process of being coordinated and updated.[12]

Local government within the Tanzanian political system is a vital part of the political process and serves to focus on political and economic development as well as on providing a two-way channel of access from the center to the people. There are some 7000 village development committees, 13 town councils, and 58 district councils. Members of the government bureaucracy, the party, and the people meet at all levels. Representatives of the Ministries

[11] *Ibid.*, Section 57 (2).
[12] For an in-depth analysis of the legal framework of Republican Tanganyika, see J. S. R. Cole and W. N. Denison, *Tanganyika: The Development of its Laws and Constitution* (London: Stevens and Sons, 1964).

of Regional Administration and Economic Affairs and Development Planning, TANU, and the local community are involved. As mentioned earlier, the 17 regional and 60 area commissioners, appointed by the President, are critical links between the government and the people: they serve as members of the government bureaucracy, act as party secretaries, and chair the elected councils. They are, thus, in a position to pass information and decisions both upward and downward within a variety of political institutions.

In addition to the local assemblies, which are open to all, there are parallel structures for TANU members. There are some 1500 local party cells, as well as district and regional conferences (each with a standing executive committee) leading up to the biennial National Conference and the National Executive Committee. The party structure thus augments local governmental bodies and is itself, likewise, a blend of direct and indirect representation that helps to make Tanzanian local government a complex and multidimensional operation, characterized by extensive participation and a pattern of leadership choice.

Although there has been no attempt at a complete amalgamation of the party and the government, there is a blending and harmonizing of the two institutions through interaction and cross-membership; and civil servants are encouraged to become members of TANU. The President and Vice-President of TANU are the President and Second Vice-President of the Republic. The party membership, first through its district conferences and finally through the National Executive Committee, preselects the candidates for the National Assembly and screens the nominees of the national institutions. Members of the National Assembly are likewise members of the TANU National Conference, so that, at all levels, the party feeds its members into the representative bodies (whose memberships, particularly at the village and district level, may include non-TANU personnel). TANU also acts to sustain the political system, for as William Tordoff has written, "It is after all the party which, through its contact with the people, confers legitimacy on the Government." [13] "*TANU yajenga nchi*" say the Tanzanians, "TANU is building the nation."

The party maintains a national Central Committee which used

---

[13] William Tordoff, *Government and Politics in Tanzania* (Nairobi: East African Publishing House, 1967), p. xiv.

to consist of the President of TANU, the Vice-President, Secretary General, and Treasurer, as well as nine persons appointed by the President, but is somewhat smaller now, the posts of Secretary General and Treasurer having been abolished in 1967. The Central Committee meets weekly and acts as a sounding board for the government's proposals. Of more importance is the larger National Executive Committee (NEC) made up of the Central Committee, 17 regional chairmen and their secretaries, 17 delegates chosen by the National Conference to represent the districts, 1 representative each from the national institutions, and 2 from the TANU Youth League. Although the proceedings of the NEC (as well as those of the Central Committee) are not public, it seems clear that the National Executive Committee plays an important role in policy formation as well as in the selection of National Assembly candidates. It often causes a reassessment of the executive proposals.[14] On occasion, the debate within its membership is vigorous and the criticisms hostile, although, by the time a policy decision has been made public or presented to the National Conference, most difficulties have been resolved.[15] It is difficult at the present time to pinpoint exactly where major national decisions are made except that they result from the interaction of the President and the leaders of the National Executive Committee and to a lesser extent, those of the National Assembly.

The National Conference, now held every 2 years, is of less importance in the process of decision making, although it selects the party and national presidential nominees. It consists of 400 delegates, including 300 voting members, and is made up of the members of the National Assembly, the Central Committee, 17 at-large members of the National Executive Committee, 1 representative from each of the national institutions, and 60 district party secretaries. Its primary function is to serve as a public forum and to provide contact between the national personnel and their local counterparts. Because of the difficulties of communication,

[14] Henry Bienen, *Tanzania: Party Transformation and Economic Development* (Princeton: Princeton University Press, 1967), p. 185. Bienen's book is one of the finest pieces of political analysis dealing with Africa yet to appear.

[15] Tordoff, *op. cit.*, p. 16. Nick Georgulas, "Post-1964 Trends in the Tanzania Unions: A Brief Commentary," paper delivered at the African Studies Association Meeting (November, 1967), p. 9.

the dispersed nature of the population, and the free-floating character of the national offices (which lack ethnic or regional bases of support), this function is of considerable importance in stimulating a feeling of solidarity, in making opinions and policies known, and in linking the national center with its political as well as geographic periphery.

In addition to providing political representation, TANU and the government also serve to direct national institutions such as the army and the bureaucracy, and, hence, to mute the centrifugal forces that have proven so divisive to other political systems. The techniques and strategies adopted by the leaders of the Tanzanian political system are worth noting, for these institutions are used both as instruments of political power and national politics and as channels of information. Subgroup autonomy is reasonably well established in Tanzania, and the political center seems inclined to interfere with their operation only if the institutions or groups in question threaten the system or jeopardize its primary goals. Guidance, not control, is the operational intent.

The case of the Tanganyikan Federation of Labor (TFL) is illustrative. During the late 1950's, the trade union movement grew rapidly, increasing its membership from 9,000 in 1956 to 80,000 in 1960. The Tanganyikan Federation of Labor, led by Rashidi Kawawa, worked closely with TANU to bring selective pressure on the colonial authority. However after independence, despite the fact that Kawawa was brought into the government (first as Minister without portfolio, then as Prime Minister), labor continued to press for its demands, seemingly regardless of the social and economic consequences of those demands for the entire country. (A similar phenomenon occurred in Niger between the *Parti Progressiste Nigerien* and some of the country's unions). The government then tried to co-opt the labor leadership by making M. Kamaliza Minister of Labor (and later Secretary General of NUTA) and C. S. Tumbo High Commissioner to Great Britain, and by passing the Trade Disputes (Settlement) Law of 1962 which, in effect, made strikes illegal. Despite these measures, labor resentment surfaced during the army mutiny of January 1964, and the government was forced to arrest 500 workers. The decision was then made to implement closer supervision of the labor movement. Consequently, the government dissolved the Tanganyikan Federation of

Labor, merged its members with the still independent unions to form the National Union of Tanganyikan Workers (whose secretary general was nominated by the President) in 1964, and in 1967 set up a permanent labor tribunal to mediate employee-employer negotiations. Despite the fact that organized labor has but 240,000 members, (1967), it continues to play an important, although supervised, role in the life of Tanzania.

Similar, although less drastic, measures were taken to insure the loyalty and political involvement of the bureaucracy. Because of the British curb on civil servant political activity, the large number of expatriates in positions of authority (in 1961, only 1170 out of 4452 middle- and senior-grade positions were held by Africans) and the perceived need to stimulate economic and political development simultaneously, the government moved to alter the status of the bureaucracy.[16] It opened TANU membership to civil servants, abolished the native authorities, and, by Legislative Act No. 1 of 1962, replaced the nonpolitical provincial and district commissioners with regional and area commissioners who were members of TANU. In an attempt to insure technical as well as political competence, however, specialists were retained at each of these positions. At the time, there was fear that the politicalization and centralization of the bureaucracy would curtail its usefulness.[17] Although manpower problems and frequent shifting of personnel have, on occasion, resulted in local intransigence, at present the politicalization of the bureaucracy seems to have aided, rather than inhibited, both political and economic development at the district level.

As will be seen in the section on the regulative capacity of the system, the government and TANU were forced to undertake a fundamental reorganization and reorientation of the army in order to curtail its dysfunctional activities. The army mutiny in January of 1964 shook the system to its core and indicated the need for close political supervision of yet another institution in the society. The degree of party and government control can easily be overstated, however. In stressing the relationship between these interest

[16] Bienen, *op. cit.*, p. 124.

[17] Anthony H. Rweyemamu, "Managing Planned Development: Tanzania's Experience," in H. E. Smith (ed.), *Readings on Economic Development and Administration in Tanzania* (Dar es Salaam: Institute of Public Administration, 1966), pp. 411–424.

groups and the government party, it should be remembered that these organizations enjoy more autonomy than did similar groups under the Convention People's Party in Ghana or the Communist Party in the Soviet Union, and wider recruitment patterns than comparable groups in South Africa. It has been a major policy of the government, the party, and in particular, the President to encourage "internal democracy" within the groups, the party, and the government, and there are major differences of opinion in all three on such issues as the pace of Africanization, nationalization, foreign policy, and industrialization, even though this opposition is seldom formally constituted.

There are other reasons for the continuing autonomy of interest groups, local areas, and individuals. As Henry Bienen has pointed out in his excellent analysis of Tanzania, TANU is neither monolithic nor strongly centralized. In fact, "TANU is a complex of interacting organizations," for it lacks a powerful, central organization to supervise its 1500 local branches and 7000 village committees. There are less than 25 full-time officials at party headquarters in Dar es Salaam and no central filing system.[18] Looked at in perspective,

> . . . there is no mechanism through which all TANU members can be kept constantly in touch with a political ideology as it changes to meet new needs and situations, and there is no means for TANU leaders to institutionalize their view of reality and enforce it within their organization.[19]

Whether this inability is due to the nonauthoritarian character of the leaders, to the limited resources available to them for party development, to the scattered nature of the population, or to a combination of all three, is not totally clear, but a lack of trained manpower is obviously a hindrance. TANU has a membership of over 3 million, but not all are active, and the demands on its membership are substantial. The village committees, for example, need nearly 140,000 persons, and, although not all of these are TANU personnel, many are.[20] Partially by design and partially by

[18] Bienen, *op. cit.*, pp. 2–10.
[19] *Ibid.*, pp. 204–205.
[20] Tordoff, *op. cit.*, p. 120.

default, the political system of Tanzania is distinguished by a party that has mass roots but is loosely organized and generally sympathetic to subgroup autonomy. Moreover, the leaders of the system have worked with diligence to insure wide participation in the decision-making process.

The Presidential Commission and TANU persistently stressed the "channel" functions of the various party and governmental institutions and indicated that participation lies at the heart of the political process.

> There shall be the maximum possible participation by the people in their own government and ultimate control by them over all the organs of State on the basis of universal suffrage.[21]

From its inception, TANU stressed that this participation was to be meaningful and not of the fleeting type often associated with plebiscites.

> It is also necessary to have a strong political organization active in every village which acts like a toll way, all weather road, along which the purposes, plans and problems of the Government can travel to the people, at the same time as the ideas, desires and misunderstandings of the people can travel direct to the Government.[22]

These views are mirrored in reality, for the political culture of TANU and Tanzania are open to all, and decision making is carried on at all levels of government and party by many citizens (although post-Arusha developments have tended to reduce participation somewhat). The TANU Youth League has been open to members of every race since 1956, as has TANU since 1963. From December 1961 until December 1963 residents of Tanganyika could become citizens automatically and, although since then application has to be made, citizenship remains within easy attainment. Leaders within the party and the system are chosen from a broad spectrum of socio-economic groups, and recruitment patterns are far more

---

[21] J. K. Nyerere, *Freedom and Unity: Uhuru na Umoja* (London: Oxford University Press, 1967), p. 262.

[22] Lionel Cliffe (ed.), *One Party Democracy: The 1965 Tanzania General Elections* (Nairobi: East African Publishing House, 1967).

achievement-oriented than in South Africa, for example. Ascription is not a critical factor. During the elections of 1965, few constituencies were decided on tribal grounds.[23] Non-Africans, such as the Asian Minister of Finance, Amir Jamal, and the European Minister of Agriculture and Cooperatives, Derek Bryceson, have been freely chosen by the population over African opponents, and there is a greater percentage of non-Africans elected to the National Assembly than exists in society as a whole.[24] Nor is age a limiting factor—59 of the 101 elected members of the National Assembly are under 35.

The achievement orientation of politics in Tanzania and the population's realization of this are reflected in the operation of the system. According to what surveys we have, there are high levels of involvement on the part of individual citizens and a strong belief in the efficacy of political activity.[25] Voters seem to feel that their votes count and that the government is responsive to their interests and desires. Participation has increased steadily. During 1962 only 20% of the eligible voters registered and voted, while in 1965, 50% of the population registered and 76% of those registered voted; and over 3500 political meetings involving over 2.25 million people were held.[26] A brief examination of the 1965 general elections will illustrate the kinds and levels of participation.

After the election dates (September 21 for President, September 26 for the National Assembly) were announced, nominations began. There was to be a single presidential nominee, selected by the electoral conference of the party, but if in the general elections he did not receive a majority of "yes" votes, other candidates would be chosen until one received a majority. For the National Assembly, any 21 year-old citizen who was a member of TANU and accumulated twenty-five signatures of qualified voters, could apply for nomi-

[23] *Ibid.*, p. 360.

[24] Several writers have, however, pointed out the apolitical character of the Indians in East Africa and their generally low levels of political efficacy: Barton M. Schwartz (ed.), *Caste in Overseas Indian Communities* (San Francisco, Calif.: Chandler Publishing Co., 1967), pp. 267–320, and Yash Tandon, "A Political Survey," in Dharam P. Ghai (ed.), *Portrait of a Minority: Asians in East Africa* (Nairobi: Oxford University Press, 1965), pp. 65–89.

[25] Kenneth Prewitt and Goran Hyden, "Voters Look at the Elections," in Cliffe (ed.), *One Party Democracy*, p. 277.

[26] Cliffe, *op. cit.*, p. 236.

nation. It was decided that each constituency would have two candidates wherever possible to insure a voter choice, but the number was held at two in order to insure that no minority candidate would be elected. If there were more than two petitioners, the respective candidates were questioned by the TANU regional conference which then ranked the candidates in order of preference and sent their names to the National Executive Committee, which selected the final contestants. Six candidates ran unopposed, so that the committee chose 202 candidates out of the 803 aspirants to contest the 101 seats. TANU's selection of candidates did not favor party stalwarts. Cliffe estimates, for example, that 74% of those chosen were "merely card-holding members with no special status in TANU." [27]

By the Election (Amendment) Act of 1965, the two candidates in each constituency campaigned as one, sharing transport and expenses. Oration had to be conducted in Swahili with each candidate given the same opportunity to speak. "Private" competition was discouraged and candidates were not allowed to claim special TANU support. There were also restrictions on the use of racial or ethnic competition and the discussion of foreign policy issues. The basic nonracial, socialist character of the system and its foreign policy objectives were not open to debate. Because perhaps 90% of the electorate is illiterate, each of the candidates was given a symbol, either a hoe (*jembe*) or a house (*nyumba*) in their constituency. These symbols did not turn out to be totally neutral, but their allocation apparently was.[28]

Julius Nyerere was elected President on September 21, with a majority of 97%, doing slightly better on Zanzibar (which participated in the presidential elections but not those of the National Assembly) than on the mainland.[29] The elections for the National Assembly were held 5 days later, and the results were surprising. Not only were the elections free and indicative of polyarchal decision making, but the voters defeated so many incumbents (including 2

---

[27] Cliffe, *op. cit.*, p. 267.

[28] Angela Molnos, "An Attempt at a Psychological Analysis of the Role of 'Symbols' in the Tanzanian Elections," in Cliffe (ed.), *One Party Democracy*, pp. 410–430.

[29] Figures differ on the exact number of votes; Tordoff (*op. cit.*, p. 38) gives Nyerere 2,519,866 out of 2,612,225, while Cliffe (*op. cit.*, p. 359) lists 2,520,903 out of 2,636,040.

ministers, 6 junior ministers, 13 district chairmen, and 16 of 31 former members of parliament who ran) that the election could quite properly be classified as a "sweeping turnover" which few political systems anywhere could match.[30] It seems clear that members of the National Assembly had lost touch with their constituents and that since most races were decided on the basis of local issues, the leader alteration did not reflect a rejection of the system. If this were the case, it seems likely that the vote for Nyerere would have reflected that rejection.

In attempting to assess the political system of Tanzania, it should be remembered that this was the first election under the new reforms and may not constitute a pattern. But on the basis of the available data, it does seem to represent an important beginning and to offer a clear indication that democratic politics need not be confined to wealthy, developed countries or to multiparty systems. Within the framework of a single party, the voters chose most of their leaders including the President. Their involvement in decision making seems ongoing as well, through the operation of the TANU party cells. Although the next national elections are not scheduled until 1970, some tentative judgements are in order. The present Tanzanian system seems to be a unique constitutional form, offering both central direction and substantial amounts of polyarchal decision making, within both the party and the entire system, on the local as well as the national level. Taken as a whole, the system does contain some bargaining elements (such as the compromises between TANU and the Afro-Sharazi Party which resulted in Zanzibari overrepresentation (in terms of population) in Parliament and the cabinet, and retention of control over the internal affairs for Zanzibar and Pemba), but these do not seem to be crucial. Were it not for the unfortunate use of the phrase "guided democracy" by the Sukarno regime in Indonesia, this might well adequately describe the Tanzania system which combines elements of central guidance with genuine and democratic choice of leaders by nonleaders.

Representatives of the people in TANU choose the party con-

[30] Ruth Schachter Morgenthau, "African Elections: Tanzania's Contribution," *Africa Report* (December, 1965) 16. For an in-depth view of one such surprise, see Bismark Muansasu and Norman N. Miller, "Rungwe: Defeat of a Minister," in Cliffe (ed.), *One Party Democracy*, pp. 128–154.

ference, which in turn chooses the presidential candidate; final authority rests with the population as a whole. Representatives of the people in TANU choose among the petitioning applicants, but the population ultimately decides between the final two candidates selected. The elected members of the National Assembly form a majority of that body. There is also evidence that the National Assembly is playing a more important role in policy formation than it did when there was a well organized TANU parliamentary party in 1964 to mute public debate. Even in the process of nomination to the National Assembly, the public is considered. For example, in October 1965 the National Executive Committee of TANU rejected the nominees of the national institutions on the grounds that they were members of those institutions (TANU wanted less parochial representation) and because many of the nominees had previously been defeated in the September elections.[31]

Thus a characterization of the Tanzanian political system as both democratic and egalitarian does not seem unwarranted. The National Ethic and the Creed of TANU, calling for individual freedom as well as social solidarity, seem operative. Observers have commended the antiauthoritarian style of Tanzanian leadership and have described the operation of the system as "exceptionally honest." [32] Information and decision making seem to flow both upward and downward along both the government and the party structures. There seems little reason to suppose that an organized, formal opposition, which proved so meaningless during the 1961–65 period, would more effectively insure the democratic functioning of the system. Generalized support for TANU has always been so overwhelming (more so than that enjoyed by the Convention People's Party in Ghana or the *Parti Democratique de Guinée* in Guinea), that de jure recognition of a de facto situation and subsequent democratization of the political process within a single-party framework may well have, as its proponents claim, opened up the decision-making process to more meaningful levels of participation.

Not that the system is without flaws. One may well wish for more widespread appreciation of and participation in the major

---

[31] Nyerere did select Paul Bomani as a representative at large in order to use his financial talents in the Ministry of Commerce, Economic Affairs, and Development Planning.

[32] Cliffe, *op. cit.*, p. 229.

foreign policy decisions, and one would like to see a more formal institutionalization of a Bill of Rights and other safeguards which could not be overridden by some capricious future leader. But in light of the persistent erosion of democratic politics throughout the Third World, the accomplishment of Tanzania seems well worth noting. It seems to have evolved, in a few short years, a system designed to prevent political fragmentation and to curb the centrifugal forces which threaten so many other regimes, at the same time preserving a democratic core which ensures, indeed encourages, meaningful and widespread participation. As we shall be arguing in the concluding chapter of this work, the Tanzanian system may well serve as a model for other single-party regimes seeking controlled democratization of their political culture and an increase in the representative function of the central government. Clearly it could have a good deal of relevance for existing regimes of this type in Europe, Latin America, and Asia, as well as, in Africa.

There are of course, some factors in the social, economic, and political context which have aided this experiment in basic democracy. There are few Europeans within the system and little land alienation. There is also a marked lack of "tribal" tension. The largest ethnic group is that of the Sukuma, which has over a million members, but there are a dozen groups with hundreds of thousands of persons, such as the Nyamwezi, Makonde, Haya, Chagga, Gogo, Ha, and Hehe, so that there is little danger of numerical domination. Also, as was suggested in Chapter III, the traditional African political systems which now fall under the jurisdiction of the Tanzanian government, generally speaking, lacked strong, centralized authority, and this has had a salutary effect on the growth of non-tribal politics.[33] One has only to compare the role played by the

[33] There are reams of material on the ethnic groups of Tanzania. Much of the data, however, suffers from the difficulties outlined in Chapter III: Hans Cory, *The Indigenous Political System of the Sukuma* (London: Oxford University Press, 1953); Kathleen Stahl, *History of the Chagga People of Kilimanjaro* (London: Mouton and Company, 1964); C. F. Dundas, *Kilimanjaro and Its People* (London: Witherby, 1924); A. I. Richards, *East African Chiefs* (London: Faber and Faber, 1960); R. Young and H. Fosbrooke, *Smoke in the Hills: Political Tension in the Morogoro District of Tanganyika* (Evanston, Ill.: Northwestern University Press, 1960) and *Land and Politics among the Luguru of Tanganyika* (London: Routledge and Kegan Paul, 1960); P. H. Gulliver, *Land Tenure and Social Change among the Nyakyusa* (Kampala: East African Institute of Social Research, 1958); R. G. Abrahams, *Political Organization of Unyamwezi*

powerful, centralized kingdom of Buganda (relatively the same size
as the Sukuma) in the post-war history of Uganda or that of the
Ashanti in Ghana to those of the Tanganyikan groups to see the
importance of the traditional political structures. Many traditional
systems in Tanzania are either acephalous lineage segments (such
as the Kutu or Luguru), independent village systems (Zaramo,
Kwere, and the Swahili groups of the coastal region), or age-set
segments (Masai). Other groups had chieftains before 1963, but
these were divided into multiple, often small units (Nyamwezi,
Nyakyusa, Sumbwa, Kimbu, Konongo). Even if there were paramount chiefs over these small groups (as are found among the
Vidunda, Zigula, and Shambala), they enjoyed little political power
over their subordinates. There were some peoples with ruling dynas-
ties and identifiable class stratification, as the Haya and Ha, but
these groups are confined to the north-west corner of the country
near Lake Victoria and are politically unimportant.

In short, judging from the data we now have, the traditional
political systems of Tanzania were characterized by diffused political
powers and authority fragmentation. When the British tried to institute a process of indirect rule, they found over 120 units (which
by 1950 had 435 recognized native authorities).[34] TANU and the
independent government of Tanganyika did nothing to create or
enhance tribal authority—in fact they abolished it in 1963 [African
Chief Ordinance (Repeal) Act]. The political leadership has been
able to move ahead with its proposals for a modern system without
major blockages from the traditional authorities. Because of the
lack of sufficient manpower resources, TANU did on occasion use
some of these former authorities as individuals within the party and
the bureaucracy, but this was done on a highly selective basis.[35]
There seems little question that the traditional African systems
provided a suitable environment for the present system and that
long traditions of internal democracy and opposition to arbitrary

(London: Cambridge University Press, 1967); and several monographs in the
Ethnographic Survey of Africa: A. H. J. Prins, *The Coastal Tribes of the North-
eastern Bantu*, and Mary Tein, *The Peoples of the Lake Nyasa Region*.

[34] Cole and Denison, *op. cit.*, p. 82.
[35] Norman N. Miller, "The Political Survival of Traditional Leadership,"
Journal of Modern African Studies, Vol. VI, No. 2: 183–201.

rule facilitated the development of the present system. The formation of a Tanzanian political system has also been aided by the
existence of a national language, Kiswahili, and a quasinational culture (which, at the very least, contributed a few central reference
points, such as communal cooperation, welfare concerns, and a
social obligation to work).

Finally, there is the matter of national poverty. As we indicated
in Chapter II, generalizations beyond individual countries are difficult to make and of doubtful validity pending exhaustive cross-
comparison. Nevertheless, Bienen has made a substantial point in
recognizing that the very low levels of wealth that inhibit the formation of a strong central party and, hence, rapid economic development, also mean that the system qua system is not faced with many
entrenched socio-economic oppositions. The low levels of income,
the dependence upon subsistence agriculture, and the scattered, rural
nature of the population means that a stage-three, "modern" government has been superimposed on a stage-one socio-economic context. The lack of socio-economic differentiation and the relative
classlessness of Tanzanian society do seem to facilitate the formation of an egalitarian, democratic political system.

The astute leadership of Tanzania is also a factor. We have
deliberately down-played the role of Julius Nyerere in reaction to
many of the highly personalized political accounts of other African
political systems but also in order to indicate the historical and
societal underpinnings of the present system. Nevertheless, his vision
and foresight, his commitment to a nonracial, democratic government, and his rational guidance may well have provided the necessary impetus to ensure the present accomplishment of at least a
modified polyarchal political system.

Capabilities Analysis

In terms of the survival and development of the Tanzanian
political system, it is just as well that it enjoys not only these advantages, but also the widespread support of its citizens that stems
from their political participation. For with the possible exception
of the symbolic capacity, its capabilities are both quantitatively and
qualitatively unimpressive.

REGULATIVE CAPACITY

The regulative capacity is limited by a lack of both human and natural resources.

Along with the British Westminster political system, the independent government of Tanganyika inherited an army trained, equipped, and led by the British—three battalions of the King's African Rifles. These had fought well during World War II in Burma and the Horn of Africa, but served the new government less well. There seems to have been a good deal of resentment at the postindependence pay scales and the fact that two-thirds of the officers were still British by 1964. In any case, after the revolution on Zanzibar during January 1964, the army mutinied, putting their officers under guard and demanding reforms. It now appears that the revolt had little political motivation, but its repercussions were dramatic. The President went into hiding, local security forces permitted a week of looting in Dar es Salaam, and members of the Tanganyikan Federation of Labor took to the streets to dramatize their demands. The government was forced to call in British troops, who restored order with little loss of life. Although the TANU–government political infrastructure remained in place during the crisis and although life went on as usual outside the major cities, the mutiny underscored the weak regulative capacity of the central government and resulted in a substantial reassessment of the relationship between the armed forces and the government.

In particular, the previous apolitical character of the army was called into question. Once order was restored, the Tanganyikan government sought to dramatically alter the make-up and ideological inclination of its security forces. It imprisoned the leaders of the army and dismissed most of the rank and file. TANU opened up its membership to both the army and the police, and sought to inject its own personnel into the security forces. A new People's Defense Force, under the direction of the Second Vice-President, was formed and its members underwent extensive political indoctrination. Because of limited funds, the size of this force is currently limited to 3000, and a reserve has been created by giving weapons and training to elements of the police, the National Service Corps and the TANU Youth League. A new field force of military police with strong paramilitary capabilities has also been formed, and seems to form the basis for any ready reaction operations.

The British instructors were replaced by a variety of foreign specialists. Communist China now trains the army, Canada the fledgling air force, West Germany the navy, and Israel the police. It remains to be seen, however, whether these security forces, with their diverse training, often unclear regulatory assignments, and minimal control from the center will function effectively in a period of national stress. They have not yet been tested in a major crisis. Until they are, the basic assumption that the Tanzanian regulatory capability remains weak is warranted. The government has, however, taken two steps which seem to offer an increased potential. First, the army is no longer allowed to ruminate in its barracks, but has been put to work on such nation-building projects as village development and roadwork. Secondly, since the development of the cell system of TANU, it seems likely that these local units may be able to provide information and, if necessary, to play a quasi-security role at the local level.

The Tanzanian political system also employs two techniques, rustication and preventive detention, which have been used selectively to date, but could serve as a basis for a more extensive regulatory system. During 1966, for example, the government proposed that all secondary and university students participate, upon graduation, in a National Service Corps for a 2 year period. There would be 6 months of training and 18 months of service in the countryside. Many students, especially those at the University College at Dar es Salaam, protested against the idea, refused to participate, and demonstrated against the government. The government reacted by banning the National Union of Tanganyika Students and expelled over 300 students. These were sent to their home villages to rusticate and rethink the implications of their positions. After several months away from the capital, most students apologized and were allowed to return. This tactic was also used with some effectiveness against some labor leaders such as Victor Mkello during 1963–64 and against some of the army personnel involved in the mutiny of 1964.

Tanzania also has a preventive detention act. Passed in 1962 to "safeguard" national life from persons "threatening" the security and stability of the state, it has been used but rarely. After the army mutiny, some labor leaders were held, and in 1968, after Oscar Kambona went into exile, some of his relatives were arrested; but, in general, the government has avoided using this act—apparently recognizing the potentially harmful aspects and implications of its continuous or widespread use.

Censorship is also used sparingly. Under the direction of the Ministry of Information rather than the Ministry of Justice or Home Affairs, it is directed primarily against foreign firms, although some Kenyan newspapers were briefly banned during the disorders of 1964 and during October 1968. The government has generally relied upon the promulgation of its views and a steady flow of propaganda, rather than upon the suppression of information, to promote its policies. Taken with rustication and the preventive detention act, the use of censorship in Tanzania does seem to indicate a regulatory pattern. The central government does not like to use these methods and, wherever possible, avoids them. At the same time it is clear that the leaders will not endanger the safety of the regime and the system in order to avoid their use. Generally speaking, miscreants have not been sentenced to permanent banishment or capital punishment for crimes against the state (in fact, many persons in Tanganyika complained about the light sentences meted out to the mutineers).

There is, however, one area where governmental regulation is significant, and that is in the economic sector. TANU has always felt strongly on this point:

> . . . it is the responsibility of the state to intervene actively in the economic life of the Nation so as to ensure the well-being of all citizens and so as to prevent the exploitation of one person by another or one group by another, and so as to prevent the accumulation of wealth to an extent which is inconsistent with the existence of a classless society.[36]

We have already alluded to government direction of organized labor and its regulation of collective bargaining. It has also sought to control the commanding heights of the economy through such governmental agencies as COSATA (retail cooperatives), INTRATA (export-import agency), and TANESCO (national development cor-

---

[36] *Constitution of the Tanganyikan African National Union*, preamble.

poration). Despite its goals of Pan-Africanism and its commitment to an East African Federation, Tanzania has not hesitated to act in a more parochial fashion economically. By 1965 Tanzania was running a $30 million deficit with her partners in the East African Common Market, Kenya and Uganda. The government, then, introduced a new currency to replace the East African monetary units, established an independent central bank, and imposed trade restrictions.[37]

In recent years, the government has taken an even more active role in economic matters. The Arusha Declaration of February 1967, coming after a reexamination of the relationship between the government and the still private sector of the economy, announced its commitment to a "truer" form of socialism. The government proceeded to take a controlling interest in many firms, and totally nationalized others. The banks, insurance companies, flour mills, breweries, cement factories, and those food-processing firms which purchased food through the National Agricultural Board were all affected. In October 1967 the action was extended to the various sisal plantations in which the government took a controlling interest.

This action seems to have been more a matter of principle than of economic expediency, since Tanzania pledged to reimburse the affected firms out of her scarce foreign exchange and appointed a Danish economist to calculate the cost and plan the implementation of repayment:

> In all cases we have stated quite clearly and categorically that we shall pay full and fair compensation for the assets acquired, and that we shall honor all existing commitments—with special reference to commitments to employees.[38]

The relationship of the government to economic life, especially to the private sector of the economy, seems to be motivated by the ideology of African Socialism (as seen in Tanzania) and a belief in both grass roots development and the virtues of self-reliance.[39] It is

[37] Paul Bomani, "A Central Bank for Tanzania," *Readings on Economic Development and Administration in Tanzania*, pp. 120–124.

[38] *Sunday News*, Dar es Saalam: February 12, 1967.

[39] Martin Lowenkopf, "The Meaning of Arusha," *Africa Report* (March, 1967), 8–13.

felt that only the government and TANU, working in consort, can control the economic progress of the country and ensure the equitable division of the wealth which will result from development. But running an economy is a large task and, as in other spheres of life in Tanzania, it remains to be seen whether the lack of trained manpower and capital will not militate against the attainment of these goals to the extent that it seems to operate against others. It would appear that for the foreseeable future, a weak control apparatus and an underdeveloped regulatory capacity will continue to be distinguishing characteristics of the system.

EXTRACTIVE CAPABILITY

The extractive capability of Tanzania is likewise minimal. Tanzania is one of the poorest countries in Africa, with a gross domestic product of $700 million and a per capita income in 1965 of $64.[40] Most of the country consists of dry savanna; much of it covered by the tsetse fly. Only 10% of the total land is in use, and 90% of the population is engaged in subsistence agriculture. In spite of these handicaps, Tanzania is heavily dependent upon the production of primary agricultural products for its export revenues of which sisal, coffee, and cotton amount to 80%. The island of Zanzibar is even closer to being a monocrop economy, with 90% of its exports being derived from the sale of cloves and coconuts. The potentially harmful implications of this dependence on agricultural products which are subject to the vicissitudes of a world market have been underscored in recent years. Because much of Tanzania's development plan from 1964 to 1969 was predicated on sustained earnings from these products, the severe erosion of world prices, particularly of sisal (due to competition from synthetic fibers), has called into question the possibility of Tanzania's achieving those goals, and has placed in jeopardy many of the socio-economic schemes upon which the nation was to be based.

The rest of Tanzania's resource base is likewise scanty. There are some diamonds, gold, tin, and coal, but these account for but 20% of exports, and the coal deposits cannot be commercially mined. In

---

[40] *The United Nations Statistical Yearbook 1967*, p. 577. A comparable analysis is to be found in Andrew M. Kamarck, *The Economics of African Development* (New York: Frederick A. Praeger, 1967), p. 251.

general, Tanzania lacks the mineral deposits that elsewhere in Africa have stimulated foreign investment and economic take-off. It also lacks an internal market of sufficient size and wealth to warrant rapid industrialization. There is almost no heavy industry and the manufacturing section accounts for but 4% of the gross domestic product.[41] Tanzania does have a variety of good ports, such as Mtwara, Lindi, Tanga, and Dar es Salaam, and has railroad links between Dar es Salaam and Lakes Tanganyika and Victoria, Tanga and Moshi, and Mtwara and Nachingurea. Since the Rhodesian Declaration of Independence in November 1965, there has been a plan to link Zambia with the existing rail net. The 1000 mile project, now under Chinese auspices, is currently in the survey stage. Tanzania also has nearly 30,000 miles of roads, but, given the size of the country, this makes for one of the lowest per-square-mile ratios in all of Africa.

There seem to be two possible areas of development that could aid the economy over time: tourism and game ranching. Neither of these has been fully exploited. With the largest herds of wild animals left in the world, Tanzania could develop both solid tourist and meat-processing industries. Kenya has found that the potential for tourism is almost unlimited, and her earning of several hundred million dollars annually is curtailed only by the lack of accommodations. Similar largesse could be Tanzania's were adequate tourist facilities available. Likewise, the farming of game, which has a higher yield per acre than cattle ranching, could have an important nutrient impact on diets of rural Tanzanians. These hopes lie in the future, however, and it is not clear that either project will receive the kind of priority necessary to insure its attainment without massive outside aid.

The human resource base of the Tanzanian political system suffers from the handicaps normally associated with severe underdevelop-

[41] Kamarck, op. cit., p. 257; Hance, op. cit., pp. 374–431. A less than objective account of the economy of Tanzania is to be found in Gilbert L. Rutman, The Economy of Tanganyika (New York: Frederick A. Praeger, 1968). A more balanced view is from the International Bank for Reconstruction and Development, The Economic Development of Tanganyika (Dar es Salaam: Government Printer, 1961). Some authorities have suggested that the manufacturing sector could be best strengthened by more complete processing of raw materials (Arthur D. Little Inc., "Tanganyika Industrial Development," Readings on Economic Development and Administration in Tanzania, pp. 269–284).

ment. Life expectancy is just over 35 years; the literacy rate is but 10%. There are high birth and death rates, and the yearly population increase seems to be holding firm at 1.9%.[42] Although there is some overpopulation near Lake Victoria and on parts of Mt. Kilimanjaro, the population is generally scattered with a density of 35 per square mile. Only 4% of the people of Tanzania are urbanized, and 45% of the population is under 16, placing a heavy burden of dependence on those old enough to support others. The work force currently employed is estimated at only slightly more than 3%, and has actually declined since independence.[43]

In 1964, the government of Tanzania launched an ambitious development program to improve the life conditions of its citizens and to stimulate economic growth, but falling prices for export commodities and a lower inflow of foreign investment and aid than anticipated have forced the curtailment of many of the capital-intensive projects once envisioned. Nevertheless, Tanzania hopes to finance additional development through self-generation and by a reliance upon indirect taxes on imports and customs duties, and a greater emphasis on the use of manual labor.[44] It seems clear however, that Tanzania's interest in preserving her "independence" and her socialistic ideology have cost the system foreign investment capital. The Tanzanian growth rate has been a respectable 4% a year but this is only 60% of the rate of the Ivory Coast which does accept foreign investment almost irrespective of its political and diplomatic repercussions. (There are compensations, of course: Tanzania does seem able to project a far more independent stance in the international community.)

DISTRIBUTIVE CAPABILITY

Because both the regulative and extractive capabilities of the system are weak, the reward pools of goods and services available for distribution by the system are not abundant. Nevertheless (and this is a definite support for the regime), the political system seems committed to allocating the rewards it has on the basis of equality and merit. The circumscribed nature of the private sector

[42] *The United Nations Statistical Yearbook 1967*, p. 99.

[43] Tordoff, *op. cit.*, p. 153.

[44] Government of Tanzania, The Treasury, *Budget Survey 1965–66* (Dar es Salaam: Government Printer, 1965), pp. 33–40.

of the economy and the commitment of the government to welfare projects and African socialism do, of course, place limits on individual attainment, but, within these boundaries, a decidedly egalitarian distribution of rewards occurs:

> We have declared that we wish to build our economy on the basis of the equality of all citizens, and have specifically rejected the concept of creating a class system where one group of people owns the means of production for the purpose of getting personal profit and another group works for them.[45]

The government has taken an active role in distributing land, wealth, and education. Land, for example, has been regarded in many traditional African systems as communal property with individual "ownership" permitted only during the period of actual use. In those areas where land was held on a more feudal basis (such as the *nyarubaja* system of the Haya), the government has worked to abolish it. Only about 1% of the land encompassed by the Tanzanian political system is held by non-Africans and although there is some freehold land among such groups as the Chagga and Meru, most land is controlled by the government. Land is currently "leased from the state for life," as long as it is used.[46] The government has, through its various village development schemes, encouraged the communal workings of existing family plots in order to promote the "greatest good for the greatest number." Nationalization of property has also worked against the development of a freehold, peasant class (as in nearby Kenya). While this policy may have political and ideological validity, it does prevent industrial entrepreneurs from using land as collateral for loans and may actually inhibit economic development.

Attempts are also underway to distribute the existing national wealth more evenly. Africans constitute 98% of the population but

[45] Julius K. Nyerere, "The Costs of Nonalignment," *Africa Report* (October, 1966), 63.

[46] Government of Tanganyika, *Proposals of the Tanganyika Government for Land Tenure Reform* (Dar es Salaam: Government Printer, 1962), pp. 1–13; and Aaron Segal, "The Politics of Land in East Africa," *Africa Report* (April, 1967), 49–50. See also Krishan M. Maini, *Land Law in East Africa* (Nairobi: Oxford University Press, 1967).

share only 70% of the gross domestic product, for example, and the government has increased the rate of Africanization in such areas as the civil service and put pressure on the Arabs and Asians in the retail trade to include Africans in their operations. This is particularly true in the case of noncitizens, and many have already left the country. Equalization, however, is not simply directed toward non-Africans. The present government, recognizing the inequity between the rural and city situations and the tendency for government employees to live far beyond the means of the average person, has stated quite clearly:

> We must not forget that people who live in towns can possibly become the exploiters of those who live in the rural areas. All our big hospitals are in towns and they benefit only a small section of the people of Tanzania. Yet if we have built them with loans from outside Tanzania, it is the overseas sale of the peasant's produce which provides the foreign exchange for repayment.[47]

Impressed by the fact that urban wages have increased 50% since independence while those of the agricultural workers are only 5% higher, the government has moved to correct the situation and promote a more equitable distribution of, at least, the government-dispersed wealth. During 1966, for example, the President cut his own salary and those of the ministers by 20%, and those of civil servants by 10%. This was followed by the Arusha Declaration of February 1967 which stressed the opposition of the party and the government to the development of a privileged class, even if that class consisted of government workers and party officials:

> No TANU or Government leaders should hold shares in any company.
> No TANU or Government leaders should hold directorships in any privately-owned enterprises.
> No TANU or Government leaders should receive two or more salaries.
> No TANU or Government leaders should own houses which he rents to others.[48]

---

[47] *Arusha Declaration*, February 5, 1967, Part III, published as Tanganyika African National Union, *The Arusha Declaration and TANU's Policy on Socialism and Self Reliance* (Dar es Salaam: Government Printer, 1967).

[48] *Ibid.*, p. 31.

This is not to say that there are no classes in Tanzania or that no government officials use their positions to amass wealth, but these exist in spite of government policy not because of it (as in the Ivory Coast). There can be little question that governmental dedication to the doctrine of *Uhuru na Kazi*, freedom and work, and the lack of conspicuous consumption helps to stress the positive relationship between the government and the people and that in this way, poverty seems to contribute to and provide support for the regime.

Just as the political system takes a rather instrumental view of the land and wealth it distributes, so education is allotted on the dual basis of national need and merit, with the national need taking priority. Education is regarded as a means of positive socialization and as a way of supplying the needs of the system but with this proviso: "the educated elite of East Africa is an elite of attainment rather than ascription." [49] In short, the needs of the nation are expected to come before the needs of an individual.

REJUVENATIVE CAPABILITY

We have already dwelt at length on the process of political participation and the widened recruitment patterns that help to reinforce the system. The general trend observed in the distribution sector seems to carry over into this area. Europeans and other non-Africans are perhaps overrepresented in commerce and in the government bureaucracy, but the government seems committed to more Africanization in order to redress the balance only if it will not jeopardize the development of the nation as a whole.

The process of political socialization in Tanzania may be observed in three general areas: education, communications, and the political process, the last area being the most important in terms of positively reinforcing the citizens' commitment to the system. Education is also of importance, for Tanzania has concentrated on the premise that "education be regarded primarily as a means of supplying the manpower requirements of the nation." [50] Soon after independence, the

[49] Idrian N. Resnick, "Manpower Development in Tanzania," *Journal of Modern African Studies* (1967) Vol. V, No. 1: 107; and David Koff and George von der Muhll, "Political Socialization in Kenya and Tanzania—a Comparative Analysis," *Journal of Modern African Studies* (1967) Vol. V, No. 1: 34.

[50] Resnick, *op. cit.*, p. 107. See also Robert L. Thomas, *Survey of the High Level Manpower Requirements and Reasons for the Five Year Development Plan 1964-65–1968-69* (Dar es Salaam: Government Printer, 1965).

system made a firm commitment to the educational process, allocating 24% of the budget to education through 1969 and channelling the students into needed occupations and skill groups by a system of controlled scholarships and encouragement of specific careers.[51] Attempts have been made to develop a national school system of seven primary grades and four lower and two upper level secondary grades, all linked with national syllabi and examinations. Students could then go on to study at the University of East Africa with its three colleges—Makerere in Uganda, University College in Nairobi, Kenya, and University College in Dar es Salaam.

The results to date have been mixed. Perhaps two-thirds of the primary and secondary schools are still run by missions (although the government controls the curriculum) and two-thirds of the university students continue to study outside the country.[52] School dropouts have been a serious problem in the lower grades, and the nonreturn of overseas students has also caused concern. Even more importantly, the high cost of education (Nyerere estimates that it takes the per capita income of fifty people to keep one student in college) and the problem of securing adequate employment for those who leave school with insufficient skills have caused the government to question some of its priorities in the field of education and to cut back on some of the "crash" educational programs. The reaction on the part of the students to the National Service Corps proposals, for example, indicates the need for the inculcation of more "egalitarian" material and "education for self reliance."

On the other hand, the government-sponsored Kivokoni Adult College, which was founded in 1961, seems to have worked out quite well, and Tanzania is now placing greater stress on adult education and on a program of politicalization for the population as a whole than on the young, because "our children will not have an impact on our economic development for five, ten or even twenty years."[53] Government and party officials, as well as individual citizens, take short courses of a political nature, and many interesting ideological notions have come out of the sometimes lively discussions held at

[51] Resnick, *op. cit.*, p. 116.

[52] Cliffe, *op. cit.*, p. 264. See also Helen Kitchen (ed.), *The Educated African* (New York: Frederick A. Praeger, 1962), pp. 145–160.

[53] Julius K. Nyerere, *Address to the National Assembly*, May 12, 1964.

Kivukoni.

Communications are not under total governmental control, although the government operates the Tanganyika Broadcasting Company and TANU publishes two daily newspapers through the Mwananch Publishing Company: the *Nationalist* (an English-language paper with a printing of 6,000 and a claimed readership of 22,000) and *Uhuru* (a Swahili paper with an 11,000 printing and a readership of 100,000).[54] These express the government position on most matters (although often reflecting different points of view within it): *"We preach and exhort about 40% of the time, if we don't exhort, who will?"* [55] There are also two private papers, the *Standard* (an English-language medium with a printing of 17,000 and a readership of 51,000 as well as a Sunday edition, the *Sunday News*) and *Ngurumo* (which is in Swahili and totals 14,000 and 50,000 respectively). Foreign papers are also available, so that at least in the capital, there is a wide selection and reasonably good coverage of world events. But Dar es Salaam consumes half of all the papers, leaving few for the 12 million persons in the rest of the country. Illiteracy and the difficulties of distribution clearly hamper the dissemination of information, whether government or private, and thereby substantially reduce the opportunities for communication and/or control.

Thus, it is neither the educational system nor the government use of communication that gives the political system its major thrust in terms of rejuvenation. In the total life experience of the individual, political activity seems to play an important role in shaping his levels of identification with the government. Elections seem to have heightened both national consciousness and a feeling of solidarity within the system.[56] Participation in the decision-making process, contact with elections which are regarded as honest and observable patterns of dissent-protection, probably do more to reinforce the central government and the political system than any combination of propaganda, censorship, or enforced regulation of individuals' activities.

[54] John C. Condon, "Nation Building and Image Building in the Tanzanian Press," *Journal of Modern African Studies* (1967) Vol. V, No. 3: 336.
[55] *Ibid.*, p. 352.
[56] Cliffe, *op. cit.*, p. 241.

SYMBOLIC CAPABILITY

In spite of decidedly weak regulative, extractive, and distribution capabilities and a currently uneven rejuvenative capacity, Tanzania demonstrates a strong symbolic capability. This is true despite the fact that, like so many other African states, it lacks many national symbols. Like others, it does have a flag and a national anthem (a Swahili version of "God Bless Africa," *Mungu iBariki Afrika*), but it is doubtful that these have much meaning for most of the population. There is also a Ministry of National Culture and Youth which emphasizes the use of Swahili and other aspects of "African" culture, but its impact to date has been negligible.

Julius K. Nyerere and TANU are perhaps the most significant national symbols. Nyerere is *Baba Wa Taifa*, father of the nation; he is the leader and the *Mwalimu* or teacher. He adds an element of charisma (although he discourages a cult of personality and has refused the position of life President). His image is, of course, bound up with that of TANU—the party of independence, the anticolonial, antiimperialist force that supports the system and gives the government meaning. The system clearly enjoys a legitimacy based on a frugal, honest, almost humble, style of national leadership. Nyerere, the grass roots nature of TANU, widespread participation in the political life of the nation, and the equality of the distribution system, all seem to reinforce the political system as a whole and help to establish its credibility.

Behavioral studies of these legitimacy patterns are not exhaustive, but at least a small sample does seem to indicate a basic support for the system. A high percentage of students "trust" the government and are "interested" in matters of state, because they regard it as *their* system.[57] Another study indicates that the average citizen believes in the effect of his participation and the exercise of his choice, and that most exhibit a greater level of identification with, and faith in, the government than has been measured in such developed countries as the United States.[58]

The political system of Tanzania also seems to benefit from the existence of a quasinational ideology which, however diffused and unspecific, provides a basic set of supports for the government. The

---

[57] Koff and von der Muhll, *op. cit.*, 23–25.
[58] Prewitt and Hyden, *op. cit.*, pp. 273–298.

term African Socialism has been used to describe some of its facets, but since this phrase has also been applied with regularity to systems as diverse as those of Mali, Kenya, and Senegal, it is best to use it with caution. In the case of Tanzania, or at least among the political elite of Tanzania, African Socialism is often equated with *Ujamaa* or familyhood:

> It is opposed to capitalism, which seeks to build a happy society on the basis of the exploitation of man by man; and it is equally opposed to doctrinaire socialism which seeks to build its happy society on a philosophy of inevitable conflict between man and man.[59]

As Fred Burke has suggested, *Ujamaa* is not universally known in Tanzania: it has tended to mean different things to different people, and seems at best to form a "state of mind" rather than a precise ideology as Marxist-Leninism or the capitalism of Adam Smith.[60] At the same time, the writings of Nyerere, the contents of both the National Ethic and the TANU Creed, and, most recently, the statements of the Arusha Declaration, all indicate a generalized philosophy which seems to strike a resonant cord in many Tanzanians and which might be summarized as a set of basic tenets.

1. an acceptance of a humanism which transcends ethnic groups and nations
2. a faith in the dignity and essential goodness of individual men
3. a strong commitment to egalitarianism in both economic and political realms
4. a social obligation to work and cooperate on communal projects
5. a welfare strain by which the old, the infirmed, and the young are to be taken care of [61]

[59] Nyerere, *Freedom and Unity*, p. 170.

[60] Fred G. Burke, "Tanganyika: The Search for Ujamaa," in William H. Friedland and Carl G. Rosberg (eds.), *African Socialism* (Stanford, Calif.: Stanford University Press, 1964), pp. 194–219. See also chapters 1, 2, and 5, and appendix II.

[61] Julius K. Nyerere, *Democracy and the Party System* (Dar es Salaam: Tanganyika Standard, 1963), and *Ujamaa: The Basis of African Socialism* (Dar es Salaam: Tanganyika Standard, 1962). For these principles in action see Rodger Yeager, "Micropolitics, Persistence, and Transformation: Theoretical Notes and the Tanzania Experience," paper delivered at the African Studies Association meeting (November, 1967) and Rene Lemarchand, "Village-By-Village Nation Building in Tanzania," *Africa Report* (February, 1965), 11–13.

This is socialism with a small "s," a basically humanistic philosophy which reminds one more of Mazzini than of Marx.

This philosophy, whether actualized or not, adds to the legitimacy of the system and gives meaning and purpose to the sacrifices demanded of individual Tanzanians. In light of the government's attempts to actualize its tenets, the philosophy (and the system) seems both worthwhile and believable:

> The justification of socialism is man; not the State, not the flag. Socialism is not for the benefit of black men, nor white men, nor yellow men. The purpose of socialism is the service of man, regardless of color, size, shape, skill, ability or anything else.[62]

Goals of the Political System

For a poor, militarily weak country struggling to emerge from its economic predicament, Tanzania exhibits an interesting set of goal priorities. Despite the polyarchal aspects of the decision-making process on the local and national level, goal formation seems most often to be the prerogative of the leaders of the system, particularly the President, Julius K. Nyerere. These goals may reflect the "general will" of the people of Tanzania, but at this time we do not have data to support such a proposition. Although interest articulation on foreign policy was definitely lacking during the September 1965 elections and most contests were settled on the basis of local issues, international issues are of major importance in the goal hierarchy of Tanzania.

The first of these is freedom. While there is little question that such a goal has domestic ramifications, its orientation is by definition reactive and outward-looking. The attainment of freedom for the political system of Tanzania (and by extension the black populations of southern Africa) is the central goal of both the regime and the system. Nyerere put the matter quite bluntly:

> Not even for the sake of our national security or our economic development can we allow our nation to succumb to outside control—direct or indirect. We do need outside financial and technical help. But we did not struggle

[62] *The Nationalist*, February 14, 1967.

for our independence in order to sell it to the highest bidder.[63]

It is true that the leadership of many newly independent nations have made similar statements, but few have followed such a course of action if the political, diplomatic, and economic rewards dictated the wisdom of downplaying one's independence. The Ivory Coast is an obvious case in point. For Tanzania, however, it is not mere rhetoric. Here the pursuance of independence and search for freedom have taken the form of an almost xenophobic reaction to any attempts (and seeming attempts) to circumscribe the action of Tanzania. In 1961, for example, Tanganyika, along with Ghana, brought pressure to bear on Great Britain concerning the application of South Africa for membership in the Commonwealth as a republic. Despite the need for British financial assistance and the importance of the Commonwealth market for its goods, Tanganyika threatened to leave that organization if South Africa were allowed to enter:

> We believe that the principles of the Commonwealth are betrayed by an affirmative answer to South Africa's application for re-admission as a Republic. Inevitably, therefore, we are forced to say that to vote South Africa in, is to vote us out.[64]

In this instance, South Africa's withdrawal of her application obviated any test of Tanganyika's commitment, but Tanganyika proceeded to cut off all trade with South Africa and to prohibit the recruitment of her citizens for contract labor in the gold mines. Diamonds from the Mwadui mines, however, continue to be marketed through the Anglo-American Corporation which is essentially a South African and British firm. In December 1965 Tanzania did face a situation in which there were definite costs concomitant with following her principles. After Great Britain failed to crush the rebellious European minority government of Rhodesia, Tanzania broke off diplomatic reactions with Great Britain and thereby lost use of a $21 million loan. Diplomatic relations have since been restored, but Tanzania continues to pay a large portion of the burden of "liberating" southern Africa. The government takes care of over 40,000

[63] Julius K. Nyerere, *Speech to the National Assembly*, August 24, 1964.
[64] Nyerere, *Freedom and Unity*, p. 112.

refugees from that region and the Congo, and has allowed Dar es Salaam to serve as the headquarters for the various exile groups. It sponsored the Pan-African Freedom Movement for East, Central, and South Africa (PAFMECSA) until 1963 when the functions of that organization were taken over by the Liberation Committee of the Organization of African Unity, which is now based in Tanzania. Training facilities, schools, and hospitals are currently provided for many exile groups, although the commitment is perhaps the most pronounced in the case of the *Frente De Libertaçao de Moçambique* (FRELIMO) of Mozambique.

The exact costs of this independent course and the persistent concern over "foreign" domination are difficult to assess, but we can say that Tanzania has gone to great length to avoid taking sides in the Cold War or the Sino-Soviet split.[65] After the merger with Zanzibar (which already had diplomatic relations with the German Democratic Republic), Tanzania (which had diplomatic relations and an extensive aid program with the Federal German Republic) reacted strongly to West German pressure to break relations with East Germany. When West Germany cancelled its military aid, Tanzania peremptorily refused to accept nonmilitary aid. In 1965, largely on the basis of a misunderstood phone conversation, Tanzania expelled two U.S. diplomats. When the United States protested, Tanzania recalled its ambassador from Washington, jeopardizing both the existing and future aid programs.

This independence, regardless of economic and diplomatic cost, is not confined to Tanzanian relations with the West however. Despite the large amounts of Soviet aid (over $40 million since independence), Tanzania has encouraged a large Chinese presence (also amounting to $40 million of promised aid); but her leaders have not hesitated to object to some of the revolutionary views of China and have in fact resisted the suggestion that China totally replace Taiwan at the United Nations (although Tanzania favors the seating of China). Ideologically, her position runs counter to the prevalent Chinese philosophy:

> We have to make a fundamental change in the conditions under which our people live. That is what revolution really

[65] Julius K. Nyerere, "The Costs of Non-alignment," *Africa Report* (October, 1966), 61–67.

means; bloodshed is irrelevant to it; the political changes of independence are only a precursor to it. A revolution in underdeveloped countries like the United Republic means an economic revolution if it is to mean anything.[66]

Tanzania currently receives financial aid and technical assistance from Great Britain, China, the USSR, the U.S., Japan, Israel, both Germanies, Yugoslavia, Canada, Denmark, Sweden, and the World Bank, with the first four countries mentioned supplying the major portion of that aid.[67] This gamut of donors is not in itself remarkable, but Tanzania's apparent commitment to an independent course of action despite all manner of aid and her success in adhering to that commitment is.

Within the African context as well, Tanzania has pursued an independent course. Aiding the liberation movements of southern Africa and opposing such actions as the French nuclear tests in the Sahara and the United States paratroop operation in the Congo, Tanzania has the company of many African states. At the same time, Tanzania was the first African state to recognize the breakaway regime of Biafra and, despite African opposition to her stand (which seems to line up Portugal, France, the Ivory Coast, Gabon, Zambia and Tanzania against the rest of the African states), continues to champion the Biafran claims to nationhood. Tanzania has maintained that Biafrans have lost faith in, and identification with, the Nigerian government and the decline in unity cannot be redressed by violence.

Taking these various stands and actions together, Tanzania seems to be pursuing a course of independence and to be making an attempt at freedom while exhibiting a fear of foreign domination and influence. In the process, the leadership has often sacrificed economic gain and political expediency for that stance—a course of action that contrasts most dramatically with that of the Ivory Coast, but appears similar to that of Somalia.

A second major goal of the system, and one which has been pursued with vigor by the leaders of Tanzania, is that of political development. The implementation of the constitutional reforms con-

[66] Nyerere, quoted in *Africa Report* (August, 1964), 5.
[67] Government of Tanzania, *Budget Survey 1965–1966* (Dar es Salaam: Government Printer, 1967).

stituted a major commitment in terms of time, energy, and manpower (as the elections of 1965 illustrate). We have already alluded to the widespread participation in the decision-making process and to the accent on polyarchal leadership choice. There are other signs of increasing political development as well. There is growing linkage through the mechanisms of the village development committees and the TANU party cells. The newly introduced district commissioners act as linkage agents between the center and local authority, between the government and the population. National integration of ethnic and economic groups into the body politic has already taken place, and the beginnings of a national ideology as personified by the national party creeds are discernible. Participation has demonstratively widened, and the government and TANU have worked to keep channels of access open to the people. In addition, the leadership has demonstrated a refreshing willingness to admit past mistakes and to experiment with new political and economic techniques.

Tanzania also exhibits an external facet of political development which appears as a willingness to enter into larger and more viable economic and political groupings. The political merger with Zanzibar, the relations with the East African Common Market, the hesitant steps toward an East African Federation, and a continued commitment to Pan-Africanism all indicate that political development is a major goal of the system.

Even prior to independence Tanganyika demonstrated a willingness to sacrifice its national interests for such development:

> I believe, however, that it is in the best interests of Tanganyika as well as of the other territories that we should unite into a Federation. I also believe that the attainment of complete independence by Tanganyika alone would complicate the establishment of a new political unit. If the British Government is willing to amend their timetable for the constitutional changes of the other territories and then those territories expressed a desire for Federation, I would be willing to ask the people of Tanganyika to join that Federation with the others.[68]

Great Britain was unwilling to advance the timetable for Kenya's independence, and the Buganda region of Uganda had serious reser-

---

[68] Nyerere, *Freedom and Unity*, p. 86.

vations about such a union so the idea was temporarily dropped. But Tanganyika's willingness to hold back independence in order to facilitate the formation of an East African Federation seems an indication of its seriousness of purpose. Certainly, when Tanganyika merged with Zanzibar it paid a high price in terms of overrepresentation for the offshore islands, their continued local autonomy, and a hierarchical form of government. This observation should not be pushed too far, however, for when the East African Common Market countries drifted apart during 1964 and 1965, Tanzania finally resorted to unilateral action in order to redress a serious trade deficit with Kenya and Uganda. Tanzania's introduction of her own currency and central bank did stimulate Kenya and Uganda to redress that deficit and Tanzania subsequently moved to form a more permanent economic union with them.[69] In short, Tanzania is not willing to sacrifice everything for external political development, but has shown a willingness to sacrifice some national advantages for such a union.

During June 1967 the three states moved once more toward regional cooperation and signed the Treaty for East Africa Cooperation, thereby setting up a formal community. Although the organization is essentially economic, the inclusion of three East African ministers and several on-going political committees seem to hold up the prospect of future political development:

> Behind the treaty's approach to unity is the acceptance, at least for the foreseeable future, of a kind of supra-nationalism which falls short of a fully integrated system and which reconciles established national interests for certain limited technical and economic progress.[70]

[69] For a variety of points of view on the steps and missteps toward East African Federation, see Ali Mazrui, "Tanzania versus East Africa," *Journal of Commonwealth Political Studies* (November, 1965) Vol. III, No. 4: 209–225; A. J. Hughes, *East Africa: The Search for Unity* (Baltimore, Md.: Penguin Books, 1963); Joseph Nye, *Pan-Africanism and East African Integration* (Cambridge: Harvard University Press, 1965) and "Patterns and Catalysts in Regional Integration," *International Regionalism* (Boston: Little, Brown and Company, 1968); and Donald Rothchild, "A Hope Deferred: East African Federation, 1963–1964," in Gwendolyn M. Carter (ed.), *Politics in Africa* (New York: Harcourt, Brace & World, 1966); Richard Cox, *Pan Africanism in Practice, PAFMECSA 1958–1964* (London: Oxford University Press, 1964).

[70] Donald Rothchild, "Experiment in Functional Integration," *Africa Report* (April, 1968), 45.

The prospects of a true common market with the economies of scale, as well as the diplomatic and political advantages of regional cooperation (vis-à-vis other groups and continents), seem to have an appeal for other countries in the area, and Somalia, Ethiopia, Zambia, and Burundi have all expressed a desire to participate, particularly in light of the community's decision to seek association with the European economic community after 1969.[71] There are many hindrances to the accomplishment of a federation in East Africa, but Tanzania's commitment to the concept is not one of them.

In stressing international goals and in showing a preoccupation with political development, Tanzania has not forgotten economic development and welfare concerns. These, too, are regarded as important, although as we have seen, economic development in particular has been sacrificed for freedom. The current 5 year plan budgets nearly $700 million for investment (including $325 million from private and foreign sources), most of it directed toward a variety of social welfare and economic development projects with a heavy emphasis on the creation of a physical infrastructure and large-scale agriculture projects.[72] The lower than anticipated flow of capital, both from foreign and domestic sources, has necessitated a reorientation of some of these projects toward less capital-intensive aspects and toward local, cooperative investments of human time and toil.[73] The cooperative movement in particular has become a primary goal in the eyes of the government for it fits in well with the ideology of African socialism and the virtues of self-reliance.

> It is the Government's intention to extend the co-operative movement into every town, every village and every hamlet in Tanganyika, and to enable those societies to undertake every kind of enterprise which can be run by co-operative effort. . . .[74]

Such a program of local development through individual participation

71 Gerald K. Helleiner, "East African Community: Approaching the EEC," *Africa Report* (April, 1968), 37–42.

72 Smith, *op. cit.*, p. 185.

73 In addition to the Lemarchand and Yeager works mentioned earlier, the reader should consult Alexander MacDonald, *Tanzania: Young Nation in a Hurry* (New York: Hawthorn Books, 1966), chapters V–VIII.

74 Nyerere, *Freedom and Unity*, p. 185.

and governmental guidance would, if successful, enable the government to link its two goals of political and economic development while encouraging social solidarity and preventing the unwanted development of dysfunctional socio-economic struggles.

Freedom, political development, democratic decision making, welfare, and economic development, then, rather than stability or hierarchical decision making, distinguish the political goals of Tanzania. They are impressive, not only for their intent, but in light of the formidable obstacles which seem to hinder their attainment. It seems unlikely that they will be realized in the lifetime of the present leadership of the system, if at all, but one cannot help but wish that leadership well in the attempt. Faced with staggering problems in literacy, communications, economic development, and manpower, Tanzania has, nevertheless, pioneered the development of a political system that features a grass-roots, participatory, democratic ethos within a framework of national unity and cohesion. Although post-Arusha political developments may or may not reinforce the democratic achievements already logged, the system seems to enjoy widespread and meaningful popular support.[75]

BIBLIOGRAPHY

Bienen, Henry, *Tanzania: Party Transformation and Economic Development* (Princeton: Princeton University Press, 1967).

Cliffe, Lionel (ed.), *One Party Democracy: The 1965 Tanzania General Elections* (Nairobi: East African Publishing House, 1967).

Friedland, W. H., and C. G. Rosberg (eds.), *African Socialism* (Stanford, Calif.: Stanford University Press, 1964).

Nyerere, J. K., *Freedom and Unity: Uhuru Na Umoja* (London: Oxford University Press, 1967).

[75] *The Nationalist*, December 31, 1968, for example, declared that all members of the TANU Youth League "must declare themselves to be militant adherents of the principles of socialism as embodied in the Arusha Declaration or their membership in the TYC will be terminated." See also, Ali A. Mazrui, "Anti-Militarism and Political Militancy in Tanzania," *The Journal of Conflict Resolution* (September, 1968) Vol. XII, No. 3: 269–284. Hugh Stevens is particularly persuasive that there is a "discernible pattern" of centralization and governmental supervision of society. See his *The Political Transformation of Tanganyika 1920–67* (New York: Frederick A. Praeger, 1968), pp. 156–175.

———— *Essays on Socialism* (London: Oxford University Press, 1969).

———— *Freedom and Socialism: Uhuru Na Ujamaa* (London: Oxford University Press, 1969).

Smith, H. E. (ed.), *Readings on Economic Development and Administration in Tanzania* (Dar es Salaam: Institute of Public Administration, 1966).

Stevens, H. W., *The Political Transformation of Tanganyika: 1920–1967* (New York: Frederick A. Praeger, 1968).

Taylor, J. C., *The Political Development of Tanganyika* (Stanford, Calif.: Stanford University Press, 1963).

Tordoff, William, *Government and Politics in Tanzania* (Nairobi: East African Publishing House, 1967).

CHAPTER VI

The Somali
Political System

The present state of the Somali Republic encompasses 246,000 square miles and is thus the size of France. Although there has never been a reliable census, the population within its internationally recognized borders is estimated at over 2.7 million, including several thousand non-Somali Africans, 40,000 Asians and Arabs, and 4,000 Europeans. The rest are Somalis. Beyond its current frontiers, however, are more than a million persons who are also Somalis. Forty to sixty thousand of these are in the French Territory of the Afar and Issa, 250,000 in Kenya, and a million in Ethiopia. These inhabit another 125,000 square miles of territory. Because this population is linguistically, ethnically, and culturally part of the Somali nation, because their demands upon and supports for the central government are so pervasive, and because the present leadership of Somalia is so dedicated to their eventual inclusion in an enlarged Somali state, it is difficult not to consider them at least a part of the Somali political system.[1]

[1] This, of course, is a matter of some debate. The Ethiopians and Kenyans obviously see the boundaries between their countries as less permeable and more permanent than do the Somalis.

The Somalis were not the original inhabitants of this area. Fragmentary evidence suggests that the Horn of Africa was originally populated by bushmanoid peoples who were gradually absorbed by the Bantu-speaking groups who arrived from the south. These in turn were inundated by successive waves of pastoral peoples who migrated from the Arabian peninsula as early as the 7th century A.D.[2] While these groups—who were later to become the Afar, Galla, and Somali —moved inland, Yemenite Arabs set up city states such as Zeila, Berbera, Brava, and Merca along the coasts of the Red Sea and the Indian Ocean. Linked at various times with the Swahili trading system to the south (outlined in Chapter V), these cities carried on substantial commerce with Arabia, India, and China.

> Proceeding coastwise towards the Red Sea there is a very great Moorish town called Mogadishu; it has a king over it, the place has much trade in divers lands, by reason whereof many ships come hither from the great kingdom of Cambay, bringing great plenty of clothes of many sorts and divers other wares, also spices. . . .[3]

As in East Africa, these coastal towns were eventually conquered by the Portuguese in the 16th century and recaptured by various Arab groups in the 17th. These conquerers were replaced in turn by the

[2] The history of this area is by no means complete. The interested reader should consult I. M. Lewis, "The Somali Conquest of the Horn of Africa," *Journal of African History* (1960) Vol. I, No. 2: 213–229, and his *The Modern History of Somaliland* (New York: Frederick A. Praeger, 1965) and *Peoples of the Horn of Africa: Somali, Afar and Saho* (London: International African Institute, 1955) as well as H. S. Lewis, "The Origins of the Galla and Somali," *Journal of African History* (1966) Vol. VII, No. 1: 27–46; G. W. B. Huntingford, *The Galla of Ethiopia* (London: International African Institute, 1955); J. S. Trimingham, *Islam in East Africa* (London: Oxford University Press, 1952); and Norman DeMattos, *Ethiopia, Eritrea and Somaliland* (London: Victor Collancz, 1915).

[3] Manzel Longworth Dames, *The Book of Dwarte Barbosa* (London: Hak Luyt Society, 1918), quoted in Davidson, *The African Past* (New York: Grosset & Dunlap, 1967), p. 135. Davidson also has an extensive bibliographical account of the older sources in his *Lost Cities of Africa* (Boston: Little, Brown and Company, 1959). Of particular interest is Wilfred H. Schoff, *The Periplus of the Erythraean Sea* (New York: Longmans, Green and Company, 1912). As late as the middle of the 19th century, Richard Burton was able to comment on the extensive trading process in his *First Footsteps in East Africa* (London: Longmans, Green and Company, 1860).

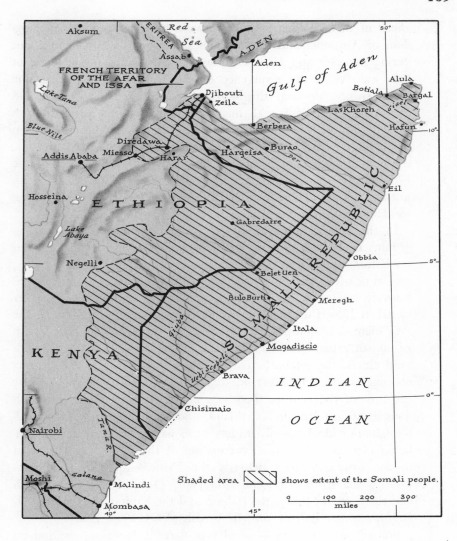

Shaded area shows extent of the Somali people.

Turks, the Egyptians, the Sultan of Zanzibar, and finally by the colonial powers of Western Europe.

While the city states were developing, the pastoral Somali clans moved south and east into the Horn, pushing the Galla peoples ahead of them. When fighting between the Coptic Christian kingdom of Abyssinia and the Moslem states on the coast broke out during the 14th and 15th centuries, Somalis joined in the *jihad* or holy war. With the resurgence of the Abyssinian empire in the 16th century however, this northern expansion was checked and the main thrust of Somali migration continued to be southward. Somali pressure was in part responsible for Galla movement into the Ethiopian plateau. When the Galla peoples captured this area, the Somalis moved in behind them, so that by the middle of the 19th century the Somalis occupied most of the Horn of Africa up to the Ethiopian plateau, absorbing the remaining Galla and Bantu-speaking groups in the process.

In the face of powerful exogenous forces, however, Somali hegemony over the Horn was never secure. Their nomadic life, their small numbers and segmented political structure, as well as their incessant tribal wars militated against the formation of a united front to oppose foreign intrusion. After the opening of the Suez Canal in 1869, European interest in the strategic possibilities of the area increased. European involvement in the Horn coincided with Ethiopian expansion under Menelik II and protection treaties with local chiefs, the establishment of refueling rights, and the gaining of concessions led, rather inexorably, to physical occupation. By the turn of the century there was a French Somaliland, a British Somaliland, an Italian Somaliland, and an Ethiopian Ogaden. Although individual Somali leaders were party to many of the protection treaties, the formal occupation of the Horn was actualized in the various treaties between the French and the Ethiopians (1887), the British and the Ethiopians (1887, 1897), the British and the French (1888), the Italians and the Ethiopians (1889, 1891, 1897), and the Italians and the British (1894, 1905, 1924).

Somali opposition to colonial rule flared into open rebellion on occasion, the most famous and long-lived instance being the *jihad* of Sayid Mohamed Abdullah Hassan.[4] From 1900 until 1920, the religious-nationalistic movement which he led struggled against the

[4] Government of Great Britain, *Correspondence Relating to the Rising of the Mullah Abdulla in Somaliland and Consequent Military Operations 1899–1902* (London: His Majesty's Stationary Office, 1903); O. Jardine, *The Mad Mullah of Somaliland* (London: Herbert Jenkins, 1923); E. Monroe, *A History of Ethiopia* (Oxford: The Clarendon Press, 1955).

Italians, Ethiopians, and most persistantly, the British. After his death in 1920, the colonial authorities reasserted control. We have already described the British and Italian colonial styles in Chapter III.[5] In the case of British Somaliland, the British confined themselves to doing as little as possible. The Italians did introduce plantation agriculture to Somalia and developed a modest physical infrastructure, but their resources and energies were diverted into their Ethiopian operations after 1935. After the conquest of Ethiopia, the Italians administered the Somali-inhabited Ogaden from Mogadiscio, Italian Somaliland. When they likewise occupied British Somaliland after the outbreak of World War II, the Italians brought the Somalis under a single government for the first time in their history. Thus despite the colonial overtones, this brief period is remembered by the Somalis as evidence of their essential unity as a people.

In a counterattack the British eventually retook the area during 1941. Uninspiring as subsequent British rule was economically, it did permit, even encourage, political activity, particularly of an anti-Italian variety. The Somali Youth Club and the Patriotic Benefit Union sprang up in 1943 and became the Somali Youth League and the *Hisbia Digil Mirifle*, respectively, in 1947. The British in the person of Ernest Bevin, then Foreign Secretary, also stimulated Somali ambitions by proposing the creation of a "Greater Somalia" to unite all the Somalis in the Horn of Africa. However desirable this plan might have been from the Somali point of view, it was opposed by the other colonial powers (as well as by the British Colonial Office) and undercut by the British-Ethiopian agreements of 1942 and 1944 and the beginnings of the Cold War.[6]

[5] For the relevant works in Italian, see the bibliographies of I. M. Lewis, A *Pastoral Democracy* (London: Oxford University Press, 1961), A. A. Castagno, Jr., *Somalia* (New York: Carnegie Endowment for International Peace, 1959), and Robert Hess, *Italian Colonialism in Somalia* (Chicago: University of Chicago Press, 1966). For a primarily physical overview and a comprehensive listing of tribal groupings in British Somaliland, see J. A. Hunt, A *General Survey of the Somaliland Protectorate 1944–1950* (London: Crown Agents for the Colonies, 1951) and Lord Rennel of Rodd, *British Military Administration of Occupied Territories in Africa during the Years 1941–1947* (London: His Majesty's Stationary Office, 1948).

[6] The definitive study of the forces that coalesced against the idea of a "Greater Somalia" has not yet been written. The Somalis themselves have some definite ideas as to who was to blame: Republic of Somalia, *The Somali Peninsula: A*

Eventually the Ogaden region was returned to Ethiopia (1948), as were the Haud and the Reserved Area of British Somaliland to the same power in 1954, control of British Somaliland having reverted to Great Britain in 1941. When a Four Power Commission could not agree on the future course of the former Italian area, the matter was turned over to the United Nations. In 1950 the General Assembly approved a trusteeship agreement whereby Italy would administer the territory, now known as Somalia, for 10 years under United Nations supervision. The instructions to the administering authority, the *Amministrazione Fiduciaria Italiana della Somalia* (AFIS) were clear:

> Foster the development of free political institutions and promote the development of the inhabitants of the Territory towards independence; and to this end shall give to the inhabitants of the Territory a progressively increasing participation in the various organs of Government.[7]

Italy and the United Nations are widely credited with encouraging both political and economic development and with maintaining a stable arena within which multiparty, democratic politics could take place.[8] Suffrage was eventually extended to all and Somalis gradually

---

New Light on Imperial Motives (Mogadiscio: Government Printer, 1962). British-Ethiopian relations that directly influenced events are documented in C. Potholm, *The Struggle for Ethiopia 1941–1944* (Unpublished M.A.L.D. Thesis, The Fletcher School of Law and Diplomacy, 1965) and three reports by the Government of Great Britain, *Agreement and Military Convention between the United Kingdom and Ethiopia* (CMD 6334, 1942) *Agreement between His Majesty in Regard of the United Kingdom and His Imperial Majesty the Emperor of Ethiopia* (CMD 6594, 1944), and *Report of the Somaliland Protectorate Constitutional Conference* (CMD 1044, 1960). Italy's role is underscored in G. H. Becker's *The Disposition of the Italian Colonies 1941–1951* (Annemasse: Imprinerre Grandchamps, 1952), while that of the various international organizations is covered in the Council of Foreign Ministers, Four Power Commission of Investigation for the Former Italian Colonies, *Report on Somaliland* (London: mimeographed by the Commission, 1948) and Benjamin Rivlin, *The United Nations and the Italian Colonies* (New York: Carnegie Endowment for International Peace, 1950).

[7] United Nations, *Draft Trusteeship Agreement for the Territory of Somaliland Under Italian Administration* Supplement No. 10 A/1294 (1950), p. 5.

[8] Those interested in an examination of this period should consult Lewis, *The Modern History of Somaliland*, chapter VII; Castagno, *Somalia*, chapters I and II; and Saadia Touval, *Somali Nationalism: International Politics and the Drive for Unity in the Horn of Africa* (Cambridge: Harvard University Press, 1963),

took over control of the army, police, and the civil service. Politics throbbed and a plethora of parties sprang up. In the series of municipal, district, and national elections which took place during the decade from 1950 to 1960, the Somali Youth League emerged as the most powerful and widely supported of the parties. One of its leaders, Abdullahi Issa, headed the first Somali government and served as Prime Minister during the period of internal self-government (1956–60). At independence, July 1, 1960, the former Italian area merged with British Somaliland which had attained independence 5 days before to form the Republic of Somalia. The new state did not accept its provisional boundaries and chose for its national flag a five pointed white star on a blue background, signifying its commitment to the union of all Somalis including those in the other three territories. It was a significant choice, for the national goal which it symbolizes has not yet been attained and continues to influence the course of politics in Somalia and the Horn of Africa.

We have passed over the colonial and trusteeship periods rather quickly because an understanding of the underlying dynamics of the present political system of Somalia is more likely to result from an analysis of traditional Somali political and social processes than from an elaboration of the institutions and laws of the colonial period. Stimulated by their traditional, "tribal" ethos, the Somalis took easily and enthusiastically to the concept of international statehood, national political institutions, and polyarchal decision making.[9]

---

chapter VII; as well as Laurence S. Finkelstein, *Somaliland under Italian Administration: A Case Study in United Nations Trusteeship* (New York: Woodrow Wilson Foundation, 1955); Mark Karp, *The Economics of Trusteeship in Somalia* (Boston: Boston University Press, 1960); Gilbert Ward, "Somalia: From Trust Territory to Nation 1950–1960," *Pylon* Vol. XXVI, No. 2: 173–186; and Robert Gavin, "Economic and Social Conditions in Somaliland Under Italian Trusteeship," *International Labor Review* (September, 1952) Vol. LXVI, No. 3: 25–26. There are ample documents from the United Nations: *Report of the United Nations Visiting Mission to the Trust Territories in East Africa, 1951, on Somalia Under Italian Administration* T/1033 (1952); *Report of the United Nations Visiting Mission to the Trust Territories in East Africa, 1954, on Somalia Under Italian Administration* T/1143 (1955); and *Report of the United Nations Visiting Mission to the Trust Territories in East Africa, 1957, on Somalia Under Italian Administration* T/ 1344 (1958).

[9] I. M. Lewis, "Modern Political Movements in Somaliland," *Africa* (July, 1958) Vol. XXVIII, No. 3: 344–364 and "The Northern Pastoral Somali of

After a brief examination of the present institutional framework of the Somali political system, we shall analyse in detail both the traditional impulses and their more modern counterparts which seem to determine the course of politics in Somalia today.

Participation in the Decision-Making Process

The Somali Republic is a unitary state. There is a President who is head of state and commander-in-chief of the armed forces. He is chosen by the National Assembly for a period of 6 years and may serve but two terms. On the first two ballots, election to the office of President requires a two-thirds majority of the Assembly.[10] Thereafter, a simple majority suffices. The President summons and dismisses Parliament, calls and retires the Cabinet, and ratifies treaties. Upon completion of his national service, the President becomes a National Deputy for life.

The National Assembly consists of 123 members who are elected for 5-year terms by universal adult suffrage. Deputies must be at least 25 years old. Legislative authority is vested in the Assembly although bills may be introduced to that body by the President, any deputy, or 10,000 voters.[11] There is a Prime Minister and a Council of Ministers who are responsible to the National Assembly. There are currently fifteen ministries plus three ministries of state, one each for the Presidency, Somali Affairs, and Planning. Many political parties are represented in the National Assembly. The governments of Somali since independence have reflected the views of a variety of parties as well as different positions within the major party, the Somali Youth League (which includes an active parliamentary opposition group). As of January 1969, Abdirashid Ali Shermarke of the Somali Youth League was President of the Somali Republic and Mohamed Hagi Ibrahim Egal was Prime Minister. Mr. Egal is now a member of the Somali Youth League although he was formerly

the Horn," in *Peoples of the Horn of Africa*, pp. 319–361; and A. A. Castagno, Jr., "The Republic of Somalia: Africa's Most Homogeneous State," *Africa Special Report* (July, 1960) 2–3, 8–11, 15, and "Somali Republic," Coleman and Rosberg (eds.), *Political Parties and National Integration*, pp. 512–559.

[10] Government of Somalia, *The Constitution of the Somali Republic* (Mogadiscio: Government Printer, 1963), Article 70.

[11] *Ibid.*, Article 60.

head of the Somali National League and Prime Minister of British Somaliland.

An extensive bill of rights was written into the constitution. It provides for the freedoms of association, assembly, speech, and private ownership.[12] The "republican and democratic" aspects of the constitution cannot be amended. There is an independent judiciary and a Supreme Court with "civil, criminal, administrative, and accounting" jurisdiction. No special courts may be established.[13] The legal framework of the country is supposed to reflect Islamic law and the provisions espoused in the United Nations' Universal Declaration of Human Rights.[14] In reality, the legal fabric is a blend of the Moslem *shari'* code, Italian common law, British military provisions, and various trusteeship regulations. Although many of the laws have been codified since independence and the government has sought to replace the traditional courts, application of local customary law continues, particularly among the nomads who occupy the border areas.

Local government consists of municipal and district councils. There are thirty-six districts and forty-eight municipalities, both publicly elected. The municipal councils are the more important of the two and enjoy the greatest autonomy, although governmental secretaries are appointed to serve as both channels of communication and policy formulators. The role of the district councils is more consultative in character than that of the municipal councils. District councils generally confine themselves to the settlement of local disputes over grazing and water rights, while the municipal councils are more likely to be concerned with local ramifications of national issues and rule application. Because of the small size of the population, the responsive nature of the political institutions, and the pervasive aspects of clan linkages, politics in Somalia are often simultaneously national and local in character.

The vibrancy of national political life in Somalia and the responsiveness of the central government, as well as the basically egalitarian and democratic nature of present-day Somali society are the reflection of basic societal patterns deeply ingrained in the Somali past. This traditional social setting is distinguished by two

[12] *Ibid.,* Articles 8–46.
[13] *Ibid.,* Articles 95, 96.
[14] The State Religion is Islam however.

diverse strands of behavior and belief. The first is the accent the Somali people place on the fundamental oneness of all Somalis. The Somalis exhibit an almost unique characteristic in sub-Saharan Africa, a deeply felt sense of nationhood. This is not a feeling shared only by the elites or a concept that national leaders are attempting to instill into their people, but an emotional, cultural, and historical experience shared by all Somalis.

> Somali nationalism stems from a feeling of national con-
> sciousness in the sense of 'we' as opposed to 'they' which
> has existed among the Somalis for many centuries. It was
> nurtured by tribal genealogies and traditions, by the Is-
> lamic religious ties and by conflicts with foreign peoples.[15]

Many observers of the Somali scene, and to a certain extent the subsequent analysis found in this chapter, emphasize another aspect of Somali life: a tendency toward cleavage and division, toward individualism and ethnocentricity. It should be remembered, how-ever, that the feeling of commonality, of basic kinship, of unity is as much an explanatory and motivating factor in Somali national life as is the second. And in terms of the goals of the political system, it is of great and lasting consequence. Language, culture, and history, even the history of fragmentation, tend to unify the Somalis over and against the fissiparous tendencies of their society.

Counterpoised to this feeling of oneness is a sense of genealogical and occupational distinctions which divide the Somalis. There is, for example, a pronounced difference between the Somalis who think of themselves as Samaales and those who think of themselves as Sabs. The majority Samaales are essentially nomads who occupy the areas south of the Uebi Scebelli river and north of the Giuba. The Sabs are the descendents of those Somalis who settled between the rivers, intermarried with the Bantu-speaking and Galla peoples, and became over time farmers who kept livestock rather than true pastoralists. In addition, the Sabs are distinguishable from Samaales linguistically.[16] The broad distinctions between the two can be over-drawn however. There are, for example, among the Samaales some

---

[15] Touval, *op. cit.*, p. 84.

[16] Castagno, "Somali Republic," 517 describes the difference as like that be-tween Italian spoken north of Rome and Italian spoken on Sicily. Lewis (*A Pas-toral Democracy*, p. 13) suggests that the contrast is somewhat greater.

sedentary Hawiyes and farming Isaqs. Over-all, 70% of all Somalis are pastoralists, 20% are primarily engaged in agriculture, and 10% in commerce and government.[17]

The Sabs and the Samaales are themselves broken down into clan families, clans, primary lineage units, and dia-paying groups.[18] There are two major Sab clan families, the Digil and the Rahanweyn, and four Samaale groups, the Darod, Hawiye, Dir, and Isaq. Generally speaking, each clan family is able to trace its ancestors back thirty generations and ranges in size from 500,000 persons (Dir) to over 1.5 million (Darod).

Somali clans are smaller, ranging in size from 10,000 to 100,000 persons, and trace their common ancestry back perhaps twenty generations. Examples of clans would be the Dulbahante of the Darod clan family, the Iise of the Dir, and the Galgial of the Hawiye. Although many of the Sab clans have a territorial base, Samaale clans do not have as rigidly defined territories and move across the Horn of Africa in search of grazing land and water.

Clans are further divided into primary lineage groups or subclans. These are able to trace their lineage back six to ten generations. As was outlined in Chapter III, there are seldom formal offices of leadership among the primary lineage groups. Marriage usually takes place outside the primary lineage group but within the clan or clan family. Society is basically patrimonial and patrilocal although the husband often uses the grazing and water rights of his wife's lineage.

Below the subclan is the dia-paying group. "This is the fundamental political unit in northern pastoral Somali society." [19] Depending upon its location and the ecological situation, the dia-paying group may range in size from 120 to 9000 males. By the late 1950's there were over 650 recognized dia-paying groups in Somalia plus 361 in British Somaliland.[20] Dia-paying groups were originally fighting units of Somali males, consisting of "close kinsmen united by

[17] Lewis, *A Pastoral Democracy*, p. 267. Many of Lewis' generalizations are meant to apply primarily to the Somalis of British Somaliland but most have validity for Somalia as well.
[18] This section is distilled from the relevant portions of Lewis, "The Northern Pastoral Somali of the Horn" and *A Pastoral Democracy*, and from Castagno, "Somali Republic."
[19] Lewis, "The Northern Pastoral Somali of the Horn," p. 325.
[20] Castagno, "Somali Republic," p. 517.

a specific contractual alliance whose terms stipulate that they should pay and receive blood compensation (Arabic, *diya* [Somali, *mag*]) in consort." [21] Blood compensation is based on the stipulations of Islamic law as applied by the Somali. There are three specific types of offenses: *dil* (homicide), *goon* (wounding), and *dalliil* (loss of face).[22] *Dalliil* is compensated for by *haul* (damages), *goon* by *goomall* (wound compensation), and *dil* by *mag* (blood compensation). In the harsh struggle for life in the Horn of Africa, where the margin of survival was seldom wide and every able bodied man was needed, the Somalis tended to use compensation of camels and other livestock wherever possible. Joining a band to reduce one's liability was essential. By accepting a common share of the fortunes of a dia-paying group an individual would no longer stand alone, he would have protection, status, and a place in the society. The process of identification with one's dia-paying group is centuries old and has not died out with the thrust of modernity, for the dia-paying group represents the primary building block of Somali society.

Quite obviously, kinship is of vital concern in placing an individual in society and providing him with a reference point. To this extent, the Somali system remains essentially ascriptive. But there is another side to life as a Somali. Somali males are born into genealogies over which they have no control, but they also enter into contracts or compacts which bind them to other persons and social clusters which link societal segments together by specifying the kind and degree of interaction.[23] Contracts are made, and broken, between individuals and groups and between groups. Allegiances shift, alliances are formed and dissolved. There is also a strong achievement orientation to Somali life, even though ascriptive elements place broad limits on the process. Struggling in a hostile environment, the Somalis are highly competitive. They are, generally speaking, active not passive, and conditioned to accept achievement as well as birth as social determinants.

With this qualification—and it is an important one—clan and kinship may well be viewed as the primary forces that shape Somali

[21] Lewis, *Modern History of Somalia*, p. 11.

[22] A more extensive examination of this aspect of Somali life is found in Lewis, *A Pastoral Democracy*, pp. 162–167.

[23] I. M. Lewis, "Clanship and Contract in Northern Somalia," *Africa* (July, 1959) Vol. XXIX, No. 3: 274–293.

social and political life. The links of kinship are both vital and pervasive:

> No other single line of communication and common interest connected so directly and incontravertably the pastoral nomad in the interior with his kinsman in the civil service, in the National Assembly, or in the Cabinet itself. No other bond of mutual interest had so many far-reaching ramifications in all aspects of private and public life.[24]

Yet the importance of kinship has not, as in other societies, led to social stratification or the formation of socio-economic classes. In traditional society, all Somali males were either *waranleh* (warriors) or *wadaad* (religious figures). There were no age sets or organized military castes (except for brief periods among those Somalis who came under the direct influence of the Galla). There were a few occupational castes such as the *midgaans, tumaals,* and *yibirs* who worked with leather or iron. There was also a social bias against persons of non-Somali ancestry, African or European. Generally speaking however, in terms of the Somali people themselves, society was and is undifferentiated and egalitarian. In terms of political authority, the various kinship groupings enjoyed autonomy. Power was decentralized among and within clan families, clans, subclans and dia-paying groups. The few formal political offices that existed were not of a hierarchical nature. Political officials were chosen. Among some groups of British Somaliland, there were elected leaders called *akils* and among the Sabs a more formal political apparatus existed, but on balance, traditional Somali politics were characterized by democratic decision making which took the form of adult males sitting face to face. Males were considered worthy of political participation after age 15 and allowed to speak at the ad hoc councils (*shirs*) that were called to deliberate on matters of concern.

> Naturally, however, the words of different men carry different weights, for respect is given to such factors as wealth, inherited prestige, skill in oratory and poetry, political acumen, wisdom and age.[25]

[24] Lewis, *Modern History of Somaliland*, pp. 166–167.
[25] Lewis, "The Northern Pastoral Somali of the Horn," p. 345.

Action was usually taken on the basis of majority opinion, expressed through a formal vote or by a consensus which emerged from the sense of the meeting.[26] What political authorities existed were chosen in the same fashion and generally regarded as leaders rather than rulers even though there were some hereditary positions.[27] Thus prior to the development of a national arena, Somali traditional political forms and processes reflected the egalitarian, decentralized, essentially democratic ethos of their society.

Some of these political patterns as well as the absence of transclan political institutions were a matter of some concern to the various United Nations visiting missions.[28] Actually in the postindependence period, the Somali traditional political culture seems to have been a crucial element in the maintenance of a vibrant, multiparty political system with widespread participation in the decision-making process. Comparisons with the situation in Tanzania come readily to mind in the sense that decentralized, segmented political authority in traditional society did seem to aid in the development of national politics. And the initial postindependence elites in Tanzania and Somalia (particularly in the Somali Youth League) both sought to curtail "tribalism" as a force in the politics of the nation. For the reasons outlined in Chapter V, those in Tanzania were able to accomplish this. In Somalia, however, because of the basic homogenity of Somali culture, "tribalism" was not as potentially dysfunctional as it was in Tanzania and other sub-Saharan countries, and in the sense of traditional political patterns, proved highly resistant to change. In fact, the Somalis were able to adapt their traditional politics to new forms and new arenas:

> Thus modern party political forms have been most successfully adopted but they have, of necessity, been accommodated to the indigenous pastoral pattern. Moreover, the introduction of party politics and of representative government has, if anything, widened the sphere of action of traditional politics. Nationalism itself has provided a new stage on which, in the same roles but new costume, traditional lineage interests are played out.[29]

---

[26] Castagno, *Somalia*, pp. 363 and 342.
[27] Lewis, *A Pastoral Democracy*, p. 209.
[28] UN T/1033 (*Visiting Mission, 1951*) p. 328.
[29] UN T/1143 (*Visiting Mission, 1954*) p. 63.

Equally important, the traditions of individual participation, political segmentation, and shifting tribal alliances have insured that Somali politics are characterized by a variety of political parties, a succession of government coalitions, and widespread disagreement over the methods and tactics of goal attainment (even though there is substantial agreement among the leaders and the peoples as to those goals). Tribal lineage groups have been instrumental in providing the linkage necessary to maintain the system; and the webs of influence which are such an integral part of Somali society have provided an element of cohesion as well as an opportunity for communication and decision-making influence.

Given the fragmented and undifferentiated aspects of Somali society and the lack of political centralization, it is not surprising that the clan groups represent and, in fact, function as interest groups. Less than 14% of the population is urbanized, fewer than 5,000 persons belong to labor unions, and only a small percentage of the population is directly involved in the cash sector of the economy. It may well be that as time goes on, kinship groups will be supplanted by more associational groups (although at the present it seems more likely that, rather than being replaced, the ascriptive groups will themselves change). The character of these groups is already in a process of mutation. Political alliances are now made between dia-paying groups of different clans. Political expedience often overrides genealogy, and the surge for political authority divides agnatic kinsmen. Various kinship groups combine for interest articulation and interest aggregation on some issues only to move apart on others. Yet national politics in Somalia do retain strong overtones of "tribalism" even though the government has with recent electoral laws sought to reduce the large numbers of lineage parties by accenting the need for political candidates to obtain a representative quotient of the vote in their districts.

There has also been a process of natural selection in that the series of national and local elections have winnowed the plethora of parties. However, there are at least four that have demonstrated major vote-getting ability and widespread popular support among various groups. The most important of these is the Somali Youth League (SYL). Formed in the 1940's, it underwent a period of Hawiye-Darod hegemony to become a national coalition encompassing a wide variety of ethnic groups. During its initial formation, it enjoyed British support, not only in British Somaliland but in Italian Somaliland and Kenya as well. In contrast to British policy in Tanganyika, civil servants were allowed, even encouraged to participate in politics. When the Somali Youth League publicly pressed for Four Power rather than purely British control over Somalia, however, Great Britain banned the SYL in Kenya and incarcerated its leaders.

The Somali Youth League was initially led by the more progressive townsmen in the territory and opposed "tribalism" even though it subsequently modified its stand on this issue and ultimately adopted a policy of "ethnic balance." It stood categorically for the union of all Somalis irrespective of existing international frontiers:

> We wish our country to be amalgamated with the other Somalilands and to form one political, administrative and economic unit with them. We Somalis are one in every way. We are the same racially and geographically, we have the same language and the same religion. There is no future for us except as part of a Greater Somalia.[30]

The SYL has always been the most national of the parties and its strong showing in the early elections of the 1950's enabled it to form the first Somali government in 1956. Since that time, its leaders have generally formed the majority of the decision-making elite although it has shown a remarkable ability to change that elite internally and to absorb a variety of counterelites and leaders of would-be pressure groups. In fact, the internal dynamics of the SYL have provided as much a basis for national politics in Somalia as has the interplay between the SYL and the other parties. Each president and every prime minister since independence has belonged to the SYL at the time of their selection even though several came from other parties initially. The SYL relies heavily on the clan organizations to provide its party organization at the local level.

A second party of note and the one Somali party with a transnational rhetoric and ideology is the Somali Democratic Union. Formed by Haji Muhammad Hussein in 1962, the Somali Democratic Union (SDU) has adopted a basically socialist platform and would seek to replace the tribe with the state as the basic welfare

---

[30] Touval, *op. cit.*, p. 95.

institution in Somali society. In this regard, it has generally urged the confiscation of foreign investment in Somalia and opposed Somali contact with the European Economic Community. Haji Hussein was himself a president of the SYL during 1956–57 but for personal as well as ideological reasons, he quarrelled with Abdullahi Issa, who was Prime Minister, and the chairman of the legislative council (and later President of the Republic), Aden Abdullah Osman. Haji Hussein then formed the Greater Somali League (GSL) which in turn was split over Hussein's militant espousal of Pan-Arabism and socialism. Haji Hussein was subsequently joined by some members of the Somali National League and the United Somali Party (each of which was a coalition of parties from the former British Somaliland). The new party was called the Somali Democratic Union. Although Hussein and his various parties are reported to have received aid from a variety of foreign sources including the Italian Communist Party and the People's Republic of China, the Somali Democratic Union remains a national party and forms a substantial part of the opposition. The GSL won 36 seats in the municipal elections of 1958 but boycotted the National Assembly elections of the next year, charging political harassment. The SDU won 15 seats in the March 1964 general elections. Even though the SDU is unable to match the appeal of the SYL in the countryside, it continues to play the role of devil's advocate and to offer policy alternatives to the electorate. Because it challenges some of the fundamental assumptions of the ruling coalition, it undoubtedly enriches the political context of Somalia.

A third major party is the Somali Independent Constitution Party or the *Hisbia Destour Mustaquil Somali* (HDMS). Founded as the *Hisbia Digil Mirifle* (HDM) in 1947, this party has acted as a major pressure group representing the interests of the Sabs. Based among the riverine peoples, it originally urged the administering authority to adopt a federal constitution for Somalia, one which would have protected its agricultural interests from pastoral hegemony. When this effort failed, the HDMS attempted to broaden its appeal to non-Sab groups and changed its name to the Somali Independent Constitution Party. This tactic was not an outstanding success: the party has not enlarged its political position since it won 13 national seats in 1956. Along with the GSL, the HDMS boycotted the 1959 elections. Nevertheless, some of its leaders ran for public office, were elected, and subsequently joined the SYL-dominated government of 1960. Although the HDMS did win 9 seats in the 1964 national elections, its strength has not increased further and it continues to function primarily as a Sab-orientated pressure group. It votes for or against government proposals depending upon how they would impinge upon the area between the Uebi Scebelli and the Giuba rivers.

Another major party which is in some disarray is the Socialist National Congress (SNC). It is the heir to the Somali National League which emerged as the dominate party in British Somaliland and which originated as the Somaliland National Society of 1947. The SNC won 20 of 33 seats and 52% of the vote in the preindependence election of 1960, defeating the northern branch of the SYL, the National United Front, and the Darod and Dir-based United Somali Party. Since the union of the Somaliland and Somalia, the leaders of the SNC have played major roles in various governments. Ibrahim Egal, for example, who was Prime Minister of Somaliland from June 26 to July 1, 1960 subsequently became Minister of Defense and later Minister of Education during the Somalia government of Abdirashid Ali Shermarke (1960–64). Egal left the government in 1962 along with the other principal northern politicians such as Jama Abdullahi Galib in a protest over the "second class" treatment accorded the north after the merger. These northern dissidents eventually aided in the defeat of the SYL government of Abdirizak Haji Hussein in 1967. Under the new President of the Republic, Abdirashid Ali Shermarke, Egal formed the government and this "national" coalition was elected by the largest majority ever attained by any Somali government (119 to 2). It remains to be seen, however, whether the inclusion of northern politicians into the present regime will totally undercut the existence of the northern based parties such as the SNC, for the differences between political groups in Somalia continue to be personal, regional, and ethnic rather than ideological.

A brief description of the course of politics in Somalia since independence is necessary in order to show how the Somali Youth League has emerged to play a dominant, but not dominating role in the political life of the nation and to illustrate the continuing patterns of widespread participation, regime alteration, and political divisiveness. The growth of political awareness and the expansion of participation in the decision-making process proceeded quite rapidly during the 1950's and 1960's.[31] During the 1954 municipal elections, 37,697 men voted. Two years later over 614,904 participated and after suffrage was extended to women in 1958, over 1 million Somalis voted in the 1964 general election. The number of political parties increased from eight in 1950 to twenty-one in 1954 to over one hundred by 1968. The United Nations observers who had feared for the democratic process if the suffrage was too rapidly extended were both surprised and pleased: "The high degree of political party activity throughout the Territory is without doubt one of the most unique and impressive aspects of the Territory's political life." [32]

In Somalia, the Somali Youth League demonstrated early that it had a national following, winning 141 of 281 seats and 48% of the vote in the 1954 municipal council elections. The HDMS captured 57 seats while the Somali African Union and the Somali National Union won 28 and 5 seats, respectively. Smaller local parties won the rest. Politics in British Somaliland were stimulated both by the developments in Somalia and by the British decision in 1954 to return the Haud and the Reserved Area to Ethiopia the following year. Ethiopian claims to these regions had been established on the basis of the 1897 treaty with Great Britain and reaffirmed in the 1942 and 1944 agreements. The British government was itself divided over the return, the Foreign Office being in favor of it and the Colonial Office generally opposing it. The Colonial Secretary himself seemed to be chagrined by the provisions of the 1897 treaty but found that it was "impossible to undo it." [33] Reaction was not long in coming. The northern branch of the SYL with its support among the Darods and the newly formed Somali National League, which drew its strength from the Isaqs, cooperated briefly in the Somaliland National Front in a vain attempt to oppose the British action. After the first flush of unity, both groups went their own ways although the Front lingered on as a separate entity. De-

---

[31] Lewis, *Modern History of Somaliland*, chapters VII and VIII, and Castagno, "Somali Republic," 524–558, analyse in some detail the course of party politics. For more descriptive accounts of Somalia in this period, see E. A. Bayne, *Four Ways of Politics* (New York: American Universities Field Staff, 1965) and the earlier account by Margaret Laurence, *New Wind in a Dry Land* (New York: Alfred A. Knopf, 1964).

[32] UN T/1344 (*Visiting Mission*, 1957) p. 16.

[33] Lewis, *Modern History of Somaliland*, p. 152.

spite the fact that all Somaliland parties opposed the British action and all championed the unification of all Somalis, the Somali National League emerged as the most organized and effectively led organization, combining with its allies in the United Somali Party to form the independence government in 1960.

In 1956 national elections were held in the trust territory of Somalia for the newly created Territorial Assembly which succeeded the older, largely appointed Territorial Council. Some distillation of the parties took place, due in part to the perceived need to compete across the country as a whole. The SYL emerged as the major force in national politics, winning 43 of the 70 elected seats and 54% of the vote. Ten seats in the Assembly were reserved for various other ethnic groups, 4 Italians, 4 Arabs, 1 Indian, and 1 Pakistani. The renamed HDMS captured 13 seats, the Somali Democratic Party 3, and the Marehan Union 1.

The Somali Democratic Party is illustrative of the processes in Somalia during the 1950's and 1960's whereby political parties were formed, split, coalesced, and reformed, changing names all the while. The Somali Democratic Party was itself a union of four smaller parties that had won 66 seats between them in the 1954 elections —the Somali Progressive League, the Somali African Union, The National Somali Union, and the Somali Patriotic Union. Led by Muhammad Sheik Osman and Abdullahi Hagi Mohammed, it amassed 80,000 votes in the 1956 general elections and later merged with two smaller parties to form the Liberal Somali Youth Party. Yet by independence the party had melted away, some of its supporters gravitating toward the Greater Somali League, others to the SYL. Despite the fact that its program approximated that of the SYL, the SYL's greater organizational power and position at the center of the decision-making process attracted many of Somali Democratic Party members, particularly after Abdullahi Issa of the SYL became acting Prime Minister and Aden Abdullah Osman became President of the Territorial Assembly.

Yet the very tendencies toward amalgamation, in the personal and ethnic ethos of Somali politics, produced tensions within the SYL as new members joined and diluted the already loose control the leaders of the SYL were able to maintain over the rank and file. After the disagreements outlined above, Haji Muhammad Hussein formed the Greater Somali League prior to the 1958 municipal elections and gained a measure of Darod support. Despite these defections, the SYL won 51% of the vote and 416 seats to 175 for the HDMS, 36 for the Greater Somali League, and 27 for the Liberal Somali Youth Party. These successes were followed by the strong showing of the SYL in the Territorial Assembly elections of 1959. It won 61 seats uncontested and 22 of the 29 contested seats. The Liberal Somali Youth Party captured 2 and the HDMS dissidents 5. As mentioned earlier, the HDMS and GSL boycotted the election on the grounds of SYL harassment and voting fraud but individual members of the HDMS gathered 40,857 votes to 35,769 for the Liberal Party and 237,134 for the SYL.

Despite their commanding majority in parliament, the leadership of the SYL made overtures to HDMS personnel in an attempt to unify the country behind the government. Two prominent leaders of the HDMS, Muhammad Abdi Nur "Juju" and Abdulcadir Muhammed Aden "Zoppo" did in fact join the government. A. A. Castagno feels that this was due to Sab fear of eventual Darod hegemony and the perceived need to work with the Hawiye elements in the SYL, which were in control after the Haji Hussein defections.[34] It could also have been due to a realization of where personal political power lay. The parliament itself was roughly one-third Sab, one-third Darod, and one-third Hawiye and the overtures by the SYL did cause some discontent within the Darod wing of the SYL and among those SYL leaders such as Dr. Abdirashid Ali Shermarke who opposed "tribalism." It is interesting to note, however, that when Dr. Shermarke formed several governments during the 1960–64 period, he judiciously applied the much maligned principle of "ethnic balance."

Early in 1960, as previously agreed by the SYL and SNC, the Legislative Council of Somaliland and the Territorial Assembly of Somalia voted for unification of the two areas; on July 1, 1960 the two states became the united Republic of Somalia. The thirty-three members of the Somaliland council joined the ninety members of the Somalia assembly to form the National Assembly of the Republic, and political developments continued at a rapid rate following independence and unification. Aden Abdullah Osman, a former President of the SYL, became provisional President of the Republic

---

[34] Castagno, "Somali Republic," pp. 538–539.

until he defeated Sheik Ali Jumale in the presidential elections of
July 1961. Dr. Abdirashid Ali Shermarke formed a new government
which was in effect a coalition between the SYL and the two dominant northern groups, the Somali National League and the United
Somali Party.[35]

The entrance of the northerners into the cabinet did not eliminate
the general sense of dissatisfaction which grew in the former British
territories. The difficulties centered around the differing colonial
backgrounds, legal codes, tariff rates, and languages as well as the
sense of power deflation that accompanied the shift of the capital
from Hargeisa in the north to Mogadiscio in the south.[36] The June
1961 plebiscite to approve the union showed that a large number of
northerners opposed the merger even though, over-all, it was approved by a vote of 1,760,540 to 182,911.[37] Later in the year, during December, there was an army mutiny among northern officers
stationed at Hargeisa. Strictly speaking, the disturbance was not an
attempted coup: no effort was made to take over the government,
and by the time troops arrived from the south, the disorders were
over. However, the incident served to underscore the dissatisfaction
rife in the north as did the resignations of Egal and the other
northern politicians in 1962. Their formation of the Somali National
Congress in 1963 signalled the existence of formidable opposition
in that region. They were joined by the SYL followers of Sheik Ali
Jumale, the defeated candidate for President.

Although Prime Minister Shermarke was able to form a new
government, opposition continued until after the 1964 elections.[38]
These elections, by Somali standards, were a massive exercise involving twenty-one parties, 973 candidates for 123 seats, and over
a million voters. Competition was keen and the SYL faced its

[35] Ibid., p. 546.
[36] Touval, op. cit., chapter IX, and Lewis, Modern History of Somaliland,
chapter V.
[37] Touval, op. cit., p. 120.
[38] Analysis of the Somali scene since 1963 has been somewhat sketchy. I. M.
Lewis, "The Somali Republic Since Independence," The World Today (April,
1963) Vol. XIX, No. 3: 167–174; Jeanne Contini, "The Somali Republic
Politics with a Difference," Africa Report (December, 1964), 3–8; and "Somalia
Walks The Tightrope," New York Times Magazine (August 8, 1965), 14–46;
as well as C. J. Martin, "The Somali Republic," The British Survey (February,
1966) No. 203: 1–20, provide some clues to the contemporary workings of the
political system.

strongest opposition to date as the northern based Somali National Congress won 22 seats, the Somali Democratic Union 15, the HDMS 9, and the various other parties 8. There was a high turn-over of deputies with 68 new members elected out of 123. Soon after the elections, 20 members elected under other party banners crossed the aisle and joined the SYL forces. Despite the command-ing lead enjoyed by the SYL, President Osman apparently felt that the nation was ready for a change and urged Abdirizak Haji Hus-sein to form a government.

Abdirizak Haji Hussein then sought to interject a more "progres-sive" (i.e. detribalized) ethos into the operations of the government but opposition coalesced around his plans to enlarge the cabinet and curtail the expansion of the army. An SYL faction led by Dr. Shermarke and Secretary General Yassin Nur Hassan joined with members of the SDU and SNC to bring down the government after only 6 weeks in office. Inner turmoil within the SYL led to a protracted governmental crisis and Abdirizak Haji Hussein was un-able to form a government that was acceptable to all sides for 2 months. The government he eventually formed lasted 3 years but was constantly under attack. Crossing and recrossing of party lines and the shifts of personal and ethnic loyalties occurred throughout the life of the government.

Ironically enough, Abdirizak Haji Hussein was chosen Secretary General of the SYL in February 1967, becoming the first man ever to hold the two offices of secretary general and prime minister simultaneously. Six months later he was voted out of office. He then formed a new party, the Democratic Action Party, with some SYL dissidents. In the presidential elections of 1967, the National Assembly chose Dr. Abdirashid Ali Shermarke to replace Aden Abdullah Osman, and Shermarke in turn asked Muhammad Ibrahim Egal to form a government. The inclusion of Egal brought in many former members of the SNC and the Egal government received the largest vote of confidence ever accorded a Somali government. Both in terms of personnel and domestic policy, the Egal govern-ment did not differ markedly from the previous governments. Only in the area of foreign policy did the government seem to move in new directions, and even here it seemed to be less a change in goals than in tactics.

Without renouncing the goal of eventual union of all Somalis, the Egal government sought a détente with Kenya and Ethiopia in an attempt to gain by negotiation what Somalia had been unable to accomplish by supplying various Somali insurgent groups in both countries. Since the Arusha accords of October 1967, Somalia has attempted to normalize relations with Kenya and Ethiopia. This development will be analyzed in detail under the section on goals but it should be mentioned in this connection that there was widespread opposition to this change in tactics.

There is no reason to assume that there will be any diminution of political activity, factionalism, or switching of allegiances in the future. There are over 130 registered parties, and it remains to be seen how strictly a new electoral law stipulating that parties must obtain a certain percentage of votes in order to be represented on the national level will be enforced. As this brief survey of Somali politics has indicated, the Somali Youth League will continue to play an important, even dominant, role in the life of the nation. And much of the decision-making activity will remain in the hands of the SYL central committee (consisting of the president, deputy president, secretary-general, comptroller, and the executive committee) and its parliamentary party. But the League and subsequent Somali governments will also continue to be conditioned by the personnel and demands of the other parties. Because the SYL is linked directly to the countryside by the network of clan alliances outlined above, both interest groups and pressure groups will continue to have access to the national decision-making apparatus. It is within this context that the compromises so vital to the reconciliation of various ethnic and regional factions will continue to be worked out.

Institutionally, the National Security Council has played an important role in the decision-making process, particularly under the administration of Abdirizak Haji Hussein.[39] Consisting of the prime minister, the ministers of interior, foreign affairs, defense, and finance as well as the heads of the army and the police, the National Security Council served as a demand articulating and policy formulating institution which operated in private. With the Egal regime, the Council has fallen into disuse and has been surplanted by

---

[39] James D. Farrell, "The Somali Army: A Time of Testing," paper delivered at the African Studies Association meeting (November, 1967), p. 7.

a larger, less powerful, public forum, the National Advisory Council. Broader participation has diluted somewhat the decision-making character of the body while increasing the opportunity for public debate, and curtailed the role of the army.

Decision making in the Somali political system is open to all and, because of the fluid nature of national political life, large scale involvement in politics is continually possible. The Somali political system also exhibits several characteristics that, according to the criteria outlined in Chapter II, indicate a high degree of political development. In fact, the Somali experience offers a substantial amendment to much of the developmental theory outlined in that chapter, for it has the lowest economic and literacy bases in the world. Regime alteration, rehabilitation of defeated personnel, responsiveness to public demands, and a demonstrated ability to withstand periods of national crisis—despite the "tribal" and ethnic aspects of the political system [40]—all point to significant achievement in the area of political development.

REGIME ALTERATION

Although the Somali Youth League has been in power, either independently or in consort with other parties, since independence, there has been a discernible pattern of regime alteration in terms of personnel. That this has been done without bloodshed and without force is in itself a major accomplishment. There have been two presidents, Aden Abdullah Osman (1960–61 and 1961–67) and Abdirashid Ali Shermarke (1967–69), and four prime ministers, Abdullahi Issa (1956–60), Abdirashid Ali Shermarke (1960–64), Abdirizak Haji Hussein (1964–67), and Muhammad Ibrahim Egal (1967–69). Further, a series of regularly scheduled elections on the municipal, district, and national level, as well as within the party bureaucracy together with virtually unrestricted participation in the political life of the nation insure fairly frequent alteration of decision-making personnel on all levels. The Somali Youth League, for example, elects its president and secretary-general on a yearly basis and there have been literally dozens of changes in its top posts since 1956.

These facets of the Somali political experience help to maintain

[40] See, for example, Castagno, "Somali Republic," p. 531.

the democratic ethos of the system and to insure that individuals and groups do not view politics as a zero-sum game.[41] The Somalis are encouraged, and the entire system buoyed by the fact that should various parties, individuals, or groups lose a particular election there will be future opportunities to attain one's goals and achieve elected office. Hence individuals and groups take a more relaxed view of the electoral process and tend to adopt maximum-minimum strategies rather than attaching an all-or-nothing connotation to each election. Individual commitment to the political system as a whole is enhanced by the ongoing opportunity to participate in the political process and by the regularized procedures for attaining political office.

REHABILITATION OF PERSONNEL

A corollary to the process of regime alteration and one which underscores the level of political development and sophistication already attained in Somalia is the rehabilitation of personnel. Even when an individual has been voted out of office or has made a political mistake of considerable magnitude, he can expect to subsequently have the opportunity to redress the mistake and eventually play an active life in the political activities of the Republic. Defeated candidates for major political office are not shot, exiled, or jailed: they continue to participate in politics. For example, Abdullahi Issa, who was Prime Minister from 1956 to 1960, became Foreign Minister under the man who defeated him for that office, Abdirashid Ali Shermarke. Sheik Ali Jumale, who lost the presidency to Aden Osman in 1960, then participated in the Shermarke government. Abdirashid Ali Shermarke himself, after being Prime Minister from 1960–64, was voted out of office, eventually left the SYL, and then came back to be elected President of the Republic in 1967. Ibrahim Egal participated in the 1960–62 government, went into the opposition for 5 years and subsequently became Prime Minister. After even more serious mistakes, those northern officers who staged the December 1961 mutiny at Hargeisa were jailed, but after a period in prison were allowed to rejoin the army and fought against the Ethiopians. They have subsequently rejoined society and are regarded as members in good standing.

[41] Elections, for example, are not characterized by the all-or-nothing spirit among the political parties so prevalent elsewhere in Africa.

We have chosen only the most prominent examples of this process which, for want of a better term, we have labelled rehabilitation. Other instances of a local nature could be adduced to support the proposition. What seems most important, however, is that the responsiveness of the Somali political system results in part from the maintenance of an ethos where the losers can afford to take a relaxed view of the eventual consequences of their political defeats. When deferred hopes and aspirations, not exile or imprisonment, are the result of a political loss, individual actors are far less inclined to view politics as a zero-sum game or to act in such a way as to undermine the entire system.

RESPONSIVENESS

Widespread participation in politics, the pattern of regime alteration, and the rehabilitation and subsequent integration of politically defeated personnel help to sustain the Somali political system by increasing levels of identification with it and its leaders. The system also seems highly responsive to the demands placed upon it by individuals and groups. It is easy to overestimate the dysfunctional aspects of clan politics and to speak of governmental responsiveness to ethnic and group pressures as if they were totally improper and a hindrance to progress.[42] Yet because of the basic homogeneity of Somali culture and the uniformity of the clan networks, the process should not be regarded as totally pejorative. Clan organizations and ethnic groups do, in the Somali context, operate as both interest and pressure groups and provide an important, in-place feedback mechanism which provides vital linkage between the central government and the society as a whole. Further, the tensions between the "modern," "detribalized" elite and their traditional counterparts have been muted by the very process of bargaining among different ethnic groups:

> Tribal differences have not prevented political party leaders from focusing attention on national goals and spreading the thought patterns of nationalism. Nor have these differences prevented them from viewing and resolving problems in their national context.[43]

[42] Touval, op. cit., p. 85, for example, states that Somali politics are "essentially tribal" in character.
[43] Castagno, Somalia, p. 360.

We are not suggesting that the Somali case refutes the experiences elsewhere in Africa where tribalism has proven to be, on occasion, highly disruptive. It may well be that because of the basic societal homogeneity and the widespread agreement on the goals of the political system one finds in Somalia, the system can afford the luxury of particular and local attachments. The fact that there is basic agreement as to where the system is going means that local interest groups that seek to place their demands ahead of the nation are less disruptive than they would be in other systems where the degree of agreement on basic goals is far less. There is fragmentation in Somali society and in Somali politics, but this fragmentation is not of a centrifugal nature. To say that the Somali political system is responsive to tribal or ethnic pressures is not, and should not be interpreted, as being an indication, ipso facto of a lack of political development.

RESILIENCE

Another aspect of the Somali political system that indicates a high degree of political development is the resilience of the system to periods of sustained crisis. We outlined in Chapter II the pressures that can develop as a result of economic development and demographic change, and the need for a system to "grow" in order to meet these stresses. As will be outlined in the section on capabilities, Somalia has not yet faced its hours of maximum crisis but the system has already undergone significant levels of stress. During 1961, 1964, and 1967, for example, there were considerable periods of time when a minimum of governmental business was carried out due to constitutional crises. Yet the system survived and the very fact that it did added greatly to its legitimacy, reinforcing Somali faith in the system as a whole, even though Somalis lost faith from time to time with particular governments.

The decision-making process in Somalia can thus be characterized as essentially polyarchal in scope even though there are strong patterns of intergroup bargaining once these leaders are chosen. Participation in the system is multidimensional in character. There is extensive freedom of speech, assembly, and association and vibrant subgroup autonomy. Politics are viewed as the proper concern of all men and an integral aspect of life. There is also a strong commitment on the part of most Somali groups and political parties to the existing political structure and the system as a whole.

However, the system is not without flaws. Politics in Somalia often reflect excessive concern with local, even parochial interests. Nor is corruption unknown. There is far less prohibition against the use of public office for private gain than we encountered in Tanzania (although the President of the National Assembly, Sheik Ahmed Absiyeh Mohamed, was removed from office in 1966, allegedly for malfeasance). There is also a tradition of inflated voting counts, selling of votes, and block voting by local leaders, and a persistent strain of violence in the society.[44]

In addition, there is the problem of the military as shown by the abortive mutinies in Hargeisa (December 1961) and Mogadiscio (February 1967). Because of the priority attached to the union of all Somalis and the perceived need to use force to attain that goal, the military in Somalia has become a powerful, expensive institution. There is the distinct possibility that any lasting détente with Kenya and Ethiopia or reduced Somalian military budgets could promote a hostile military reaction. Thus one cannot say with assurance that the military will not intervene in Somali politics. What can be said, however, is that the notion of military rule, or the rule of any group not elected, runs counter to the Somali political heritage as well as to the course of its political life since independence. A coup could occur in Somalia, but the evidence suggests that it would be neither welcomed nor enduring.

Capabilities Analysis

Like Tanzania, but unlike the Ivory Coast or South Africa, the Somali political system is distinguished by weak extractive and distributive capabilities but a strong symbolic capacity. Its current power in the regulative and rejuvenative areas is limited but improving. Only in the symbolic area is the Somali system particularly strong. The accomplishments attained by Somalia in the fields of

[44] This subject is covered by Castagno, "Somali Republic," p. 531, UN T/1344 (Visiting Mission, 1957) p. 38, and The Somali National Police Academy, *The Somali Police Force: A Brief Report on the Functions and Activities of its Various Branches* (Mogadiscio: Government Printer, 1968), p. 159.

democratic decision making and political development should be evaluated in this context.

REGULATIVE CAPABILITY

The political system of Somalia possesses effective instruments of regulation for use in law enforcement and the preservation of societal order. Its police force consists of 6000 men, including a police air wing and a highly mobile patrol force of 1500 men, the *Darawishta Poliska*. Organized into nine territorial divisions, forty-nine stations, and seventy-two posts, it is well trained and fully integrated. No societal or clan groups dominate its organization although Samaales make up a majority of its members.[45] All officers undergo a stiff 9 month training course at the National Police Academy; additional training is provided in the United States, Italy, West Germany, and Switzerland. There is a refreshing emphasis on the retraining of personnel at periodic intervals and supervision of their performance in the field. The former commander of the police force General Haji Mohamed Abshir Musa, has with dispatch and vigor, infused the police with a strong sense of professionalism and encouraged them to safeguard the basic civil liberties so important in Somali society.[46] As a further check on the arbitrary use of power, the force as a whole is answerable to the various "organs of Justice" even though it is under the control of the Ministry of Interior.[47] For all of these reasons, the Somali police force is widely regarded as one of the most effective and equitable regulatory establishments in sub-Saharan Africa.[48] It is a critical element in the maintenance of a stable, orderly society within which democratic politics can transpire.

The well trained and well equipped army, headed by General Mohamed Siad Barre, is composed of 10,000 men, including an air force of 1500 men and a navy of 180. This defense establishment is

[45] Castagno, "Somali Republic," p. 532.

[46] Somali National Police Academy, *The Somali Police Force*, p. 7. It remains to be seen, however, whether this professionalism will survive his ouster early in 1969.

[47] *Ibid.*, p. 6.

[48] For a comparison of the Somali Security establishment and other law enforcement agencies in sub-Saharan Africa, the interested reader may consult C. Potholm, "The Multiple Roles of the Police as seen in the African Context," *Journal of Developing Areas* (January, 1969) Vol. II, No. 2: 139–158.

large, particularly for Africa.[49] With one-third the population of Tanzania and about the same as the Ivory Coast, Somalia has three times the armed forces of each. In terms of the percentage of total population in the armed forces and the percentage of gross national product spent on military affairs, Somalia is close to the levels attained by South Africa. The Soviet Union has provided over $30 million worth of arms and conducted an extensive training program, although the amounts of modern weapons and the degree of Soviet influence have been exaggerated in many reports.[50] The large size of the defense establishment is explained by the primacy of the goal to unite all Somalis under one flag and by the fear of substantially larger Ethiopian forces. As long as this goal remains of paramount importance to the Somalis, and Ethiopia, Kenya, and France prevent its attainment, it seems likely that the armed forces will continue to absorb 20% of the national budget. Since the accords of 1967 and the scaling down of military aid to the Somalis in Kenya and Ethiopia, the army has been used on a variety of national building projects such as the construction of roads, the digging of wells, and the building of barracks.

The police and the army give the Somali political system a firm security capability, but that capacity is used sparingly. Most police work, for example, centers around antismuggling operations along Somalia's 1500 mile coast and undefined borders and the curtailment of tribal feuds over grazing and water rights, rather than around political regulation.[51] Law enforcement is often locally generated among the Samaale nomads in remote areas and usually only major disturbances are brought to the attention of the central authorities. In addition, punishment for crimes is often light, and during national holidays many criminals are released or have their sentences reduced. Not even treason is punished by death. During 1968, for example, the former Foreign Minister of Somalia, Ahmed Yusuf Dualeh, was given only a prison sentence for passing state secrets to a foreign power.

In fact, the Somali political system and its leadership take a sur-

[49] Whether it will be expanded depends on the outcome of political deliberations now in progress and upon future foreign support.

[50] The Somali Air Force, for example, has 3 Mig 15's and 7 Mig 17's. *The Economist* on August 13, 1966 stated that the Somalis had 150 Migs.

[51] Somali National Police Academy, *The Somali Police Force*, pp. 158 and 159.

prisingly laissez-faire attitude toward the society they govern. On all levels, there is less direction from the political center than one finds in South Africa, Tanzania, and the Ivory Coast, and less administrative structure. As in Tanzania, the public administration is not particularly extensive (although the government employs 16,000 persons) and does not penetrate deeply into the countryside. Communications and travel difficulties also curtail the ability of the government to regulate the daily lives of the Somalis. But the major reason for a minimum of governmental regulation lies in the nature of Somali society and the fact that the central political authorities reflect that society. There is no preventive detention act, for example, no governmentally controlled trade unions, no organized institutions designed to insure that the desires of the government are superimposed on society. Some of the leadership of the Somali Youth League or the Somali Democratic Union may well view themselves as the vanguard of society, but there is little evidence to indicate that they act as if they are. We have already stressed the free and open nature of politics. Information too is freely gathered and freely disseminated. There are several official government publications, including the English language weekly *Somali News*, the Italian language daily, *Corriere delle Somalia,* and a fact sheet of the Somali Youth League *Union,* but other parties, groups, and individuals as well, publish newspapers in Italian, Arabic and English.

Likewise, the economic sphere is supervised only in the most general of fashions. There was a 5 year plan which ended in 1967 and there is now a 3 year plan for 1967–70 that seeks to diversify the economy and achieve self-sufficiency in food. But there is little regulation of foreign investment and the National Economic and Labor Council which advises the government on economic matters has encouraged laws that promote such investment. New industries are tax exempt for 10 years and by the Foreign Investment Code (1961) and the Investment Guarantee Program (1964) companies may repatriate up to 15% of their annual profits per year and the original value of the investment is freely transferable after 5 years. Although the SDU has advocated the expropriation of some of the large, Italian owned plantations, Somalia has not nationalized any foreign firms to date and has generally avoided competition with the private sector of the economy (except to offer relatively cheap loans for development purposes through such governmental avenues as the National Bank of Somalia as the *Credito Somalo*). The government relies on such indirect means as tax laws and import duties to influence the course of economic development rather than on central planning or control.

EXTRACTIVE CAPABILITY

Somalia, like Tanzania, has a markedly underdeveloped extractive capability. Its physical attributes are unimposing. Most of the country, from the Ethiopian highlands to the coastal plain, consists of dry bush which receives only 2.15 inches of rainfall per year. Fully 40% of the total area of Somalia is unsuited for grazing and nearly 90% is unfit for dry farming. Irrigated farmland moreover amounts to but 0.033% of the land.[52] Drought and locusts are significant and persistent threats.

The Somali population is likewise underdeveloped. A large number, perhaps a majority of the Somalis live out their lives in small nomadic bands. Population density is but eleven persons per square mile. Illiteracy is estimated at 90% and the per capita income, at $62 per year, is even lower than that of Tanzania.[53] Its gross national product now stands at $150 million. Fourteen per cent of the Somalis are urbanized primarily in the four major cities, Mogadiscio (200,000), Hargeisa (40,000), Chisimaio (30,000), and Berbera (20,000). According to the latest United Nations figures there are but sixty-seven doctors and two dentists for the entire country or an average of 30,000 patients per physician. The government is seeking to improve the health, education, and income levels of the population, but the handicaps to be overcome are substantial and the population remains in a highly undeveloped state.

The current physical infrastructure of the country is not adequate for major economic development. It has perhaps best been described by the Somalis themselves as "ramshackle."[54] There are 8000 miles of roads, only 367 miles of which are paved.[55] There are no railroads.

[52] Hance, *op. cit.*, p. 369. For a discussion of the Somali economy in general, see Hance pp. 365–374 and Mark Karp, *The Economics of Trusteeship in Somalia*, Chapters II–VIII and *International Financial Statistics* (November, 1968) Vol. XXI, No. 11: 272.
[53] *The United Nations Statistical Yearbook*, 1967, p. 576.
[54] *Africa Report* (November, 1966), p. 28.
[55] *The United Nations Statistical Yearbook*, 1967, p. 411.

Somali ports, such as Mogadiscio, Merca, and Brava, are of notorious quality, dependent upon costly and inefficient lighterage, although most are in the process of being improved. Two modern deep water ports, Chisimaio and Berbera, are now nearing completion. Only Mogadiscio and Hargeisa have 24 hour a day electricity. The economy of Somalia is currently based on the raising of livestock and the growing of bananas. These products accounted for 90% of export revenues in 1965. There are, according to government figures, 24 million sheep, 6 million goats, 16 million camels, and 3 million head of cattle.[56] Meat and other animal products are exported to the United Arab Republic and the Arabian peninsula.

Plantation agriculture is centered in the area between the Uebi Scebelli and the Giuba. There are few other streams in the country and only the Giuba flows to the sea (the Uebi Scebelli peters out into a swampy area south of Mogadiscio). Bananas and sugar are the two principal products although some rice, citrus fruits, and cashews are also grown. The sugar crop is used internally while the bananas are exported to Italy. The bananas are sold above world prices through the Italian banana monopoly *Azienda Monopolio Banane* and account for 40% of the export revenues. Most of the production is in the hands of Italian firms such as the *Società Azionaria Concessionari Agricoli* (SACA) and the *Società Agricoltori Gueba* (SAG). The Italian subsidy of Somali bananas was due to end in 1969 but, because of the closing of the Suez Canal during the 1967 Middle East war, it has been extended to 1971. Somali bananas are not now competitive with those produced in Latin America or West Africa although major revampment of the industry is in progress. Despite the shift in recent years to a greater emphasis on the production of sorghum, corn, and beans, Somalia today remains a net importer of food.

Industrialization has been downplayed by the Somalis although there is some light industry in the form of sugar mills, a meat-packing plant, cotton gins, an oil extraction plant, a shoe leather factory, and a tuna cannery. Lack of capital, a small internal market, and a definite scarcity of labor (due in part to the cultural bias against manual labor in traditional Somali society), hamper even these

[56] Government of Somalia, *General Information* (Mogadiscio: Government Printer, 1968), p. 6.

modest endeavors. Industry and commerce together account for but 17% of the Somali gross national product. There is some hope that mineral wealth might provide the basis for future growth. There are 200 million tons of iron ore in Somalia as well as nearly 1 million tons of uranium and smaller amounts of tin, asbestos, kaolin, and lead. The uranium in particular may prove to be of value if the demand for its use in Europe continues at its present level; concessions for uranium granted to United States, Italian, and West German concerns in late 1968 could begin to realize profits as early as 1973. Oil exploration, however, has gone on since before independence and results to date have been negative. Whether or not minerals will prove a significant impetus to Somali development will depend upon the cost of extraction and transportation to the industrialized countries. At the present time, they cannot be regarded as a cure-all.

In addition to having an essentially unbalanced economy with a marked dependence on two products, Somalia also suffers from a perenially unfavorable trade balance. Since independence, exports have been running at a level only two-thirds that of imports, and Somalia remains closely tied to Italy which takes 50% of its exports and provides over 35% of its imports. The budget has been balanced only by direct grants-in-aid from Italy, China, and West Germany. Somalia has received over $500 million in grants and loans from a host of international donors—the Soviet Union, China, the United States, Italy, West Germany, the World Bank, and the European Economic Community—but, while helpful, this aid cannot be relied upon over the coming decades. Thus, Somalia's extractive capability seems destined to remain weak for the foreseeable future even though some heretofore neglected industries, such as tourism and fishing, could gradually brighten the general economic picture.

The increasing numbers of university graduates could also improve the quality of the government bureaucracies and thus strengthen the system's extractive capability, although the bureaucracies will have to be expanded with care to prevent overstaffing. From a political point of view, the strengthening of this capacity is not without relevance. Many Somalis are now moving directly from a pastoral setting into the cities, bypassing agricultural or mining occupations to become members of an unemployed, urban proletariat. Unless the Somali government is able over time to supplant the local clan organization which has functioned as the provider of basic welfare requirements, the political system itself will face substantial stresses in the future.

DISTRIBUTIVE CAPABILITY

The small resource base and the generally weak extractive capability place definite limits on the current distributive capacity of Somalia. The gross national product, for example, has not increased sharply enough to offset the population growth and may have fallen relative to that figure.[57] And as health conditions and diagnostic techniques improve, the gap will probably widen, increasing the pressures outlined above. It should be remembered, however, that material comforts are generally lacking in rural Somali society anyway and in terms of physical objects, the Somalis are poorer than their counterparts in the other political systems under review. Life is harsh and viewed as a constant struggle affecting all. There is little differentiation according to wealth in Somalia society. The size of herds are an indication of wealth but these are neither willingly nor easily translated into material comforts for the 80% of the total population that lies outside the cash sector of the economy.[58] Rising prosperity in the towns has drawn some Somalis to urban and peri-urban areas in recent years and, as in Tanzania, the government has made some attempt to use this wealth to improve the lot of all. During a serious drought in 1964, for example, the government allotted $1.1 million for famine relief, raising the revenue from taxes on luxury goods and deductions from the salaries of governmental employees. This has not been done on a systematic or permanent basis, however, and in terms of distribution of national wealth as in other areas, there is little concerted direction from the center.

Distribution of wealth in Somalia society contains elements of both ascription and achievement. We have already alluded to the basically egalitarian nature of traditional Somali society and the rise of new, educated elites in the urban areas. Yet ascription remains an important factor in Somali life. The patronage aspects of Somali politics, the importance of local clan connections, and the inability of the central government to eliminate nepotism all inhibit the

---

[57] Kamarck, *op. cit.*, p. 17.

[58] Hance, *op. cit.*, p. 372. See Karp, *op. cit.*, chapter II on the statistical difficulties in Somalia.

allocation of the goods, services, and status available to the political authority on the basis of achievement. The use of political office to enrich oneself and find positions for one's kinsmen is taken for granted. Despite occasional action by the government, there is not the attachment to austerity and grass roots sharing of wealth that one finds in Tanzania. Nevertheless, the government of Somalia has made progress in reducing racial and occupational discrimination and seems to be working, at least sporadically, toward a more achievement oriented society.[59]

With regard to land, the government has, as in other matters, allowed existing societal patterns to continue. The Sabs, for example, maintain their control over the land in the river valley and private ownership is permitted. In the areas inhabited by the pastoral Samaales, however, few persons "own" land. The use of grazing land and water are considered birthrights, ownership of land is not. There is also a cultural bias against women playing a major role in the economic and political life of the country. The government has attempted to encourage the participation of women in national life but there remains a strong male orientation to society. For example, unlike the situation in the Ivory Coast, South Africa, and to a lesser extent Tanzania, women do not generally play an important role in commerce.

In all of these areas, governmental educational policy offers promise for the future. Primary education is free and in principle, open to all. In fact, of course, the difficulties of nomadic life and the demands of family survival in a pastoral setting limit the opportunities to accept educational openings. These have increased rapidly. In 1948 there were but 1200 students on all levels. There are now 30,000 in public primary and secondary schools and 39,000 in private schools.[60] There are 4000 students at the university level, including

[59] UN T/1033 (*Visiting Mission, 1951*) p. 404.
[60] 1969 Figures by the Government of Somalia:

	Government	Private
elementary school	23,291	28,893
intermediary	5,596	7,782
secondary	1,989	2,702
	30,876	39,377

See also Helen Kitchen (ed.), *The Educated African* (New York: Frederick A. Praeger, 1962), pp. 83–108.

451 in the USSR, 226 in Italy, and 131 in West Germany. A new teacher training college opened in 1965 and it is hoped that its graduates will eventually replace the American Peace Corps and Egyptian personnel who now teach on the secondary level. One aspect of university education which militates against a totally achievement oriented distribution process is the fact that some scholarships for foreign study are disbursed to particular political parties or individuals who in turn assign them, often on a personal basis, to students.

The political system of Somalia then exhibits a weak distribution capacity. The small pool of goods and services available for allocation, the importance of ascriptive forces in that allocation, and the lack of central control over the distribution of resources all combine to reduce the effectiveness of the distributive capability. Given the self-reliant nature of the Somali people, this is not as great an impediment to the operation of the political system as it might be in other societies, but it could offer difficulty over time if a revolution of rising expectations permeates the countryside of Somalia.

REJUVENATIVE CAPABILITY

The rejuvenative capability of Somalia, like the distributive capacity, suffers from the tensions between an ascriptive view of society on one hand and achievement orientation on the other. It may well be that the rising numbers of educated "modernists" will be able to gradually reduce the ascriptive forces and dampen the power of local authorities. The police and the army, for example, are probably more "national" institutions (in the sense of offering careers on the basis of talent) than the bureaucracy; many of the new elite attempt to stress their modernity by refusing to reveal their clan names and calling themselves simply "Somalis." [61] In the meantime, however, the political system cannot make maximum use of its human resources because of ascriptive factors.

The rejuvenative capability, in particular the educational system, is also hampered by the fact that there is no written language for Somalia. The basic asset of a common tongue which separates Somalia from most other African states is thus enervated by the

---

[61] Lewis, *Modern History of Somaliland*, p. 168. Complaints persist however; see *Somali News*, Sept. 13, 1968.

THE SOMALI POLITICAL SYSTEM *219*

burdens of translating spoken Somali into the written forms of Arabic, Italian, or English. Not only are manpower, time, and capital consumed in the process but the fact that Somali is unwritten places an additional burden on school age children by forcing them to learn a second language. The major barrier to the creation of a written Somali language has been the continuing controversy over the type of script to be used. A group of Somali scholars, the most famous of which was Osman Usuf Kenadid, developed a Somali alphabet (later called Osmaniya) in the 1920's but it was never widely adopted and was subsequently banned by the Italians. In any case, the adoption of the Osmaniya alphabet would not eradicate the difficulties of translation and might, as its critics have suggested, lead to cultural isolation. Neither Latin nor Arabic script has proven totally acceptable either, although governmental committees have been studying the problem since 1962. There has been serious religious opposition to the use of the Latin alphabet and many Somalis fear that the use of Arabic would cause Somali national culture to be submerged by the more extensive "Arab" culture and retard access to the technological and scientific knowledge of the West. English and Arabic remain the mediums of instruction "pending the selection of an official written form of the Somali language." [62] Until this dilemma is resolved, the rejuvenational capability of Somalia will continue to be mixed.

Despite the difficulties of informational transfer, the Somali system has endeavored to keep open a free flow of information. This policy has taken the form of visits, missions, and exchanges with a wide variety of countries ranging from the United States to China, from Egypt to North Korea. The Somali National News Agency (SONNA) draws upon Reuters, the Arab News Agency, the Italian News Agency and other foreign sources for its news and there are in addition, a variety of weeklies and biweeklies published in English, Arabic, and Italian. Censorship is absent. Radio broadcasting has been greatly expanded since West Germany and the USSR donated broadcasting units and transmitters, and there are daily broadcasts in Somali, Arabic, Italian, and English. Although the government used its radio facilities to attack Kenya and Ethiopia during past crises and generated a good deal of propaganda for internal con-

[62] *Africa Report* (August, 1965), p. 31.

sumption, it made no attempt to jam radio broadcasts from outside the country.

Like Tanzania, the Somali government has created institutions to promote the process of political socialization. There is a School of Public Administration which provides "broad if elementary understanding of law, administration, history and economics to potential candidates for the civil service and to future political leaders." [63] There is no over-all educational plan however, no governmental program for allocating the newly educated elite to specific positions, in short, no manpower planning for the system as a whole.

But in one sense, the task of political socialization is made easier by the sense of national unity and the high degree of consensus as to the goals of the system. Somalis, unlike Tanzanians, South Africans, and Ivoiriens, do not have to be taught to think of themselves as Somalis. Added to the positive reinforcement which participation in the political life of the nation brings, this underlying unity aids the entire system in the process of self-rejuvenation. Identification with local clan leaders and the sense of ethnic identity, the long and supportive history of the Somalis as a people, as well as the social cement provided by a common language and culture, all aid in the maintenance of the system. In fact, the very forces that inhibit some aspects of social and political change also provide major support for the rejuvenative aspects of the system and help to insure its longevity.

SYMBOLIC CAPABILITY

Despite the handicaps outlined in the preceding analysis, the Somali political system exhibits a very strong symbolic capability. In fact, this probably represents Somalia's greatest asset—the only one which most directly and cogently supports the system. Because Somalis think of themselves as Somalis and of the political system as an extension of their society the system enjoys great credibility. Coupled with a deep commitment to a set of goals with which most Somalis can identify, this sense of unity sustains the political system.

Islam too provides a good deal of cohesion. The basic cultural values of Islam are accepted and most Somalis are devout members

---

[63] Castagno, *Somalia*, p. 366.

of the orthodox *shafi'i* school of the Sunnite sect. Most adult men belong to one of the many dervish orders. It is true that because of their ecological setting, the Somalis are often pragmatic about some aspects of their religion (the women, for example, seldom wear veils). But the Somalis are deeply religious and this adds to their feeling of oneness, separating them (in their eyes at least) from the "Christian" and "pagan" groups that exist in Ethiopia and Kenya.

Despite the fact that Arabic is the medium of expression in religious training, the Somali language is of great importance in solidifying Somali society and, by facilitating political communication, in the political system. Although unwritten, Somali is spoken by nearly 4 million persons and its oral traditions are of significance in portraying a sense of shared culture. The *gabays* or long epic poems are recited over and over and the lessons of Somali society are transmitted by means of the spoken word with a feeling that borders on reverence.[64] Moreover, the Somali language both reflects and helps to promote the democratic and egalitarian ethos so intrinsic to Somali society. It is a blunt language and its few polite words and formal forms of address are largely recent borrowings from Arabic and other languages.[65]

The legitimacy of the Somali political system thus ultimately rests on the fact that the system is itself clearly a projection of Somali society. It is supported by elements earlier identified as traditional and legal. There is little in the way of charismatic support—there are no "fathers of the nation," for example. The rough and tumble aspects of Somali politics and the egalitarian nature of their society seem to inhibit the formation of any cults of personality even though individual leaders are well liked and respected. In short, Somalis tend to identify with the political system as a whole rather than with particular governments, and this in turn provides a further dimension of legitimacy. The goal orientation of the system also helps to underpin the system. As will be seen in the section on systemic goals, most Somalis agree on the major goals of the system.

[64] Jeanne Contini, "The Somalis: A Nation of Poets in Search of an Alphabet," in Helen Kitchen (ed.), *A Handbook of African Affairs* (New York: Frederick A. Praeger, 1964), pp. 301–311.

[65] C. R. U. Bell, *The Somali Language* (London: Longmans, Green and Company, 1953); B. W. Andrzejewski and I. M. Lewis, *Somali Poetry* (London: Oxford University Press, 1963); and Mussa Galaal, *Hikmaad Soomali* (London: Oxford University Press, 1956).

These are hence not the goals primarily of would-be modernizers (as in Tanzania) or a small oligarchy (as in South Africa): they are the goals of the society as a whole. Value consensus is greater in Somalia than in any of the other political systems examined in this work. It is to these goals that we now turn.

Goals of the Political System

We have already stressed the polyarchal aspects of decision making in the Republic of Somalia and indicated to what extent democratic decision making remains a widely held and deeply cherished goal. It is necessary here to but reiterate the depth of support for that goal and how opposed the Somali government and the Somali people are to any proposed pattern of command decision making.

Beyond the maintenance of the present political system and its democratic process of decision making, one goal stands out as paramount and that is the unification of all Somalis. We have indicated the reasons why the Somalis in Kenya, Ethiopia, and the French Territory of the Afar and the Issa may be thought of as an extension of the Somali political system. From this point of view, the goal of unification might be regarded as internal, as one aspect of political development. At the same time, to the world at large and to the foreign governments involved, the goal of unification has strong international overtones since Somalia can achieve the union of all Somalis only with the voluntary or forced acceptance of that goal by Kenya, Ethiopia, and France. It is precisely this thread of ambiguity and its implications for the international actors involved that make the Somali question so difficult.

The Somalis have long demanded the union of all Somalis and have, in terms of manpower and scarce resources, made the attainment of that goal a priority item.[66] It is not our intent to outline the tortured and convoluted story of the international agreements that divided the Somali people and delineated the present boundaries of Somalia.[67] Nor is it our purpose to choose between the

[66] Defense and internal security absorbed over 30% of the 1968 budget and the commitment to union is written into the constitution (Article 6).

[67] John G. Drysdale, *The Somali Dispute* (New York: Frederick A. Praeger, 1964) and Touval, *op. cit.*, have covered the entire problem in some depth as have E. A. Bayne, *Somali on the Horn* (New York: American Universities Field

case offered for unification of all Somalis and the subsequent boundary adjustments by the Somali government and the position in support of the status quo as presented by Kenya, Ethiopia, and France. In essence their points of view are irreconcilable. The Somali claim is based ultimately on the principle of self-determination for the Somali peoples, while the other governments stress the essentially juridical nature of their position, namely, that international agreements were made and their provisions legitimize the present arrangement. No side is prepared to grant the validity of the other's claim and it will be left to the reader to decide which has the strongest case.

There are additional realities which must be considered. If one accepts the Somali claim, it should be remembered that the half million Somalis in Ethiopia, the 200,000 Somalis in Kenya, and the 40–60,000 Somalis in the French Territory of the Afar and the Issa inhabit fully one-fifth the total area of Kenya and Ethiopia and one-third the territory of the French area. It is not simply a question of "gathering in" the Somalis but actually of enlarging the Somali state. As both Ethiopia and Kenya are multinational countries with many minority groups represented within their respective areas and both share a history of polycentric stresses in the past, the implications of Somali unification go beyond the sphere of the Somalis themselves. In Ethiopia, for example, a process of minority self-determination might eventually lead to the successive peeling away of various groups, leaving only an Amharic-tigren core.

To the Somalis however, these are matters of little concern. Unification of the Somalis has long been a goal of the system. Ethiopia

---

Staff, 1960) and Anthony S. Reyner, "Somalia: The Problems of Independence," *The Middle East Journal* (Summer, 1960) Vol. XIV, No. 3: 247–255, and Mesfin N. Mariam, "The Background of the Ethio-Somalian Boundary Dispute," *The Journal of Modern African Studies* (1964) Vol. 2: 189–219. See also Drysdale's "Somali Frontier Problems," *The World Today* (January, 1964); and I. M. Lewis, "Pan-Africanism and Pan-Somalism," *Journal of Modern African Studies* (June, 1963) Vol. I, No. 2: 147–161, "The Evaluation of the Dispute," *Africa Report* (April, 1967), 42–45, and "Prospects in the Horn," *Africa Report* (April, 1967), 37–40. Ethiopia's case is stated in the official government publication, *The Ethio-Somali Frontier Problem* (Addis Ababa: Ministry of Information, 1961). Somalia's position is well articulated in two government position papers: *The Somali Peoples' Quest for Unity* (Mogadiscio: Government Printer, 1965) and *The Issue of the Northern Frontier District* (Mogadiscio: Government Printer, 1963).

early appeared as the greatest obstacle to the realization of that goal when the Ogaden (1948) and the Haud and Reserved Area (1954) were returned to its control, after independence. In Addis Ababa during June of 1963 negotiations took place between the foreign ministers of both countries but little was accomplished. A series of border clashes along the as yet undemarcated boundary between Ethiopia and Somalia occurred during late 1963 and broke into open warfare early in 1964. Following the meeting of the Organization of African Unity foreign ministers in Lagos, Nigeria, representatives of Ethiopia and Somalia met during March of 1964 and agreed to a cease fire and a mutual withdrawal of armed forces. Sporadic clashes between Ethiopian security forces and Somali nomads continued for several years, even though Somali attention and energy was directed toward Kenya from 1964 to 1967.

If the Somalis had reason to be angered with Great Britain following the return to Ethiopian control of large numbers of Somalis, the same was true of Great Britain's handling of the Kenyan Somali question. Concentrated in the Northern Frontier District of Kenya (now called the North Eastern Province), the Somalis formed the overwhelming majority of the population although the area also contained some Galla and Turkara peoples. The ceding of Kenyan territory to Italy after World War I, the British occupation of the entire Horn, and the internal dynamics of preindependence Kenyan politics (the Kenyan African National Union pushed for a centralized form of government but the Kenya African Democratic Union sought a more loosely organized federal solution) all combined to offer the Somalis in Kenya the hope that they might be united with the soon to be independent Somalia. After the jailing of leaders of the Somali Youth League, the renamed Northern Province People's Progressive Party (NPPPP) acted as the spokesman for Somali interests and actively worked for union with Somalia.[68] The British decision to send a commission to the area to determine public senti-

[68] Government of Great Britain, *Report of the Kenya Independence Constitutional Conference* (CMD 1700, 1963); *Report of the Regional Boundary Commission* (CMD 1899, 1962); and *Report of the Northern Frontier District Commission* (CMD 1900, 1962). See also, Drysdale *op. cit.*, chapter XII; A. A. Castagno, Jr., "The Somali-Kenyan Controversy: Implications for the Future," *Journal of Modern African Studies* (July, 1964) Vol. II, No. 2: 165–188; and I. M. Lewis, "The Problem of the Northern Frontier District of Kenya," *Race* (July, 1963) Vol. V, No. 1: 52–54.

ment for union and the findings of that commission (which indicated that 80% of the population favored union) encouraged the Somalis to think that their goal might be realized.[69] In a rather clumsy *volte face* however, Great Britain refused to make a decision in favor of Somalia and declared that the matter could be resolved only by an independent Kenya. When Jomo Kenyatta declared that an independent Kenya would not look with favor upon secession the outcome seemed clear.

> We, and especially KANU, feel and we have put it clearly before the Somali Government that we regard the NFD as part of Kenya. We also regard Somalis who live in the NFD and elsewhere in Kenya as our brothers. They are part and parcel of Kenya and we would like them to live in Kenya in that fashion.[70]

The Somalis in the NFD then boycotted the Kenyan elections and the Republic of Somalia broke off diplomatic relations with Great Britain during March 1963. These developments also encouraged Somalia to seek Soviet aid for her armed forces.[71] With independence in December 1963, the government of Kenya declared a state of emergency and fighting broke out in the NFD region. A simmering war continued for several years with the Somali government supporting the Northern Frontier District Liberation Movement and Kenya using troops against what they called Somali *shifta*, or bandits. By December 1967 when Prime Minister Egal met with President Kenyatta in Kampala, Uganda (talks which followed an earlier meeting at Arusha), at least 4000 persons had been killed on both sides.[72] During January 1968 Somalia renewed diplomatic ties with Great Britain and established them with Kenya. The future of Somali-Kenyan relations remains in doubt, however, pending the

[69] Government of Great Britain (CMD 1900, Appendix D); Castagno, "The Somali-Kenyan Controversy," p. 179.

[70] Drysdale, *op. cit.*, p. 119.

[71] The United States, Germany, and Italy offered a $10 million arms package, the USSR $30 million. For a somewhat journalistic account of Chinese and Soviet penetration of the Horn, see John K. Cooley, *East Wind Over Africa* (New York: Walker and Company, 1966), pp. 25–37. Further documentation is contained in Zbigniew Brzezinski (ed.), *Africa and the Communist World* (Stanford, Calif.: Stanford University Press, 1963). Neither study is exhaustive.

[72] Estimates run as high as 6000.

outcome of negotiations and the ability of the present Somali government to attain any concessions concerning the eventual status of the Somalis in Kenya.

The French Territory of the Afar and Issa also contains over 40,000 Somalis, including members of the Issa clan family and some recent Isaak immigrants who are related to, but generally oppose the 60,000 Afars (Danakil), who live in the territory.[73] Somalis here have also indicated a desire for independence and perhaps, eventual unity with Somalia. Since the decision of inhabitants to continue close ties within the French Community in 1958, Somali agitation has increased. Because of the Franco-Ethiopian railroad which connects the port of Djibouti with Addis Ababa and the strategic position of the territory, neither France nor Ethiopia is prepared to see the territory come under Somali control. The non-Somali inhabitants of the area have also resisted the cry for a "Greater Somalia," fearing a decline in their living standard and a loss of political control should they be absorbed. Somali led riots during visit of General de Gaulle in 1966 prompted the French to send in additional troops and to call for a national referendum in March of 1967. The large numbers of Somali refugees fleeing Djibouti, deportees, and disenfranchised (perhaps 10,000 all told) insured that the electoral results would not be favorable to those who wished to see union with Somalia. France, as if to underscore its willingness to thwart Somali self-determination, also changed the name of the territory from French Somaliland to the French Territory of the Afar and Issa. Somali resentment could flare into open violence in the foreseeable future.

Irrespective of the relative merits of each side, the problem remains

[73] Useful background material on the French area is to be found in R. Muller, "Les Populations de la Côte Française des Somalis," pp. 45–103, M. Albospreyre, "Les Danakil du Cercle de Tadjoura," pp. 103–163, and P. Lamy, "Les Destin des Somalis," pp. 163–213, all in M. Albospreyre et al., Mer Rouge Africa Orientale (Paris: J. Peyronnet and Company, 1959). The Somali government has issued three pamphlets dealing with the former French Somaliland, French Somaliland in True Perspective, French Somaliland: A Classic Colonial Case, and French Somaliland: The Infamous Referendum (all from the Government Printer, Mogadiscio, 1967). John Drysdale has also written, "The Problem of French Somalia," Africa Report (November, 1966) 10–17; and Virginia Thompson and Richard Adloff have placed French Somaliland in its strategic setting in their Djibouti and the Horn of Africa (Stanford, Calif.: Stanford University Press, 1968).

essentially one of power. The wishes of nearly 4 million Somalis run counter to the expressed desires of the governments of Ethiopia (23 million), Kenya (10 million), and France (48 million). In addition, the Organization of African Unity has not given support to the Republic of Somalia, apparently deciding that Pan-Africanism as a principle is not to be actualized at the expense of other African territories.[74] The colonial boundaries, however unjust and irrational, the OAU has said, must stand. Hence Somalia finds itself isolated and its goal realization thwarted by powerful forces in the international community. It is against this background that the government of Prime Minister Egal sought a détente with Kenya and Ethiopia in an attempt to achieve by negotiation what it could not attain by the selective application of force. Since the goal of unity is so widely held, it is unlikely that this approach is more than a change in tactics. It is also unlikely that the Somalis will be able to achieve more than token concessions from the countries in question. During the 1969 elections, the government had to backtrack by exaggerating the accomplishments of its new policy. Given the nature of the situation, the unresolved problems in the Horn of Africa will continue to fester for some time to come and could affect internal politics in Somalia.

Curiously enough, the very exogenous forces which limit the attainment of one major goal of the system, the unification of all Somalis, make possible whatever progress has been made toward a second goal, economic development. While economic development as a goal is perhaps not as widely held or as actively pursued as the maintenance of democratic politics and the unification of all Somalis, it is a primary goal of the leaders of the system. With the tradition of UN and Italian assistance during the trusteeship period, the Somali government has sought major foreign aid for its economic development. Whether due to Somalia's strategic position, its independent stance in the international community, great power rivalry, or a combination of all three, Somalia has been the recipient of major amounts of foreign aid. By 1968, the Republic had received $336 million in loans and $196 million in grants.[75] Italy provided nearly $100 million, the United States $70 million, the Soviet Union

[74] Government of Somalia, *The Somali Republic and the Organization of African Unity* (Mogadiscio: Government Printer, 1964).

[75] Data from Brzezinski, *op. cit.*, pp. 66 and 74.

$35 million in military assistance and $58 million in economic development, while China gave a direct grant of $3 million and a loan of $18 million. In the case of the Soviet Union, this represents the highest per capita aid commitment in sub-Saharan Africa. Smaller but substantial amounts have been added by West Germany, the United Arab Republic, Saudi Arabia, and various international organizations such as the World Bank, the African Development Bank, and UNESCO. During 1968 Somalia devoted nearly 20% of its budget to various development programs even though this fell short of the desires of the Ministry of Finance: "Much as I would have liked to provide larger amounts for development, our limited revenue resources do not permit me to do this." [76] To see this figure in perspective, 6% of the same budget was devoted to education, 7% to health programs, and 30% to the security forces.[77]

Despite the amount of foreign aid, Somalia has been able to achieve a neutral stance in the international community. Its position is only slightly less independent on the major issues than that of Tanzania (by virtue of the fact that Somalia supports, unequivocally, the Arab countries against Israel), and it has kept friendly relations with the United States and China, Great Britain and the United Arab Republic, Italy and North Korea, Bulgaria and Kuwait, the Sudan and Saudi Arabia. Nevertheless, and this undoubtedly represents a major failure in terms of foreign policy, Somalia has been unable to translate this friendship into more positive support for her plans to unify the Horn of Africa.

The political system of Somalia then, despite its impressive accomplishments in the areas of political development and democratic decision making, finds itself confronted by the implications of the fact that it remains a poor and weak country in a situation where it needs both wealth and power to achieve its systemic goals. Whether the frustration that must accompany this realization will undermine or erode the achievements already logged in the first category remains to be seen.

POSTSCRIPT

After this chapter went to press, general elections were held in Somalia on March 26, 1969. Of the 123 seats, the Somali Youth League captured 73, the Socialist National Congress took 11,

[76] Government of Somalia, *Budget, 1968*, p. 36.
[77] *Ibid.*, Table 7.

the Somali African National Union 6, and the HDMS 3; twenty-three other parties won at least 1 seat. Mohamed Egal of the SYL formed the new government.

On October 15, however, President Shermarke was assassinated by a dissident policeman while on a tour of northeast Somalia. Prime Minister Egal's government was overthrown by a military coup on the day after President Shermarke's funeral. Seizing power in order to combat what it termed "tribalism" and "corruption," the newly formed Supreme Revolutionary Council banned all political parties. Although not totally unexpected, the military intervention dealt the political system a shattering blow and underscored (as indicated in Chapters II and VIII of this work) the ease with which political development may be halted or reversed, even after a decade of growth. Yet it remains our thesis that in Somalia, the democratic ethos of the society and the long tradition of polyarchal decision making will, over time, strongly influence the future course of politics no matter what its institutional framework, and should lead to the reassertion of civilian authorities in the not too distant future.

BIBLIOGRAPHY

Castagno, A. A. Jr., *Somalia* (New York: Carnegie Endowment for International Peace, 1959).

———— "Somali Republic," in James Coleman and Carl G. Rosberg (eds.), *Political Parties and National Integration* (Berkeley and Los Angeles, Calif.: University of California Press, 1964).

Drysdale, John G., *The Somali Dispute* (New York: Frederick A. Praeger, 1964).

Lewis, I. M., *A Pastoral Democracy* (London: Oxford University Press, 1961).

———— *The Modern History of Somaliland* (New York: Frederick A. Praeger, 1965).

Touval, Saadia, *Somali Nationalism: International Politics and the Drive for Unity in the Horn of Africa* (Cambridge: Harvard University Press, 1963).

CHAPTER VII

The Ivoirien
Political System

The political system of the Ivory Coast encompasses 125,000 square miles and is thus the size of Great Britain. It includes over 4 million persons of whom 10,000 are Syrians and Lebanese, and 35,000 are Europeans, primarily French. Of the remaining population, nearly a million are Africans from the nearby countries of Mali, Guinea, and Upper Volta. The rest are Africans representing the sixty ethnic groups indigenous to the Ivory Coast.[1] This "complex human mosaic" has been broken down into four major cultural groups. Thirty per cent of the population belongs to the

[1] Depending upon one's criteria, there are between sixty and one-hundred ethnic groups. The diversity of these groups is outlined in chapter III. Aristide Zolberg in *One Party Government in the Ivory Coast* (Princeton: Princeton University Press, 1964) has done outstanding research on the Ivory Coast. He concludes that it is of great significance that the "cultural cores" of these groups lie outside the borders of the Ivory Coast. See his "Patterns of National Integration," *Journal of Modern African Studies* (1967) Vol. V, No. 4: 449–467. Other ethnographic studies include B. Holas, *Les Sénufo* (Paris: Presses Universitaires de France, 1957); C. M. Assoux, *Anthropologie Economique des Gouro de Côte d'Ivoire* (Paris: Mouton and Company, 1964); M. J. Vicenti, *Coutumes Attié* (Paris: Editions Larose, 1914); and D. Paulme, *Une Société de Côte d'Ivoire d'hier et d'aujourd'hui: Les Bété* (Paris: Mouton and Company, 1962).

230

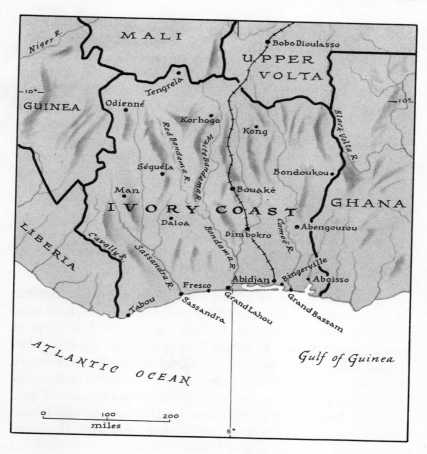

Atlantic East group which includes the various Akan peoples such as the Agni and the Baoulé. A like number are from the Atlantic West group which is made up of the Bete, Kru, and Dan people. Fifteen per cent of the population has been classified in the Upper Niger group, primarily Mande peoples such as the Manlinke and the Bambara, while twenty-four per cent are grouped with the Voltaic peoples such as the Senufo and the Lobi.

Our present knowledge of the early history of these ethnic groups is sketchy and we know less about the background of this area than about the other systems under review. There are topographical and geographical reasons for this. Because of the forest belt and its concomitant scourge of the tsetse fly, the Islamic penetration so pronounced in the savanna regions to the north did not reach the coast, while the rugged coastline and a lack of suitable harbors forestalled the European presence until the late 19th century. While these factors inhibited a variety of exogenous intrusions and spared the area the worst ravages of the slave trade, they also severely limited the quality and quantity of our written records so that much of the history of this area remains to be reconstructed.

We know, however, that during the 12th and 13th centuries substantial numbers of persons moved into the northern portion of the forest zone of what is now the Ivory Coast, but their reasons for doing so are obscure:

> Perhaps they moved in order to escape the chaos and confusion which had followed on the collapse of ancient Ghana, perhaps they were discontented with their treatment in the rising empire of Mali.[2]

In any case, there appears to have been considerable trade between this region and the empires of Mali and Songhai as well as some population exchange. During the 16th century the first waves of Senufo peoples moved south and during the 17th, some of Akan peoples from what is now Ghana moved west into the southern forest zone. Later in that century French missionaries and traders arrived although an official French presence was not established until the 1840's. Even then, French control was both sporadic and limited and the Ivory Coast did not become a colony until 1893. If we consider that the pacification of the entire territory was not completed

---

[2] Basil Davidson, *History of West Africa* (Garden City, N.Y.: Doubleday & Co., Anchor Books, 1966) p. 76. The precolonial and colonial history of the region is covered in G. Angoulvant's two works, *Guide du Commerce et de la Colonisation à la Côte d'Ivoire* (Paris: Office Colonial, 1912) and *La Pacification de la Côte d'Ivoire 1908–1915* (Paris: Larose, 1916), as well as in F. J. Amon d'Aby, *La Côte d'Ivorie dans la Cité Africaine* (Paris: Larose, 1951); R. Villamur and L. Richard, *Notre Colonie de Côte d'Ivoire* (Paris: A. Challamel, 1903); Jacques Richard-Molard, *Afrique Occidentale Française* (Paris: Editions Berger Levrauit, 1956); Henri LaBouret, *Paysans d'Afrique Occidentale* (Paris: Stock, 1953); and Bernard Schnapper, *La Politique et le Commerce Français dans le Golfe de Guinée de 1838 à 1871* (Paris: Moulton and Company, 1961). More recent events are covered in François Borella, *L'Evolution Politique et Jupidique de l'Union Française depuis 1946* (Paris: R. Richon and R. Durand-Auzias, 1958), and L. G. Cowan, *Local Government in West Africa* (New York: Columbia University Press, 1958).

until World War I, the colonial interlude was brief, less than 50 years in duration.

Nevertheless, as outlined in Chapter III, French colonial rule was to have greater consequences for the history of the Ivory Coast than did the comparable colonial experiences for Somalia and Tanzania. In large part, this was because politics in France more directly impinged upon the course of Ivoirien politics, particularly after World War II. In francophone Africa generally, but especially in the French areas of West Africa in the *Afrique Occidentale Français* (AOF), one simply cannot separate the history of the metropole from that of its overseas possessions in the way one can for Somalia or Tanzania.[3] In addition to introducing modern technology and infrastructure and providing a single language, the French colonial system allowed for political participation by Africans (however few) on three planes: the territorial level of each area (such as the Ivory Coast), the federal level of West or Equatorial Africa, and the level of national politics in France. For example, Félix Houphouët-Boigny, who became President of the Ivory Coast, held many posts within the Ivory Coast, was on various West African councils, and served in the French National Assembly from 1947 to 1957 and as a member of the government from 1956 to 1959. During the tumultuous process of politics in the Fouth Republic, Africans were instrumental in the formation of several French governments, most notably in 1956, and in some cases were a surprisingly important force in the formulation of their relationships with the metropole. This was particularly true in the case of the Ivory Coast.

It is not in our province to do more than summarize the complex interpenetration of these political forces that led to the present size and state of the Ivoirien political system.[4] What follows is

[3] Roy Macridis and Robert Ward (eds.), *Modern Political Systems* (Englewood Cliffs, N.J.: Prentice-Hall, 1968), pp. 151–280; Philip Williams, *Politics in Post-War France* (London: Longmans, Green and Company, 1954); Raymond Aron, *France—Steadfast and Changing* (Cambridge: Harvard University Press, 1960); Stanley Hoffmann (ed.), *In Search of France* (Cambridge: Harvard University Press, 1960); Herbert Luethy, *France Against Herself* (New York: Frederick A. Praeger, 1955).

[4] See Immanuel Wallerstein, *The Road to Independence: Ghana and the Ivory Coast* (Paris: Mouton and Company, 1964); Virginia Thompson, "The Ivory Coast," in G. Carter (ed.), *African One Party States*, (Ithaca: Cornell University Press, 1962), pp. 237–324; Ruth Schachter Morgenthau, *Political Parties in French-Speaking West Africa* (Oxford: The Clarendon Press, 1964),

the briefest of sketches designed to provide the reader with some background as to how the Ivory Coast rather than a larger unit came to statehood in 1960. Following the failure of the French government to implement the colonial reforms suggested at the Brazzaville conference in 1944, Africans from the francophone territories met in 1946 at Bamako in the French Sudan to form a trans-territorial party, the *Rassemblement Démocratique Africain* (RDA) in 1947. Each territory was to have its own branch under local leadership to promote political socialization and to galvanize popular support for the RDA. The RDA branch in the Ivory Coast, the *Parti Democratique de la Côte d'Ivoire* (PDCI) was led by Félix Houphouët-Boigny, one of the founders of the RDA. Because the RDA was initially supported by African and metropolitan communists and because it took an increasingly radical stance vis-à-vis France, it was harassed by the French colonial administration and opposed by those Africans who were allied with the more moderate French Socialist party (SFIO). Nevertheless, it soon emerged as the dominant political force in French West Africa. Then, in one of those antic situations so characteristic of French politics, it was the RDA which provided the votes necessary for the formation of a socialist government under Guy Mollet in 1956 after many of the Africans previously loyal to the SFIO broke with them to form a new transterritorial party, the *Indépendants d'Outre Mer*. Yet this success was to be the high-water mark of the RDA, for it became increasingly subject to centrifugal forces and by the second Bamako Conference in 1957, was in a state of internal disarray. The chief cause of the RDA's decline as a transterritorial party was the set of conflicting views held by its members concerning the future of French-speaking West Africa. While some of the territories such as Senegal and the Sudan favored the formation of a large, hopefully powerful federation, others such as the Ivory Coast and Mauritania demanded that the territories be linked individually to France.

The position of the antifederation forces was strengthened by

pp. 166–219; Félix Houphouët-Boigny, "Black Africa and the French Union," *Foreign Affairs* (July, 1957) Vol. XXV, No. 4: 593–599; Aristide Zolberg, "The Ivory Coast" in J. Coleman and C. G. Rosberg (eds.) *Political Parties and National Integration* (Berkeley: University of California Press, 1964), pp. 65–89 and "Mass Parties and National Integration," *Journal of Politics* (February 1963) Vol. XXV, No. 1: 36–48.

the passage of the *loi cadre* of 1956. Written largely by Houphouët-Boigny who was a member of the Mollet cabinet, the *loi cadre* or enabling act provided for universal African suffrage and more importantly, perhaps, extended greater authority to the individual territories, decentralizing power away from the federal structure. The coming to power of General de Gaulle in 1958 and the subsequent decision by Guinea not to remain in the French Community also undercut those who favored a federation of French West Africa. The leaders of Senegal and the French Sudan continued to push for the formation of a smaller union, however, subsequently named the Mali Federation and they were initially joined by Upper Volta and Dahomey. The leaders of the Ivory Coast, encouraged by many French officials, opposed the federation on personal, political, and economic grounds and succeeded in applying sufficient pressure to force Dahomey and Upper Volta to drop out of the Mali Federation.[5] The Ivory Coast, again with French support, then formed a looser, primarily economic union with Niger, Upper Volta, and Dahomey, the *Conseil de l'Entente*, an association that it continues to dominate.

In sharp contrast to their counterparts in Somalia, Tanzania, and many of the other French areas, the leadership of the Ivory Coast resisted the allure of independence. Only after France granted independence to the Mali Federation did the Ivory Coast and the *Entente* states drift reluctantly to independence even while maintaining the closest of ties with France.[6] When the Mali Federation broke up soon after independence in June 1960, and the *Conseil de l'Entente* remained primarily an economic grouping, the fragmentation of francophone West Africa was complete.

Participation in the Political System

The present institutional framework of the Ivoirien political system is embodied in the constitution of 1960. Centered around a strong executive branch, the new constitution replaced the earlier

[5] William Foltz has written two excellent studies of this subject, *From French West Africa to the Mali Federation* (New Haven, Conn.: Yale University Press, 1965) and "An Early Failure of Pan-Africanism: The Mali Federation, 1959–60," *Politics in Africa*, pp. 33–66.

[6] Zolberg, *One Party Government*, chapter III.

parliamentary system which the Ivory Coast had inherited from the French Fourth Republic. The President of the Ivoirien Republic is the exclusive repository of executive authority.[7] Chosen by universal suffrage for a period of 5 years, he is commander-in-chief of the armed forces. He makes all civil and military appointments, and the Council of Ministers or cabinet is directly responsible to him. There is no Prime Minister, and in addition to a veto power over acts of the National Assembly, the President may appeal directly to the people through the device of a national referendum.

The National Assembly of the Ivory Coast consists of eighty-five members chosen by universal adult suffrage from a single list prepared by the only recognized political party in the country, the *Parti Démocratique de la Côte d'Ivoire*. Members do not represent geographical constituencies but are chosen as part of a national slate. They serve for 5-year terms and are supposed to represent the country as a whole and to be concerned with national issues.[8]

According to the constitution, the judiciary is independent.[9] There is a single court system for the entire country and a new civil, commercial, and criminal code which was revamped in 1961. Based essentially on French law, the code is applied in a series of courts of the first instance and reviewed by a single court of appeal. There is also a Supreme Court which lacks the right of judicial review but which acts in an advisory capacity to the President.

Félix Houphouët-Boigny, who served as Prime Minister from 1959 until 1960, has been President of the Ivory Coast since independence. Elected in 1960, he was reelected last in 1965; there was no opposition. All members of the National Assembly since independence have been members of the *Parti Démocratique de la Côte d'Ivoire*. As there was no opposition, those elected in 1965 received 99.9% of the votes. In order to analyze the present course of decision making in the Ivory

[7] République de la Côte d'Ivoire, *Constitution de la République de la Côte d'Ivoire* (Abidjan: Les Presses de l'Imprimerie Nationale, 1960), articles 8–26. A. S. Alexander, Jr., "The Ivory Coast Constitution: An Accelerator, not a Brake," *The Journal of Modern African Studies* (1963) Vol. I, No. 3: 293–311, has analyzed the constitution in detail. He takes a somewhat overly optimistic view of the possibility of democratic politics taking place within its framework.

[8] *Constitution de la République de la Côte d'Ivoire*, articles 27–52.

[9] *Ibid.*, articles 57–66.

Coast, it is necessary to examine the rise to power of the PDCI and its leader Houphouët-Boigny and the gradual elimination of all organized opposition.

During and after the 1944 local elections, several parties sprang up in the Ivory Coast, based on one or more of the sixty ethnic groups in the country. We have already mentioned how the PDCI became the territorial branch of the RDA. It was, from its inception, essentially a coalition open to a variety of occupational and ethnic groups. Despite the radical stance of the RDA, the bulk of its early support came from the African bourgeoisie, primarily those in the planter class and their major interest group, the *Syndicat Agricole Africain* who deeply resented French domination. Ruth Schachter Morgenthau has indicated the process by which the PDCI, as a "patron" party, sought to develop into a "mass" party with widespread support: "They wanted to enroll each man, woman, and even child, and so they had to establish local branches with headquarters, regular meetings and elections for branch leaders." [10] The PDCI sought to create a "cell" in every village and every urban ward. Each cell had a central committee or *bureau* and a secretary general. The various secretary generals then met at the regional level in approximately fifty-five *sous-sections,* each of which had a *bureau* and a secretary general of its own. These, in turn, represented their districts at the national executive committee, the *Comité Directeur,* which was linked to the inner core of the party, the fifteen to twenty-five member *Bureau Politique* and the national secretary general.

Aristide Zolberg, whose *One Party Government in the Ivory Coast* has become a classic study of politics in Africa, indicates, however, that despite its modern orientation the PDCI stressed primordial ties and that linkage within the party was actually based on ethnic groups. In many situations the village and rural committees corresponded to existing ethnic groups. Where they did not, as in portions of the

[10] Ruth Schachter Morgenthau, "Single Party Systems in West Africa," *The American Political Science Review* (1961) Vol. LV, No. 2: 295. For a more complete description of the growth of the PDCI and contemporary events in the neighboring territories, see Thomas Hodgkin and Ruth Schachter Morgenthau, *French-Speaking West Africa in Transition* (New York: Carnegie Endowment for International Peace, 1960), and Ruth Schachter Morgenthau, *Political Parties in French-Speaking West Africa.* The distinctions between "mass" and "patron" parties elaborated by R. S. Morgenthau have tended to blur over time.

capital, Abidjan, new committees were created.[11] Thus, during stages of its existence, the PDCI resembled the federative systems outlined in Chapter III in that members often belonged to the PDCI through their membership in those ethnic groups rather than as individuals, although many also belonged as individuals. The use of these ethnic "building blocks" enabled the PDCI to mobilize large numbers of persons rather quickly and to galvanize popular support for its programs and personnel. It should be pointed out, however, that the PDCI was not simply a neotribal organization, one bent on preserving the status quo. Although it utilized the ethnic groups and encouraged traditional authorities to join it, only those who held "modern" views were allowed to participate in the decision-making process within the party. It was (and is) the ethnic groups, not individual tribal leaders, who are considered to be important in the Ivory Coast. This was true in the party itself, and later in the national government as well for, "In fact, though not in theory, each deputy represents his own ethnic group." [12] Moreover, economic development spurred the formation of associations and interest groups that, in turn, were also absorbed and represented, eventually forming a counterweight to the ethnic groups.

As the party with the greatest organization and the most prominent national figure, the PDCI jumped off to an early electoral lead, winning all 3 seats in the French National Assembly, all 15 seats in the Ivory Coast Territorial Assembly, and 94% of the vote in 1946.[13] However, the militant stand taken by the RDA at the federal level and the formation of a series of smaller parties weakened the PDCI's power base. These aspects, coupled with the jailing of many PDCI leaders by the French, led the party to what was to be its nadir in 1951–52, when it won but 1 of the 2 seats in the French National Assembly and 28 of 32 seats in that of the Ivory Coast on the strength of 74% of the vote.

Reacting to this decline, Houphouët-Boigny and the PDCI leadership insisted that the RDA drop its communist affiliations and expel the Secretary General, Gabriel D'Arboussier. When the RDA did this

---

[11] Zolberg, *One Party Government*, p. 116.

[12] Alexander, *op. cit.*, p. 309.

[13] Zolberg, "The Ivory Coast," 75. The figures for 1959–60 are also taken from this table.

in 1951, the PDCI set about rejuvenating itself, making its peace with the conservative elements in the political culture of the Ivory Coast by absorbing the smaller parties and their ethnic groups. By the elections of 1956 and 1957 the PDCI had regained its momentum and was again in a position of overriding strength as it won both seats in the French Assembly and 58 out of 60 seats in the Ivory Coast. Opposition within the country faded, and in 1960 the PDCI presented the only list of candidates for election for the 100 seats in the enlarged assembly and 160 local offices. Its candidate for President, Houphouët-Boigny, received 1,586,518 votes out of the 1,641,352 cast.

On the surface, there would seem to be a definite parallel between the rise of the PDCI in the Ivory Coast and that of TANU in Tanzania. While there are basic similarities to the all-encompassing nature of their successes in the national arena, there are significant differences in their central goals, their relation to society, and their process of internal decision making. Whereas TANU's history has been a search for mass involvement in the politics of the party and the nation, as well as a drive towards polyarchal participation in both, the reverse has been true of the PDCI. This is not simply an Ivoirien phenomenon but one which is discernible in many other RDA branches as well, irrespective of their ideology. Decision making and leadership selection within the PDCI have always been hierarchical. In theory, elections for party representatives take place at regular intervals. In point of fact, such elections have seldom been held and most officials have, during the history of the PDCI, been appointed by the *Comité Directeur* and the *Bureau Politique*. On the national level, moreover, there have been but four party congresses since the PDCI was founded, none during the 1950–59 period, and only one since independence. Particularly during the formative years from 1949 to 1957, all major decisions were made at the top by a small number of leaders and at no time did the rank and file directly choose either their leaders or the goals of the party. The elaborate cell system and network of ethnic committees were used primarily as a set of communication channels to carry party decisions to the population at large rather than as a method of leadership selection or policy formation. As opposition to the PDCI withered away or was absorbed, the process of hierarchical decision making within the party became intensified, so that by the time of independence the PDCI had become, in Zolberg's terms, a "political regime dispensing patronage."

In addition to a lack of democratic decision making within the party structure, the PDCI has drifted toward a similar espousal of authoritarian decision making vis-à-vis the society. Beginning as a patron party, it took on mass party characteristics in the 1950's and then evolved into a party which could be classified as one for the masses. In short, rather than encouraging mass participation in the party and the decision-making process of the political system, the PDCI by independence regarded itself as "the only valid embodiment of mass will." The PDCI in effect ruled out democracy for the party and for the society. As the views held by the organization that was to enjoy a political monopoly, these were to have profound implications for the kind of decision making that would evolve within the political system as a whole.

> Democracy is a system of government for virtuous people. It seldom works even in very mature countries. Why should we expect it to work here? We must be realistic. Our people are ignorant of the problems we face. They cannot be left to choose the solutions to our overwhelming problems but must approve the alternative debated by an elite.[14]

This view of the people and the society, when coupled with the hierarchical tendencies within the party structure, transformed the nature of the PDCI. After independence the PDCI as a party lost some of its raison d'etre. It has attained independence, secured the major political offices for its leadership, and gained control over the political system. Since it did not, as in the case of TANU, see itself as compelled to draw the population into the process of politics save at infrequent elections, it found less and less need to mobilize that population and to galvanize popular support on an ongoing basis. Without either internal or external competition in personnel or ideology, the party withered away to a certain extent after independence. Local committees, particularly in the rural areas,

---

14 For the results of this philosophy, see Martin Kilson, "Authoritarian and Single Party Tendencies in African Politics," World Politics (1963) Vol. XV, No. 2: 266. The quote is from Zolberg, One Party Government, pp. 253–254.

seldom met. Many cells existed only on paper and periodic conferences were simply not held. Observers of politics in Africa have noted these phenomena elsewhere in Africa and have stressed the blurring of the distinction between the government and the party and the development of the "party-state." [15] This seems to have been the case in the Ivory Coast. The decision-making elite in the Ivoirien political system continue to be members of the PDCI but the party as a whole plays little role in their selection or in that of the systemic goals. It is the government, moreover, which has taken over the major functions of national integration and development previously performed by the party through a greatly expanded administration.

Since participation by the general public is minimal and confined to ritualistic voting for a single slate of candidates, who, then, makes the decisions for the Ivory Coast? The PDCI as a whole does not. Local elected government, except in the major cities, is virtually nonexistent. The National Assembly does not. Decision-making authority in the Ivory Coast is concentrated in the hands of the President of the Republic, the inner core of the party, the *Bureau Politique* and the *Comité Directeur*, and a few members of the government such as the president of the National Assembly. Reinforced by the 1960 constitution (which they themselves wrote), a small group of PDCI and government officials make the basic policy decisions for the entire system and tightly control access to the decision-making apparatus. Great power is in the hands of Houphouët-Boigny who, in addition to being President of the Ivory Coast, is honorary president of the PDCI. His trusted lieutenants hold the other positions of authority, not only within the various regulative agencies such as the police and the army, but within the government and the PDCI as well. The Secretary General of the PDCI and President of the National Assembly, Philip Yacé, is his handpicked second in command. The President appoints the administrative heads of the six departments and 107 subprefectures which make up the central administration of the Ivory Coast. He selects the thirty-five members of the important advisory body, the *Conseil Economique et*

[15] Zolberg, *Creating Political Order* (Chicago: Rand McNally & Company, 1966), p. 127. Victor D. DuBois makes a similar point in his *The Party and the Government: The Role of the P.D.C.I. in the Ivory Coast and in African Affairs* (New York: American Universities Field Staff, 1962).

Social and, with the *Bureau Politique*, chooses the members of the National Assembly.

The National Assembly of the Ivory Coast merits a closer examination because it is an interesting example of an institution which could have decision-making power in the system but which does not. The tight control over the nomination procedure enjoyed by the PDCI center and the President, and the fact that the deputies do not represent regional power bases but are selected as part of a single slate by the entire country, militates against the National Assembly playing an independent, let alone opposition, role in the process of decision making. The process of rule formation is illustrative. The government generally proposes laws and submits them to a committee of the National Assembly which examines them in the presence of a government official. The bills may be slightly modified before the government submits them to the National Assembly but this is not always the case. In theory, the National Assembly may reject any proposed law; in reality, it has never done so. It has the slight power to delay passage of a particular bill by talking about it at length but observers have pointed out that even here its power is minimal and it is not even a debating society.[16]

The National Assembly does fulfill some necessary functions in the Ivoirien system, however. In the first place, its very existence helps to legitimize the system's democratic pretensions by giving "popular" approval to the laws of the land. Even though the National Assembly exercises virtually no decision-making power, the ritual of bill passage probably serves to aid the symbolic capacity of the regime. More importantly, the National Assembly serves as a patronage mechanism to co-opt would-be counterelites and insure loyalty to the leaders of the system. The salaries, privileges, housing and transportation allowances which accrue to members of the National Assembly are powerful inducements to loyalty. The President and the *Bureau Politique* are quite willing to shift membership to suit the changing political and social configurations within the system (there were, for example, thirty-seven new members in the 1965 Assembly) and to utilize its patronage to best advantage. The National Assembly also acts as a channel of communication whereby the major decisions of the government are passed on to the ethnic

---

16 Zolberg, *One Party Government*, p. 280.

and interest groups that its members "represent." As pointed out above, this representation is more symbolic than real but it does provide for a flow of information outward from the party-government center, and serves to legitimize the action of the government. These functions of the National Assembly are of importance, and aid in maintenance of order and stability, but they should not be construed to mean that the National Assembly is in any way instrumental in making the decisions for the political system.

The status of the National Assembly is illustrative of the attitude held by the political center towards groups and institutions whose personnel might seek access to the decision-making process. Subgroup authority in the Ivory Coast is limited. As in Tanzania, that autonomy is circumscribed by a skillful mixture of regulation and reward and a strong appeal to natural unity. An examination of three of the crucial elite groups mentioned in Chapter II will indicate how the political authorities are able to control those who might challenge their right to maintain political hegemony. For purposes of comparison, we have chosen those elite groups which were also the subject of analysis in our examination of the Tanzania political system.

The traditional elite, whose power in precolonial African society was greater in the Ivoirien setting than in that of Tanzania, was considerably weakened by the process of French rule. The French colonial policy of direct rule did much to sap the strength of this group and it was unable to regain its power during the decolonization process. After 1951, the PDCI did not, except for an abortive proposal in 1959 to eliminate "tribalism," pose a direct threat to the traditional authorities and even demonstrated a willingness to accept that leadership into the party and later the government if they would espouse "modern" or "national" values. Only those tribal leaders (such as the "King" of Sanwi) who sought to play a role which the political authorities viewed as dysfunctional were eliminated. In short, while the Ivoirien government was not neo-tribal, it was not antitribal either and this lack of overt hostility, when coupled with Houphouët-Boigny's skill as a politician, made the transition to independence considerably easier for the traditional elite. There remains in the Ivory Coast what amounts to an interest group for traditional authorities, the *Syndicat des Chefs*, which is headed by Houphouët and is generally docile. But the government does take the time and effort to "consult" with its members and to give the appearance of valuing its suggestions even though the traditional elite as such plays no role in the decision-making process in the Ivory Coast.

Organized labor, however, has proven to be more persistent and the government has been forced to use its regulatory capability from time to time in addition to offering rewards to those members of trade unions willing to follow the government position. The labor situation in French West Africa was more complicated than that which obtained in Tanganyika after World War II.[17] In the Ivory Coast there were at least three groups of trade unions. First, there were the small, locally-oriented labor unions with no trans-territorial affiliation. Second, there were those unions associated with the Guinea-based, Marxist-oriented international *Union Générale de Travailleurs d'Afrique Noir* (UGTAN). The pro-UGTAN unions in the Ivory Coast were led by the *Union Nationale des Travailleurs de Côte d'Ivoire* (UNTCI). Third, there were those unions such as the *Confédération des Travailleurs Croyants de la Côte d'Ivoire* associated with the *Confédération Africaine des Travailleurs Croyants* (CATC), an African offshoot of the Catholic-oriented *Confédération Internationale des Syndicats Chretiens* (CISC).

Unlike the direct relationship between the TFL and TANU, the PDCI often was in conflict with various unions in all three categories. At other times, depending upon the issues, the unions worked closely with the PDCI. In 1958, for example, over the issue of independence, the unions were themselves deeply divided. The UGTAN-oriented UNTCI was split internally with the executive supporting the position of Houphouët and many of the rank and file, especially among the civil servants, supporting that of Guinea. Moreover, in 1959 the UNTCI dissidents joined with some CATC unions to form the *Intersyndicat des Travailleurs de la Fonction Publique* which soon clashed with the government over new restrictions concerning the rights and privileges of civil servants. This hostility culminated in a strike during October of 1959 which the government crushed by arresting the union leaders and suspending

[17] Joan Davies, *African Trade Unions* (Baltimore, Md.: Penguin Books, 1966), pp. 152–158; Elliot J. Berg and Jeffry Butler, "Trade Unions," *Political Parties and National Integration*, pp. 340–382; V. Thompson, "The Ivory Coast," pp. 284–287; and A. Zolberg, *One Party Government*, pp. 296–305.

or firing 500 workers. Determined to avoid future repetitions of union independence, the government created in 1962 the *Union Générale des Travailleurs de la Côte d'Ivoire* which was without international affiliations. Those labor leaders who were quick to see that the wave of the future lay with the government were given positions within the party and the government; others were jailed or exiled. The government then went on to pass a series of laws severely limiting the right to strike, imposing provisions for submitting disputes to binding arbitration, and setting up a Consultative Committee on Labor to further regulate the course of collective bargaining.[18] Although organized labor was represented in the 1965 National Assembly, the government has prevented it from becoming an organized opposition group within the country and seems to have succeeded in curtailing some of its political aspirations. Nevertheless, there remains a good deal of labor dissatisfaction which occasionally surfaces (most recently in May 1968) as demands for economic reform and greater tangible recognition of organized labor's contribution to the economy. The fact that many lower level wage earners are non-Ivoiriens, however, gives the government a good deal of leverage in controlling them.

Student dissatisfaction is also evident, although the student movement is currently under government control. The antagonism between the students and the PDCI government run deeper than those in Tanzania and have been nurtured by the fact that large numbers (1200) of Ivoirien students study in France where they are in direct and prolonged contact with students from all over black Africa. Whereas students in Tanzania have generally identified with the government and TANU and accepted its vision for the future (even while objecting to the students' position in that vision), many in the Ivory Coast have profoundly disagreed with both the style and the direction of PDCI rule. Even during its early years, when the PDCI enjoyed the support of youth, it was not particularly oriented toward them and did not form a youth wing until 1958, long after the founding of the PDCI. Many of the Ivoirien students emotionally and ideologically supported the position of Guinea in 1958 or favored federation or objected to the "neocolonialism" of

---

[18] Gouvernement de la Côte d'Ivoire, *Journal Officiel de la République de la Côte d'Ivoire* (August, 1964) No. 44: 1059.

246 THE IVOIRIEN POLITICAL SYSTEM

France. This placed them in opposition to the thrust of the PDCI leadership, especially that of Houphouët-Boigny. And they were not mollified when, in 1958, the PDCI allowed the formation of a youth wing, the *Jeunesse Rassemblement Démocratique Africain Côte d'Ivoire* (JRDACI) which was able to extend membership separate from the PDCI. When the JRDACI took a militant pro-federation stance and began attacking the PDCI leadership, Houphouët moved against it, absorbed it into the PDCI by taking away its membership, granting privileges, and appointed several of the leaders, such as Guedé Coregnon and Bissouma Tapé, to government positions.[19]

Ivoirien students, however, particularly those overseas, continued to oppose the programs of the PDCI government. In an attempt to combat what it took to be the corrosive influence of two student associations in France, *Association des Étudiants de Côte d'Ivorie en France* and the *Fédération des Étudiants d'Afrique Noire en France*, the government formed the *Union Nationale des Étudiants et Élèves de Côte d'Ivorie* (UNECI).

UNECI students continued to take antigovernment positions, however, and friction occurred for nearly a year. Finally, during January 1965, the student leaders were brought together with their parents to a general meeting with the President and Philip Yacé. Houphouët stressed the government's desire to listen to the students but threatened to cut off scholarship support and deny government employment to those who opposed the leadership of the PDCI. He stressed the all-or-nothing character of their position:

> Equivocation is no longer possible. Either you are with us in the bosom of the party and working for national construction or you are against us and we will fight you.[20]

At this point the students seem to have capitulated and were welcomed back into the "bosom of the party," but the basic issues that had led to the opposition were not solved. The conservative cast to Ivoirien politics, the more or less closed ranks in terms of decision making, and the lack of ideological fervor continued to

[19] Victor D. DuBois, *The Student-Government Conflict in the Ivory Coast* (New York: American Universities Field Staff, 1965).
[20] *Africa Report* (February, 1965) 45.

offer major points of disagreement and trouble has flared periodically. During January 1967, for example, 315 students were arrested for antigovernment acts and in July 1968, the government first "suspended," then disbanded, the *Union Nationale des Étudiants et Élèves de Côte d'Ivorie*.

Although some dissatisfaction remains, the political center in the Ivory Coast has been successful thus far in containing potential counterelites and fragmenting their force. The position of this small number of decision-makers is reinforced not only by the regulative and distributive capabilities of the system but also by the prevailing ethos of the society they govern. The PDCI has always stressed the need for national unity in the following fashion: Unity is essential for equality, for national integration, and for economic development. Unity keeps sixty or more ethnic groups pulling together. Unity alone can prevent the tragedies such as those in the Congo or Nigeria. The PDCI government, however elitist and authoritarian it may be, provides that unity. The PDCI government is the grand coalition of ethnic groups and interest groups and "any new parties would have to be created by chipping away at this edifice and in particular, by retrieving some of its component ethnic blocs." [21] In the final analysis, the PDCI government has been very successful in appealing to this felt need for unity and has often found it useful to regard any antigovernment groups as posing threats to the unity of the nation and its not inconsiderable economic progress. The PDCI government is able to appeal to what seems to be a considerable fear within the society and to rally support on the basis of that fear.

Not that the power of the government is complete. As the situation with regard to the labor and student movement indicates, there is some dissatisfaction in the political culture. While authoritarian, the political structure is not totalitarian. There are societal values that cannot, at least at this stage, be tampered with. For example, the PDCI government could not eliminate "tribalism" in 1959 and during 1966 widespread opposition to the status of "foreigners" forced the government to drop its plans for extending dual citizenship to the population of the *Conseil* states.[22] The gov-

[21] Zolberg, *One Party Government*, p. 129.
[22] These immigrants are allowed to work in the Ivory Coast, however.

ernment remains willing to bargain with individuals and groups that are anxious to acquire a share of the spoils of the system. But the leadership of the PDCI government continues to see politics as a zero-sum game of the greatest magnitude and groups, whether ethnic or interest, will not be tolerated if they seek control of the system. There are no ongoing, organized, institutional, countervailing influences to PDCI governmental control and without any system of leadership selection or goal choice, there is not likely to be any. In short, then, the decision-making process in the Ivoirien political system is limited to a small number of participants, mostly hand-picked by the President and his closest advisers. This elite prefers buying off dissidents to regulating them, rewards to punishment, and economic largess to force. It even forgives those who make mistakes and recant if they will rejoin on the government terms. At the same time, it will brook no opposition of the type likely to supplant its preeminent position and is disinclined to loosen control over the decision-making apparatus of the system.

How, then, do we classify the political system of the Ivory Coast? Aristide Zolberg places it somewhere between a tutelary democracy and a modernizing oligarchy, seeing it as an important typology with potential importance for other systems: "Non-totalitarian, monopolistic parties, based on mass popular support, concerned with modernization and with the dissemination of equality in their societies, ultimately may have democratic consequences." [23] Virginia Thompson sees it less grandly, calling it simply a "one man, one party government." [24] Ruth Schachter Morgenthau feels that it is democratic only in comparison with the previous colonial forms.[25] Certainly the tremendous centralization of power in the hands of a small elite and the almost exclusive control over the affairs of state exercised by the President would suggest that the system could be characterized as hierarchical according to Dahl's criteria (Chapter I), even though there are on occasion some bargaining elements within the elite. Yet the Ivory Coast cannot adequately be dis-

---

[23] Zolberg, One Party Government, p. 8.

[24] Thompson, "The Ivory Coast," p. 295.

[25] Schachter Morgenthau, "Single Party Systems in West Africa," p. 307. Immanuel Wallerstein has indicated the continual challenge faced by the present elites in his "Elites in French-Speaking West Africa: The Social Basis of Ideas," Journal of Modern African Studies (1965) Vol. III, No. 1: 1–33.

missed as hierarchical for it appears to be a special type of system. In a limited sense at least, the system is responsive in that it agglomerates the demands of various socio-economic groups and satisfies them, however indirectly, through national institutions.

David Apter, while not mentioning the Ivory Coast, has outlined the characteristics of what he calls a "neomercantilist regime" which he places between the two extremes of the secular-libertarian and sacred-collectivity models and their primary prototypes, the reconciliation and mobilization regimes.[26] Apter is tantalizingly brief in his description of the neomercantilist regime but does say it is headed by a "presidential monarch" whose long term aim is the modernization of the system by nontotalitarian means. The neomercantilist regime is thus distinguishable from a stagnant, egocentric dictatorship bent simply on its own perpetuation or a true mobilization regime bent on modernization of the system at any cost. The ideology of a neomercantilist regime, suggests Apter, is over-whelmingly pragmatic and it seeks to use economic accomplishments to bolster the political system:

> It is likely to use private enterprize, controlled in some measure politically but not necessarily owned by the state. Indeed the economic mode of neomerchantilism could be labeled 'state capitalism.' [27]

The Ivory Coast seems to fit this model quite well, for as will be seen in the section on the extractive and distributive capabilities, the political system of the Ivory Coast is distinguished by these characteristics, and its accomplishments in the field of economic development do in fact provide the system with its primary supports. Further, a neomercantilist system, like that of the Ivory Coast, aims at the evolutionary rather than the revolutionary transformation of society and accepts the development of socio-economic stratification. Society is to be guided and influenced, not forced. At the same time, because of the tremendous decision-making power concentrated in the hands of a small elite and the relative lack of subgroup autonomy, the Ivory Coast cannot be termed a true reconciliation regime.

[26] David Apter, *The Politics of Modernization*, pp. 28–42.
[27] *Ibid.*, p. 411.

In comparison with the other systems under review, the Ivory Coast does not exhibit much in the way of polyarchal decision making, evidencing less participation in the decision-making process and more oligarchal tendencies than either Somalia or Tanzania. Judged on the basis of numbers of persons involved in the decision-making process, the possibility of leadership alteration within the system, and access to political authority, the Ivoirien system is closer to that of South Africa than to either Somalia or Tanzania. To understand how such a political system can continue to function effectively and to enjoy a good measure of popular support, it is necessary to examine the capabilities of the system.

Capabilities Analysis

The Ivoiren political system is distinguished by strong regulative and extractive capabilities, mixed symbolic and distributive capacities, and a weak rejuvenative capability.

REGULATIVE CAPABILITY

The regulative capacity of the Ivory Coast is based on a small but well-trained, politically reliable army and a strong police establishment. Its army of 4000 men and its security force of 2500 is under tight political control and stiffened by the presence of French personnel, including 600 troops stationed in Abidjan.[28] The French government provides the training and weapons for these security forces, including an air force and navy, and, through a series of defense agreements, retains staging, transit, and overflight privileges. In addition, the small French military presence in the Ivory Coast is augmented by the existence of a ready reaction force in southern France, the Eleventh *Division Légère d'Intervention*, which is equipped for rapid and massive deployment to sub-Saharan Africa. The government of the Ivory Coast may call upon this force at any time although France retains the power to decide as to "whether and how to intervene."[29] French military power does provide the Ivory Coast with significant levels of force with

[28] Chester A. Crocker, "France's Changing Military Interests," *Africa Report* (June, 1968) 16–24, 41–42.

[29] *Ibid.*, p. 20; similar agreements apply to the other *Conseil de l'Entente* states of Niger and Dahomey.

which to discourage would-be predators in the international community (as occurred when Guinea threatened an invasion of the Ivory Coast following the overthrow of Kwame Nkrumah in 1966). It also strengthens the regime's internal capability to control the population.

Given the spate of military coups and attempted coups which have struck at many African governments during the last 3 years and the demonstrated unreliability of any "national armies," the French presence is of enormous significance to the stability of the regime, especially when the military cooperation is coupled with extensive data-gathering and surveillance provided by the French intelligence community. In addition, the French support for the regulative capacity has meant that the Ivoirien defense expenditures have averaged less than 8% of the national budget since independence, thus preventing the military from becoming a powerful interest group with direct involvement in the politics of the state. There has been compulsory military service since July 1961, although it has not been universally applied due to the large number of volunteers. Recruits serve 1 year on active duty, 6 months of which is usually spent on civic action projects.

The Ivoirien leaders have a strong commitment to stability, law, and order and do not hesitate to utilize the regulative capacity of the system to maintain it. Houphouët-Boigny, quoting Goethe, put the matter simply: "I prefer injustice to disorder: one can die of disorder; one does not die of injustice. An injustice can be repaired." [30] Controls over the political life of the nation are numerous and civil liberties have been curtailed since independence.[31] While governmental repression has not been systematically or continuously applied, the ad hoc nature of the application of authoritarian control should not obscure the fact that the government is prepared to go to considerable lengths to maintain order and its dominant position. The Ivoirien leadership prefers to act within the law just as it prefers to co-opt counterelites rather than attack them, but it does not hesitate to act arbitrarily, or even illegally, if it feels that societal order and its preeminent position are threatened.[32] There

[30] Quoted in Zolberg, *Creating Political Order*, p. 42.
[31] Zolberg, *Creating Political Order*, p. 90.
[32] Ken Post, *The New States of West Africa* (Baltimore, Md.: Penguin Books, 1964), p. 89.

is no preventive detention act, for example, but persons accused of planning crimes against the state are often detained without warrant or subsequent trial and either imprisoned or deported.

The government's response to a series of "plots" in 1963–64 indicates both the direction and the style of Ivoirien regulation. Because of a "grave subversive threat" during January 1963, three government ministers were dismissed and hundreds of persons were arrested. The National Assembly quickly passed a bill providing that the accused be tried, not by the regular court system but by a special tribunal, the *Cour de Securité de l'Etat*. Further, the National Assembly stripped the accused of their parliamentary immunity. Judicial restraints and due process were overlooked or brushed aside. The *Cour de Securité* met in the home town of the President and tried eighty-five persons, sentencing thirteen to death. In April, another plot was discovered and six ministers, including Jean Baptiste Mockey who had presided over the earlier trial, were dismissed. Four of the accused were subsequently sentenced to death and scores more were jailed for long periods.[33]

One might conclude that the government of the Ivory Coast, by virtue of the harsh sentences meted out, felt itself to be in great danger. In point of fact, the reverse is true for none of the sentences providing for the death penalty were ever carried out, although during April 1964 Ernest Boka, the former President of the Supreme Court, committed suicide under suspicious circumstances. By 1966 most of the plotters had been released or had had their sentences substantially reduced, so that the regime seems not to have felt that these threats represented a grave challenge to the system. Today there are probably fewer than 100 political prisoners out of the 4500 persons incarcerated in the Ivory Coast.[34] Yet the government of the Ivory Coast gets considerable political mileage out of the process of rule application. In fact, Houphouët-Boigny goes to great lengths to give the appearance of being an omniscient, Olympian ruler who judges his people harshly but fairly, only to intervene and commute their sentences if they repent. Aristide Zolberg has

[33] *West Africa*, July 3, 1965, 733.

[34] Victor D. DuBois, *A Visit to an African Prison* (New York: American Universities Field Staff, 1968), p. 11. See also his *Crime and the Treatment of the Criminal in the Ivory Coast* (New York: American Universities Field Staff, 1968).

pointed out a regular scenario for the process and indicates how it is applied to political miscreants. For example, those refugees who were followers of the "King" of Sanwi, Amon N'Douffou III, who intrigued with Ghana over the formation of a Sanwi state, were eventually "forgiven" by the President in a public ceremony. In terms of preservation of order, the considerable regulatory capacity of the Ivory Coast is used skillfully with the result that it bolsters the legitimacy of the regime.

The notion that control of the political life of the system should be only as tight as necessary to insure the stability of the regime, but that tight, is also reflected in the Ivoirien regulation of information. All mass media are owned or directly controlled by the government.[35] It controls Radio Abidjan (over 200,000 receivers in the Ivory Coast) and in 1963 instituted a government-operated television network. Broadcasting for 35 hours per week, to over 2000 sets, the television network is one of the most modern in Africa and the Ivory Coast is the only country under review to have a major capability in this area. The cinema facilities in the nation are also under governmental licencing through the Department of the Interior. There is a single French language daily in the Ivory Coast, the *Fraternité Matin* which is government-controlled. *Fraternité Matin* replaced the older, French-owned *Abidjan-Matin* in 1964. Over 25,000 copies are printed daily and its readership is estimated at over 100,000.[36] The only other Ivoirien newspaper is the 10,000 copy weekly, *Fraternité*, which is the official organ of the PDCI. It, too, is printed in French. William Hachten estimates that perhaps 30–40 French newspapers and periodicals are available in the capital but few are in English or any language other than French. The government bans, seizes, and censors these, "depending upon the offence." [37] There is no vernacular press. The government press agency, *Agencie Ivoirienne de Press* (AIP), is the sole transmitter of news from abroad and the government, through its ownership of the country's printing facilities and its control of television, radio, and the press, is able to disseminate or withhold information if it desires. Although censorship is used

[35] William A. Hachten, "The Press in a One-Party State: The Ivory Coast under Houphouët," *Journalism Quarterly* (1967) Vol. XVIV: 107–114.
[36] *Ibid.*, p. 108.
[37] *Ibid.*, p. 112.

selectively, if the matter is of great enough importance, the government will not hesitate to suppress whatever information it deems necessary. At the same time, the government makes no attempt to jam foreign broadcasts from neighboring countries and does not systematically examine all incoming information.

While there is substantial regulation of the political process of the Ivory Coast and, on occasion, considerable regulation of information, there is less in the economic sphere although there have been a series of 4-year plans since independence. This should not be construed to mean a lack of capacity to alter the economy but rather, a conscious attempt to minimize the number of direct controls. The Ivoirien economy is not unplanned. In fact, it is within the context of the elaborate plans of such economic experts as Raphael Seller and his successor, Mohammad Diawara that economic development takes place. The government is opposed to the idea of a command economy, although on occasion it has sought to regulate specific facets of the economic sector. For example, during 1965, when the country was faced with a situation of marked overproduction in coffee, it forbade the creation of new coffee plantations. These are isolated instances, exceptions which prove the general rule that while setting the outer limits of economic activity and encouraging certain types of economic development, the Ivoirien government does not tightly regulate the economy of the country.

EXTRACTIVE CAPABILITY

The extractive capability of the Ivory Coast is, by African standards, impressive and is of significant magnitude to qualify as a major support for the regime and the political system. The Ivory Coast has a gross national product of over $1.1 billion and a per capita income of $220, the highest in Africa after South Africa and nearly four times that of either Somalia or Tanzania.[38]

[38] *New York Times*, January 12, 1968 and the *United Nations Statistical Yearbook 1967*, p. 576. Gabon also has a per capita income above $200. For an examination of the Ivoirien boom, see Victor D. DuBois, "Houphouët-Boigny: Francophone Africa's Man of the Year," *Africa Report* (December, 1965) 8–10; W. A. Hance, *African Economic Development* (New York: Frederick A. Praeger, 1967), pp. 250–253; and Samir Amin, *Le Developpement du Capitalisme en Côte d'Ivoire* (Paris: Les Éditions de Minuit, 1967).

Nearly 300,000 Ivoirien families earn over $500 a year, and, with the growth rate of the entire economy expected to continue at its present rate of 5–6% a year, this number is expected to grow substantially during the next several years.[39]

Physically, the country is divided into two zones, each accounting for approximately 50% of the total area. There is a northern savanna region where the major forms of activity are livestock raising and dry farming of food crops (including cassava, corn and sweet potatoes), and a southern zone, 20% of which is heavily forested.[40] In the southern zone are found the major plantation and export crops such as cocoa, coffee, bananas, and timber. In contrast to the other systems under review, the Ivory Coast is well watered, with four major rivers, the Cavally, Sassandra, Bandama, and Comoé. The Ivory Coast contains a greater percentage of arable land than any of the other three countries in this study and agriculture is the most important sector of the economy, not only for subsistence but for export as well. During the colonial era, the Ivory Coast was essentially a monocrop economy, overwhelmingly dependent on the production of cocoa which by itself provided 90% of export revenues. Since independence, the Ivory Coast has attempted to diversify its agricultural output although cocoa continues to provide nearly 40% of export revenues. The Ivory Coast is now the world's third largest producer of both coffee and cocoa and the foremost African producer of coffee. It also ranks first on the continent in terms of pineapple production and second in terms of bananas. Cotton production has increased over 100% since 1960 and forest products are up over 200%. Major development schemes have been begun for rice, sugar, and palm oil. The major export commodities are controlled by government-sponsored *caisses de stabilization.*

Unlike many other African countries, minerals have not provided major impetus toward development. There are 3 million tons of manganese and much smaller amounts of diamonds, gold, copper, and titanium but no known deposits of coal or oil. In the Ivory Coast, it has been the industrial sector of the economy which has generated the present levels of economic development. Since inde-

[39] *The Reporter*, June 16, 1966, 28.
[40] T. E. Hilton, "The Ivory Coast," *Focus* (October, 1965) Vol. XVI, No. 2: 1–6, and The United States Agriculture Department, *The Agricultural Economy of the Ivory Coast* (Washington: U. S. Government Printing Office, 1964).

pendence, the industrial portion has grown at a rate of 15% yearly, as opposed to a growth rate of 10% for the service sector and 4.7% for the agricultural. And 25,000 persons are now engaged in manufacturing. Eschewing the prestigious but often uneconomical, heavy industrial projects popular in nearby Ghana and Nigeria, the Ivory Coast has concentrated on light industries, particularly those dealing with the processing of primary products. These advances have resulted in the rapid rise of export revenues so that while the industrial index for the underdeveloped world as a whole has risen from 100 to 142 since 1960, that of the Ivory Coast has improved from 100 to 321.[41] There are now textile factories, canning facilities for both pineapples and fish, wood finishing plants and paper mills, shipyards, flour mills, cigarette and soap-producing facilities, bicycle, automobile, radio and television assembly plants, an aluminum processing facility, and an oil refinery with a capacity of 700,000 tons a year. Presently, the oil is brought from Gabon and Algeria, but it is hoped that over time, the refinery will draw upon the vast reserves located in the eastern region of Nigeria. Due to the hydroelectric facilities, production of electricity has tripled since 1960.

The physical infrastructure of the Ivory Coast has been substantially improved in recent years. In 1952, when the Vridi canal linking it with the sea was completed, the capital city of Abidjan became a major port. The 14,000 mile road net in the Ivory Coast has been overhauled and is now among the best in West Africa. There is a diesel-powered railroad linking the hinterland with the coast and a second, $22 million port has been built at San Pedro which should have the effect of opening up the southwest portion of the country.

Initial impetus for Ivoirien economic development was provided in the later 1950's when the Ivory Coast stopped contributing to the Federation of French West Africa. As the country with the second highest per capita contribution (after Senegal), this meant that the Ivory Coast was able to triple its governmental budget without additional taxation and lay the groundwork for subsequent development. The economic philosophy of the Ivory Coast has also encouraged economic development. Deciding that major amounts of

[41] *Africa Report* (April, 1967), p. 34.

foreign investment, both private and public, were necessary if the Ivory Coast was to develop, the leaders set out to create a climate where investment would feel secure:

> We have no factories to nationalize, only to create; we have no commerce to take over, only to organize better, no land to distribute, only to bring into production.[42]

In the process, they developed an ideology which has been variously called "state capitalism" or "economic liberalism." Strictly speaking, it is not state capitalism for in the Ivory Coast the state does not take over any businesses or industries. In fact, the government goes out of its way not to compete with private enterprise and while it insists on a share of the industry, it will not seek to replace the private interest at some future date. The government has seen its role as one of mediating between foreign investment and the domestic environment and insuring that investment is suitably rewarded. Toward this end, the government passed an extremely liberal investment code in 1959 which provides for tax exemptions for 5 to 25 years and virtually eliminates all restriction on the expatriation of profits. When coupled with the government's regulation of organized labor, the strong, well-managed monetary policy, and the lure of substantial profits, this has made for a very healthy investment climate. Its pragmatic, laissez-faire attitude toward foreign investment has, despite its political implications, been an outstanding economic success.

Since independence over $400 million in private investment has poured in together with $300 million in foreign aid. Despite a drastic drop in the world prices for its two primary export commodities, coffee and cocoa, over the past decade the Ivoirien economy has demonstrated a sustained growth rate of between 5 and 6%, shown a favorable balance of trade every year since independence, a balanced budget, and foreign reserves of nearly $100 million.[43] Further, it now seems likely that the boom will continue, although at a somewhat slower pace. An amount of foreign invest-

[42] West Africa, June 26, 1965, 707. See also, Elliot J. Berg, "The Economic Basis of Political Choice in French West Africa," American Political Science Review (June, 1960) Vol. LIV, No. 2: 391–405.

[43] International Statistics, pp. 342–343; Gouvernement de la Côte d'Ivoire, Budget Pour 1968 (Abidjan: Imprimerie du Gouvernement, 1967).

ment equal to the present levels has already been programmed and it is estimated that the Ivory Coast will enter the "takeoff" state where internal capital formation will be self-generating by 1970.[44] Should this occur, the Ivory Coast will be the first African state to do so and may well be the first to reach a per capita income level equal to that of a European nation.

The process of economic development is not without flaws, however, as a closer examination of the distributive capability will indicate, and the human resource base of the Ivory Coast continues to exhibit a typically underdeveloped profile.[45] Life expectancy is under 40 years, and there is but one doctor per 19,500 persons. Rates for infant mortality are unavailable and the population is increasing at the rate of 2.5% a year. Population density is 25 per square mile and the country as a whole is overwhelmingly rural with only 17% of the population urbanized. Abidjan (300,000), Bouaké (100,000), an Man (30,000) make up a major portion of this percentage. The Ivory Coast has a long way to go in order to translate its impressive extractive capability and accomplishments in the field of economic development into corresponding results in the area of human development.

At the same time, the extractive capability of the Ivory Coast is most substantial and the political system has a greater pool of material rewards, both quantitatively and qualitatively, at its disposal than either Tanzania or Somalia. So powerful is the allure of its wealth that nearly a million non-Ivoiriens are presently in the country, many of them migrant workers from Upper Volta and Guinea who work on the plantations, in trade and commerce, and in industry.

DISTRIBUTIVE CAPABILITY

The very forces that give the extractive capability of the Ivory Coast its force and vigor make the distributive capacity highly mixed in character. The substantial pool of goods and ser-

[44] Kamark, *The Economics of African Development*, pp. 239–240.

[45] R. H. Green has written a penetrating account of the Ivoirien accomplishments and has concluded that there are serious flaws in the economic structure, including "sluggish" Ivoirienization, inadequate development of national markets, and continued "external dependence": "Ghana and the Ivory Coast 1957–1967: Reflections on Economic Strategy, Structure, Implementation and Necessity," paper delivered at the African Studies Association meeting (November, 1967).

vices available for distribution provide the Ivoirien elite a good deal of leverage and a demonstrated ability to co-opt would-be counter-elites within the system. On a per capita basis, the Ivoirien system has at its command greater material rewards than the majority of black African states. The prevailing economic ethos has also produced something of an achievement orientation to the economy and the society, although the exact degree of that orientation is difficult to assess. The government often proclaims its commitment, political and economic, to careers open to talent, but the tight control over the decision-making apparatus and the arbitrary assignment of rewards militates against the actualization of these aims.

There is, for example, the matter of privileged groups. The riches of the Ivoirien system are not distributed in an equitable fashion. This is due primarily to the fact that three such groups, PDCI government employees, planters, and Europeans, because of their political and economic importance, receive a disproportionate amount of those rewards. With independence the power of the political center to disburse its rewards increased rapidly, for it was now able to provide 30,000 government jobs, interest-free loans, tax benefits, substantial salaries, and land (the government took over all unused land at independence). Development projects, particularly in the area of infrastructure, were also used as patronage: "Political considerations influenced the annual allocation of tangible projects such as schools, roads, dispensaries and public buildings to the various *cercles*." [46] Those in government service soon became a new class, easily "the most privileged group among wage earners." [47] Because of the relative affluence of the economy (as compared with Somalia) and the lack of countervailing pressures (as in the case of Tanzania), class differentiation in the Ivory Coast developed rapidly. While these new classes were not totally closed to additional members, the tight control exercised by the political center over recruitment meant that there were impediments to entering them. There is also severe economic disequilibrium between the northern and southern sections of the country.

In addition to the new government-party class, the economic de-

[46] Zolberg, *One Party Government*, p. 194.
[47] *Ibid.*, p. 299.

velopment of the Ivory Coast also served to solidify the position of the rural African bourgeois. The planter class which originally provided the basis for PDCI support became a prime recipient of the largess of the system. Encouraged to expand and diversify their production of primary products by government tax incentives and by the lure of new land and liberal credits, and aided by government regulation of labor and by the availability of large numbers of migrant workers who provided cheap, relatively docile labor, this group was able to entrench itself following independence.

There is also the matter of expatriates. As a result of the Ivoirien leadership's encouragement of a foreign French presence and a "go-slow" approach to the matter of Africanization, the number of French in the Ivory Coast has doubled from 15,000 to 35,000. While this in itself could have been a neutral phenomenon, its results have perpetuated, even increased, some of the inequities of the colonial period. It is estimated, for example, that expatriates hold from 60 to 90% of all middle and upper level managerial positions in the economy, as well as within some agencies of the administration.[48] This has been justified in the face of increasing demands for Africanization on the following grounds. First, the government has argued that many of these expatriates are governmental employees whose salaries are paid for by the French government. Hence to remove them from their positions would simply eliminate that position and mean a net loss in foreign aid. Secondly, the continued expatriate position in the economy is explained on the basis of "efficiency," for as a member of the government put it: ". . . I agree that it may not look good to have the bulk of trade in foreign hands but it works." [49] Even accepting the latter statement, the situation goes far beyond this rationale. Not only is most foreign trade handled by twenty or more foreign firms but the Europeans, who represent 1% of the population, account for 50%

[48] Efrem Sigel, "Ivory Coast Education: Brake or Spur," *Africa Report* (January, 1967), 48. Other interesting insights are to be found in Helen Kitchen (ed.), *The Educated African* (New York: Frederick A. Praeger, 1962), pp. 453–474 and Remi P. Clignet and Philip Foster, *The Fortunate Few: A Study of Secondary Schools and Students in the Ivory Coast* (Evanston, Ill.: Northwestern University Press, 1966).

[49] *West Africa*, June 26, 1965, 707.

of the industrial and commercial income.[50] When one considers that perhaps two-thirds of the 20,000 petty traders in the Ivory Coast are also non-Ivoiriens (Syrians, Lebanese, and "foreign" Africans), ascriptive factors in the allocation of positions appear not to have been ruled out. In fact, with the exception of the planters, the same groups are given preferential treatment as they were under colonial rule. Also, the "efficiency" argument which earlier might have had some validity for the operation of large scale, entrepreneurial industrial projects can hardly be applied today, particularly in the semiskilled, even unskilled areas of the economy.

> Europeans seemed to be everywhere. They still fill hundreds of jobs in the government as technical advisers; they run the schools, banks, offices, restaurants and cinemas; and there are even Frenchmen (and women) working at fish counters in Abidjan's central market and waiting on tables in hotels.[51]

It should be mentioned that these privileged groups, the government employees, the African planter class, and the expatiates have made considerable contributions to the current economic boom in the Ivory Coast and that to a certain extent their success has filtered down to other sectors of society such as the rural and urban proletariat but, with the exception of South Africa, the operation of the Ivoirien distributive capacity has resulted in the greatest amount of class differentiation of any of the systems under review. This is not only true in terms of economic rewards, but also in the dispensation of justice.[52] As in the colonial era, there are two classes of punishments, rated not as much to the nature of the crime as to the class of the person committing it. There is a *régime amélioré* for Europeans and well-to-do Africans and a *régime local* for others.

[50] Victor D. DuBois, *Social Aspects of the Urbanization Process in Abidjan* (New York: American Universities Field Staff, 1967), p. 11. Those interested in further information on the urbanization process in the Ivory Coast should consult his *Ahmadou's World* (New York: American Universities Field Staff, 1965) and Remi P. Clignet, "Urbanization and Family Structure in the Ivory Coast," *Comparative Studies in Society and History* (1965–1966) Vol. VIII: 385–401.

[51] Victor D. DuBois, *The Student-Government Conflict*, p. 5.

[52] Victor D. DuBois, *Crime and the Treatment of the Criminal* and *A Visit to an African Prison*.

There are substantial differences in the prison facilities accorded each group. Fewer privileges and less opportunity for meaningful exercise and work are provided for the *régime local* group. The educational system, too, which will be examined under the rejuvenative heading, is distinguished by a certain elite orientation which, although the government has sought to make education available to all those qualified, in fact serves to perpetuate the new classes and venerate their values rather than opening up society to different points of view. Taking into account the various aspects of wealth distribution, dispensation of justice and educational opportunities, one may well agree with Reginald Green who characterized the Ivory Coast as an "aristocratic distribution of benefits system." [53] Despite the claims to the contrary, there is considerable inequity in the way in which wealth, status, and safety are allocated. As long as the economic boom continues and there is a filtering down of the system's considerable economic benefits, the distribution capacity of the Ivory Coast can be counted on to provide the regime with a major area of support. As long as the Ivory Coast remains an elite, consumption-oriented system with discernible class and racial overtones, however, its distribution capacity will continue to be highly mixed in character, able to function well during periods of economic upswing but potentially brittle when faced with the problems of stagnation or economic decline.

The distributive capability of the Ivory Coast is currently an asset to the system but unless it is improved over time and a more equitable process of reward allocation instituted, it may eventually prove to be a liability. The government has indicated that when the economy has reached its "takeoff" stage and foreign capital is no longer of critical importance to development, the rewards of the system may be more equitably distributed. The government has also promised a vast war on "poverty, hardship, and disease" to help to equalize living conditions. Until this is actually accomplished and some of the energies and capital now spent for economic development are devoted to welfare projects, the Ivory Coast will remain vulnerable. It should be remembered, moreover, that the same forces which limit participation in the decision-making process and circumscribe the civil and political liberties in the Ivory Coast

[53] Green, *op. cit.*, p. 20.

will probably also hinder the positive transformation of its distributive capability.

REJUVENATIVE CAPABILITY

The difficulties inherent in the distributive capacity are reflected, and to a certain extent, magnified in the rejuvenative capability. The educational system, for example, is highly mixed in character. Originally designed to draw various ethnic and socio-economic groups into the life of the nation and to provide a channel for upward mobility for all, the system was greatly expanded after the *loi cadre* of 1956. Primary and secondary education were made free and 15% of the national budget was allocated for education annually. There are currently over 340,000 students at the primary level, 25,000 at the secondary level (which is differentiated into vocational, academic, and technical streams), and 1900 at the university level including those at the new (1964) University of Abidjan. Nearly 45% of school-age children are in school—one of the highest percentages in sub-Saharan Africa. Thus it is not the quantity of educational opportunity that is in question, but the quality and recruitment patterns of the system.

In *The Fortunate Few: A Study of Secondary Schools and Students in the Ivory Coast*, Remi Clignet and Philip Foster have analyzed the Ivoirien educational system in depth and have highlighted its mixed character. They maintain that despite the male, southern, and urban bias to educational recruitment, the system is essentially open, drawing from a broad base of socio-economic and ethnic groups.[54] Nevertheless, as in most African countries, the educational system is elitist in character, with but 2% of those in primary school going further; the new classes outlined above also appear to be entrenching themselves in the educational system. Although persons in the professions and government employment amount to but 2% of the working population, for example, fully 17% of the student population are the sons and daughters of those officials.[55] Further, the kind of education provided is itself a matter

[54] Clignet and Foster, *op. cit.*

[55] Remi P. Clignet and Philip Foster, "Potential Elites in Ghana and the Ivory Coast, A Preliminary Comparison," *American Journal of Sociology* (November, 1964) Vol. LXX, No. 3: 356.

of debate for observers have pointed out that the educational system is not geared to the needs of Ivoirien society:

> The school does not integrate the child into his traditional and natural milieu, but gives him the means to evade it, without permitting him, for lack of adequate professional training to insert himself into the structure of modern economic life.[56]

More serious, however, is the fact that much of the talent uncovered through education which might be used to rejuvenate the government and renovate the PDCI is disinclined to enter the political realm. Due primarily to the fact that politics is seen as a closed arena with tight control from the center and with few opportunities for careers open to talent, less than 1% of the students "even remotely contemplate political careers."[57] Political socialization in the Ivory Coast is thus not being carried out effectively and the system makes little effort to draw the youth into the process of political participation. This means that because of a lack of mobility within the PDCI government structure and a lack of governmental encouragement in the area of political participation, those with different visions for the future of the system, including the young and the radical, are simply not let in. When coupled with the lack of dissent protection and a commitment to command decision making, these factors may well prove to be highly detrimental to the future functioning of the system. The constellation of forces outlined above do insure the present stability of the system, but at the expense of the future growth and "learning" of the system.

Finally, there is the matter of the national leader. The Ivory Coast at present is heavily dependent upon one man. At the age of 64, Fèlix Houphouët-Boigny remains the Ivory Coast. A consummate politician, he has led the country to independence and through nearly a decade of substantial prosperity. He has served as a unifying force and a symbol of national unity. He has presided over economic development and national construction. Yet his very successes have prevented the system from developing institutions and processes with

---

[56] Sigel, *op. cit.*, p. 50.
[57] Clignet and Foster, "Potential Elites," 359.

which to deal with change. The delicate balance Houphouët-Boigny has maintained, between the rural and the urban, the rich and the poor, among the various ethnic and socio-economic groups, between the national and the international environments, all seem likely to offer major threats to the future functioning of the system. Upon the demise of Houphouët-Boigny, the system will be exposed to severe stresses. If this time of trial is adequately foreseen, and provision made for a smooth transfer of power, presumably with French support—à la Gabon—the system may remain substantially intact. Until such a power transmission takes place, however, the fragility of the political system and the weakness of its rejuvenative capability remain most credible hypotheses.

SYMBOLIC CAPABILITY

In contrast to the rejuvenative capacity, the symbolic capability represents a major support for the regime and the system even though it, too, revolves around the presence of Houphouët-Boigny. He is the father of the nation, *le vieux* or old one. It is he who is given credit for the abolition of forced labor in 1946, it is he who went to France, dealt with the colonial authorities, and became prominent even on their terms. It is he who took his country out of a federation which was a financial drain on the Ivory Coast and redirected the course of French West Africa in a fashion widely regarded as beneficial to the Ivory Coast. It was he who won independence on the best possible terms and who made the economic upsurge possible. Houphouët may not have done all of these things, but it is felt that he did and his substantial popularity among the general population can be traced to the aura surrounding these accomplishments.

Houphouët-Boigny embodies three different strands of legitimacy which reinforce the political system of the Ivory Coast and give it political credence. If, for example, we take Max Weber's definition of charisma as a "certain quality of an individual personality by virtue of which he is set apart from ordinary men and treated as endowed with supernatural, superhuman, or at least specifically exceptional powers or qualities," Houphouët qualifies.[58] While Houphouët-

---

[58] Max Weber, *The Theory of Social and Economic Organization* (Glencoe, Ill.: The Free Press, 1957) p. 358.

Boigny lacks the flamboyance and public personality of a Fidel Castro or a Sékou Touré, he nevertheless is a person of some magnetism and projects a forceful image, not only towards the masses in the countryside but towards others in the decision-making elite. As Zolberg has pointed out, many Ivoiriens feel that he is "destined" to rule them.[59]

Moreover, Houphouët-Boigny may be regarded also as having traditional authority. Despite the initial opposition to the RDA-PDCI among some tribal authorities, Houphouët-Boigny managed to allay their fears that modern political activity would prove inimical to their positions. In this regard, he was aided by the fact that he was a *chef de canton* in his own right among the Baoulé and had married into the Agni tribe, thus giving him a power base in two of the largest Ivoirien ethnic groups. It is also widely felt in the Ivory Coast that Houphouët is a "chief among chiefs." [60] When the paramount chief of the Baoulé died soon after independence, for example, there was no attempt made to replace him for it was made clear that Houphouët already fulfilled that role.[61] He has held that the authority of the chief is not incompatible with a modern political system if that chief holds "modern" views. Through such institutions as the *Syndicat des Chefs*, public ceremonies in which the President emerges as an almost monarchical figure, the present regime is grounded in the traditional sector of society.

But it is the rational-legal legitimacy which is of critical importance in Houphouët's symbolic capability. The charisma and traditional authority of Houphouët is important, but the President is also a symbol of modernity, an embodiment of modern values. He is a doctor of medicine, a skillful politician who is known to be as at home in Paris as in his home-town of Yamoussoukrou. He is the heir to French authority and the formulator of both a modern economy system and the "Ivoirien nation." His accent on national unity and integration and on the updating of societal values (including the abolition of polygamy and contract marriage), all give a modern stamp to the regime.

The political system also has some rational-legal legitimacy in its own right. The constitutions of 1959 and 1960 set up a legal

[59] Zolberg, *Creating Political Order*, p. 138.
[60] *Fraternité*, February 12, 1960, 1.
[61] Zolberg, *Creating Political Order*, p. 110.

framework for politics in the Ivory Coast. The new civil code also represents "modern" values, and the various political institutions such as the National Assembly, the Cabinet, the Supreme Court, however insignificant their political power, do serve to provide the system with a legal, rational grounding. The periodic plebiscites, even though they are of no direct consequence, do give the system an aura of legitimacy. The achievement orientation of the economy system and the widespread educational opportunities also give the system a rational-legal orientation and provide a source of public identification with it.

There is little symbolic flow from the political center, however. There is a national anthem, *L'Abidjanaise,* and a national flag of orange, green, and white. The orange represents the northern portions of the country, the green the south and the future, while the white stands for peace and unity but it seems doubtful that this symbolism is of much consequence, or even understood, beyond a select elite. There are few party rallies, few political slogans disseminated from the center, few attempts to mobilize the population. When coupled with the lack of participation in the political process, these elements suggest that while the symbolic capability may be adequate for the present, it, too, will have to be substantially improved if the system is to undergo a smooth or bloodless change in national leadership when Houphouët-Boigny departs from the national scene.

Goals of the System

At least three of the goals sought by the leaders of the Ivoirien political system—unity, stability, and economic development—are probably shared by large numbers of persons within the system even though their participation in the process of goal selection is minimal. To the decision-making elite, these are the major, interrelated systemic goals.[62] The decision to pursue them was made as far back as the middle 1950's and continues to be applied today. It was felt by the decision-making elite that economic development was essential to the system and that development could only occur

[62] B. Holas, *Côte d'Ivoire: Passé-Present-Perspectives* (Abidjan: Ministère de l'Education d'Ivoire, 1965), p. 1.

with substantial inputs of foreign capital. This would only be forth-coming if the political climate were stable and conducive to that investment.[63] Thus, maintenance not only of the system but of the regime has held to be directly related to economic development. The success of this strategy cannot be questioned. The expanding economy, the heightened extractive capability, and the general im-provement in the standard of living have been made possible by the attraction of over $700 million in private and public investment and it seems fair to say that the Ivory Coast is currently well on its way to the achievement of its primary goals.

The costs of this strategy are difficult to calculate. The Ivoirien leaders have been forced to sacrifice some freedom in the inter-national arena, particularly with regard to France and the European Economic Community whose development funds have so substan-tially aided Ivoirien economic development. Despite occasional dif-ferences (the Ivory Coast refused to recognize Communist China even after France did), the Ivory Coast has followed the lead of France in Africa and has taken a most modest stance against "neo-colonialism" and "neoimperialism." It should not be overlooked, however, that in many cases of Franco-Ivoirien agreement there was a genuine confluence of mutual interest (as over the breakup of the Mali Federation). Nevertheless, this agreement has put the Ivory Coast out of step with the more radical African states and Houphouët-Boigny has been the target of some criticism in the African com-munity. The leadership of the Ivory Coast feels, however, that this is a small price to pay for the levels of economic development.

The stability of the regime and the system, the major goal of the Ivory Coast, is linked directly to the concomitant (in the eyes of the leadership at least) goal of command decision making. The small numbers of decision-makers, their unwillingness to brook per-sonnel or ideological competition, and their tight control over the political powers are all justified on the basis of the need for "stabil-ity" and "unity." Political development, especially polyarchal de-cision making, is neither desired nor sought by the principal decision-makers. While the PDCI originally performed an integrat-ing function and encouraged a certain degree of political develop-ment, a decline has set in. The political arena has narrowed. There is little political linkage save bureaucratic between the center and the

[63] Berg, "The Economic Basis of Political Choice," pp. 391–405.

periphery of the system. Participation in the decision-making process, always modest, has been reduced further. Channels of communication to the political center have become clogged and the key political institutions such as the National Assembly display little vitality or vibrancy.

There is a further dimension to the lack of political development and this is the Ivory Coast's repeated opposition to any expansion of the political system through federation. For the past two decades there has been a rather persistent pattern of Ivoirien opposition to any federation, although Houphouët-Boigny has encouraged Ivoirien leadership in francophone Africa and the Ivory Coast leadership has demonstrated a willingness to enter into modest economic groupings with other former French areas.[64] In 1959, for example, the Ivory Coast formed the *Conseil de l'Entente* with Upper Volta which Dahomey Togo, and Niger subsequently joined, a grouping designed to coordinate fiscal and commercial policy and to improve common public services among the four territories. Originally offered as a counterweight to the Mali Federation, the *Conseil de l'Entente* provided the Ivory Coast with a market for its products and a supply of cheap migrant labor at a modest cost of $2 million per year which the Ivory Coast contributed to a shared "solidarity" fund. The Ivory Coast also participated in the 1961 *Union Africaine et Malgache* (UAM) which met to consider the political implications of the Congo situation, Morocco's claims to Mauritania, and the Algerian war. Consisting of the Cameroun, Central African Republic, Congo (Brazzaville), Dahomey, Gabon, Ivory Coast, Malagasy Republic, Mauritania, Niger, Senegal, and Upper Volta (Rwanda and Togo joined in 1963), the UAM was opposed by other African states such as Guinea and Ghana and was disbanded after the formation of the Organization of African Unity in 1963. Its successor organization, the *Union Africaine et Malgache de Coopération Economique* (UAMCE) was formed in 1964 to develop a common economic policy and stimulate cooperation among the members. Including the UAM countries minus Mauritania but with the addition of the Congo (Kinshasa), the OAMCE was itself replaced in 1965 by the *Organisation Commune Africaine et Mal-*

---

[64] *Ibid.* See also, William Foltz, *op. cit.*; I. William Zartman, *International Relations in the New Africa* (Englewood Cliffs, N.J.: Prentice-Hall, 1966), chapter I; and Claude Welch, Jr., *Dream of Unity* (Ithaca, N.Y.: Cornell University Press, 1966), chapter VII.

gache (OCAM) which was to encourage close association with the EEC and France. In 1966 the Ivory Coast also joined the *Union Douaniere Ouest-Africaine* (UDOA) which provides for a customs union of the francophone West African states, common external tariffs, and a Council of Ministers which is to meet periodically to "coordinate" economic policy among the members. Thus, the Ivory Coast has been willing to join in modest groupings of African states whose primary purpose is functional and which makes no attempt to circumscribe the political hegemony of the Ivory Coast. The Ivory Coast has been an important member of all of these groups and has generally espoused an anticommunist, pro-Western diplomatic stance and sought to promote an evolutionary, as opposed to revolutionary, approach to the problems of Africa although it has helped to pay for the support of the liberation movements in southern Africa. From time to time it has sought to influence other African states to adopt a similar stance, but its direct influence has generally not extended much beyond the *l'Entente* states (although along with Tanzania, Zambia and Gabon, it has recognized Biafra).

The political system of the Ivory Coast, then, has pursued its primary goals of stability, economic development, and command decision making most diligently and, especially in the economic sphere, accomplished a great deal, albeit at some social and political costs. At the present time, the system seems able to pay these costs and to maintain itself. Of the four systems under review, it places the greatest emphasis on economic matters and, next to South Africa, the least on political development. Its leadership has demonstrated great skill in maintaining the present political system but has made little provision for the future functioning of that system. Its accomplishments in the economic sphere have been considerable, however, and it is possible that its success in this area will compensate, at least for the foreseeable future, for a lack of concern with political development.

BIBLIOGRAPHY

Foltz, William, *From French West Africa to the Mali Federation* (New Haven, Conn.: Yale University Press, 1965).

Morgenthau, Ruth Schachter, *Political Parties in French-Speaking West Africa* (Oxford: The Clarendon Press, 1964).

Thompson, Virginia, "The Ivory Coast," Gwendolyn M. Carter (ed.), *African One Party States* (Ithaca, N.Y.: Cornell University Press, 1962), pp. 237–325.

Zolberg, Aristide, *One Party Government in the Ivory Coast* (Princeton, N.J.: Princeton University Press, 1964).

———— *Creating Political Order* (Chicago: Rand McNally & Company, 1966).

———— "The Ivory Coast," in James Coleman and Carl G. Rosberg (eds.), *Political Parties and National Integration* (Berkeley and Los Angeles, Calif.: University of California Press, 1965), pp. 65–88.

CHAPTER VIII

Politics in Africa:
Patterns of
Growth and Decay

In presenting a view of the functioning of each of four political systems, the foregoing analysis of South Africa, Tanzania, Somalia, and the Ivory Coast indicates the difficulties of attempting to classify African political systems along purely structural lines. One cannot tell a priori, for example, whether a particular system is democratic or nondemocratic merely by an examination of its institutional framework. Using "democratic" in the sense of polyarchal participation in the decision-making process, we have found democratic politics occurring within the multiparty system of Somalia and within the single-party apparatus of Tanzania. Conversely, "authoritarian" or hierarchical politics functioned within the single-party system of the Ivory Coast and the multiparty arrangement of South Africa. Interestingly enough, while much has been written in recent years about the possibility of democratic politics taking place within a single-party apparatus—often without sufficient data to support such a proposition—little work has been done on the hypothesis that authoritarian politics may occur in a multiparty system. Tanzania and South Africa provide substantial empirical evidence for both hypotheses.

272

This study of four African political systems also suggests the difficulties of categorizing functioning political systems on the basis of simplified, highly abstract models. During the initial phases of research, we attempted to use a variety of models in order to compare the systems under review. As the foregoing chapters indicate, we were able, on occasion, to suggest elements of analytical comparison between some models and actual political systems. For example, some facets of the neomercantilist model were found in the Ivoirien system. Nevertheless, this approach did not prove very useful over all.

This is not in any way to denigrate the accomplishments of the model builders. In addition to his substantive analysis of politics in Uganda and Ghana, for example, David E. Apter has taken a series of creative leaps in the field of political development theory. In his *The Politics of Modernization* and *Some Conceptual Approaches to the Study of Modernization,* he registers some impressive accomplishments in the titanic effort to devise a holistic and predictive theory of political development and modernization.[1] More recently he has developed four systemic models based on composites of societal norms and authority patterns: mobilization, theocratic, bureaucratic, and reconciliation.[2] His accent on the often overlooked area of "non-" or "pre-" democratic political representation, moreover, offers the hope that at some future date, refined versions of these models can be applied with profit to developing political systems. In their present form, however, most of his models are highly abstract in character and neither easily nor universally applicable to specific, functioning political systems. We say this even though we agree with his central conclusion that during a period of social modernization, political systems may be inclined to move away from democratic forms while the attainment of a modern, industrialized society may encourage the same system to move toward them. Just as the Platonic forms become sullied by their incorporation with matter, so these and other models lose their ideal character—and clarity—when applied to specific systems. The very characteristics that enable them to function as ideal types in a general theory, cir-

[1] David E. Apter, *The Politics of Modernization* (Chicago, Ill.: University of Chicago Press, 1965) and *Some Conceptual Approaches to the Study of Modernization* (Englewood Cliffs, N.J.: Prentice-Hall, 1968).
[2] David E. Apter, "Notes for a Theory of Non-Democratic Representation," in *Some Conceptual Approaches,* pp. 295–328.

cumscribe their utility in the comparison of actual political systems. In addition, most of our models of political development tend to accentuate the positive aspects of political development and often overlook the very real dangers of political decay. For many political systems, the prevention of decay is a far more pressing problem than inducing development. For this reason, a critical examination of actual, functioning political systems that pinpoints potential sources of decay will often prove to be of greater consequence and utility than the construction of abstract models.

At the same time, suggestions that such model building be curtailed, and because of the lack of data available, a process of single-factor comparison substituted seem inappropriate, particularly in light of the multidimensional character of political systems.[3] Although such an approach would enjoy the advantage of focus, the large number of variables present in any functioning political system militates against the successful categorization of any system on the basis of a single factor. What is needed is the systematic accumulation of data as well as a continual process of theory refinement, hopefully bringing the two activities closer together so that widely applicable models with strong empirical groundings may be developed. It is in this context that we chose the theoretically modest, but more inclusive conceptual framework outlined in Chapter I. From such a descriptive base we moved to an analytical comparison between functioning political systems rather than between those systems and a series of models. Until there is sufficient data available to enable us to fill in such a framework for most African political systems, it will prove difficult to engage in meaningful, continental-wide comparisons or to develop predictive theory applicable to the course of politics in Africa.

Therefore, the patterns which we have observed in four African political systems are meant to be taken as points of departure for future research, rather than as generalizations about all African political systems. Because three of the four systems reviewed in this work have been functioning as independent entities for less than a decade, it is problematical whether all of the trends that

[3] See, for example, the recent works of Michael F. Lofchie: "Political Theory and African Politics," *Journal of Modern African Studies* (1968) Vol. VI, No. 2: 3–15, and Richard L. Sklar, "Political Science and National Integration," *Journal of Modern African Studies* (1967) Vol. V, No. 1: 1–11.

we have outlined will continue. Some undoubtedly will do so. Others may be arrested or reversed. Nevertheless, on the basis of the evidence currently available, the following conclusions seem warranted. First, the impact of the colonial experience will prove to be far less enduring than has previously been imagined, particularly in the area of the international transfer of political institutions. Secondly, as time goes on, it will be the reassertion of the basic societal underpinnings of the political system, including traditional political patterns, rather than the colonial overlay, that will be of import in determining the future course of politics in Africa. This is not to say that African political systems cannot alter the societies they govern and restructure those traditional political patterns. It is to say, rather, that this will prove difficult to accomplish. Systems so inclined will not only have to take these political and social patterns more directly into account; they will also have to develop stronger systemic capabilities if they are to succeed. Finally, African political systems exhibit considerable fragility. Generally speaking, the writ of the central political authority does not cover the entire country and most systems have shown considerable amounts of political decay. Although our subsequent analysis of this proposition will draw upon contemporary developments in systems other than those under review, South Africa, Tanzania, Somalia, and the Ivory Coast do contain elements and situations which, if unchecked, could lead to a reversal of their previous patterns of political development and culminate in stagnation and decline.

In terms of the first two patterns, South Africa is something of an exception. There, the colonial age is already 300 years old and is deeply implanted within the various societies that the system controls. Thus, while it is true that the present political system exhibits some characteristics of 19th century colonialism, it is misleading to think of it as simply a "colonial" system for it is neither as superficial nor as ephemeral as those experienced by Tanganyika or Somalia. South African life—social, economic, and political—is so permeated by the experience that barring a revolution of the scope and depth of that achieved in Algeria or Zanzibar, the colonial component is likely to remain in force. It should be pointed out that to this extent at least, the present political system does, in fact, reflect some of the basic traditional patterns (i.e. European domination has been in force for centuries). Apartheid and separate development may be viewed as an attempt to reflect traditional African political structures and values in order to maintain European hegemony over the entire system. However misguided and illogical in terms of the numbers of Africans already detribalized, it represents an effort on the part of the system to deal with the basic underpinnings of its domestic environment.

With the exception of South Africa and the Portuguese controlled areas, however, the colonial interlude was short, lasting less than 80 years. The colonial experience did set the boundaries for most subsequent African political systems and interjected some linguistic and cultural values into their societies. In terms of political structures and forms, however, the colonial legacy has diminished sharply as the various political systems have moved away from the date of independence. Despite the extensive importation of political institutions, constitutions, and modes of political behavior, few European-induced forms "took" to the African environment. The widespread inability of these exogenous models to survive after independence is well documented and one can view the high incidence rate of military coups, civil strife, and domestic disorder as indications of a failure on the part of the colonial authority to select a viable political framework prior to independence and the pressing need to do so after its attainment.

Only where the European imports corresponded to existing political and social patterns (as in Somalia) or were so modified (as in Tanzania) did they function effectively. In the case of Somalia, democratic politics in a multiparty framework worked from the beginning because that framework reflected the basic societal values: decentralized political power, an egalitarian ethos, and a pattern of widespread participation in traditional politics. In short, the political system became a projection of that society. In effect, the colonial authority selected the framework after World War II and the system grew to fit it as local participatory democracy was extrapolated to the national level. Since independence, the political system has functioned effectively, aided by the basic cultural unity of the Somali people and their agreement on the primary goals of the system. This is not to say that it will always do so. A democratic political process and an egalitarian spirit are well suited to a nomadic society (and, as some have argued, to a modern, urban, literate one as well). But the very nature of economic development, the asynchronous and asymmetrical character of modernization, and the pressures inherent in the transition phase from one type of society to another may cause the system serious problems.

In the case of Tanzania, the colonial-induced framework simply did not prove adequate and the leaders of the political system had the wisdom to recognize this and the courage to experiment with a new political arrangement in an attempt to come to terms with their precolonial past as well as with the demands of political and economic development. In the process, they devised methods which take into account the societal underpinnings of the system even while they seek to propel Tanzania into new directions which will alter those underpinnings. Traditional patterns of fragmentation and the weak colonial legacy permitted extensive adjustments in the political system until, at present, the system exhibits marked signs of political development, including widespread participation in politics and a strong accent on egalitarianism and communal welfare. These directions may be reversed over time, for since the Arusha declaration the leadership of Tanzania seems to be moving toward a vanguard concept of politics and a growing concern for societal conformity. In the future, politics in Tanzania could take on a more authoritarian flavor if the society fails to respond to the directives of the central leadership (however chosen) or economic development proves impossible to achieve. Yet, even if the Tanzanian system moves away from polyarchal decision making, the idea that multiple candidates from a single party can meaningfully contest positions without raising the spectre of systemic fragmentation will, however briefly, have been actualized. In this sense at least, the Tanzanian experience may serve as a "model" for those single-party systems seeking to rejuvenate themselves or to mobilize their populations through political participation. It should be pointed out, however, that the Tanzanian concept may have more relevance for those systems that are already modernized and are now seeking to liberalize the political process, rather than to those poised on the threshold of development. In addition to the form, the style of political leadership found in Tanzania—egalitarian, frugal, and humble—is worthy of emulation. This is not to say that Tanzania is a "model" in any absolute sense, for, as was mentioned in Chapter IV, there are some contributory factors in the Tanzanian situation that may not be duplicated elsewhere. Nevertheless, the Tanzanian political system does offer political leaders, in Africa and elsewhere, an example of a way in which systemic flexibility and leadership alteration can be achieved within firmly circumscribed limits and citizen participation made meaningful in a single-party state.

The pattern of politics in the Ivory Coast is more difficult to assess. In terms of the colonial impact, substantial political, economic, and cultural ties with France remain. These bonds are not unbreakable, however, and have less to do with a basic change in Ivoirien society than with a consistent set of decisions by the Ivoirien elite to continue them. Should other leadership come to power, the colonial overlay could be drastically reduced, although at some economic cost. Yet it is precisely the colonial connection that has aided in the attainment of a major systemic goal, economic development, and provided the capabilities that permit the retention of an authoritarian political system. Unity and economic development have been achieved fcr the moment, but the future may well hold decisive difficulties. Should an economic slowdown occur or should the French alter their relationship with the government of the Ivory Coast, the system could devolve rapidly. The defects of the neo-mercantilist pattern, the evolution of marked socio-economic cleavages, and a general lack of political development beyond a stage of primitive unification are givens in the present Ivoirien situation which will have to be overcome if the political stagnation and decay that have occurred in the surrounding political systems of Togo, Dahomey, Upper Volta, and Mali are to be avoided.

Toward an Assessment of Political Decay

Concern with political development in its many forms has been a persistent theme of this work. Yet given the fragility of many political systems in sub-Saharan Africa and the nature of the pressures which impinge upon them, the possibility—even the probability—of political stagnation and decay cannot be ignored. Despite the existence of internal difficulties, the systems under review appear to be relatively "healthy" in comparison with systems such as those of Nigeria or the Congo which have suffered massive breakdowns and a host of other states where military coups and communal strife have impaired the ability of the political system to function and caused substantial devolution. In order to paint a portrait of political decay and to indicate its salient features as exhibited in postindependence Africa, it is necessary to draw upon the experiences of those systems that have stagnated or declined and to extrapolate patterns of political decay from developments within a variety of systems. It should be reiterated at the outset, however, that little work has been done on the problems of stagnation, atrophy, and decay and there remain great gaps in our knowledge of why political devolution and social disequilibrium occur. As Michael Lofchie has written, breakdown and decline often take place within a "theoretical vacuum." [4]

At the same time, the postindependence period of African politics has yielded considerable data on the process of systemic breakdown and the evidence, however scattered, offers the hope that a generalized picture of political decay may be adduced. Recently, too, political scientists have begun to turn their attention to the process of political decay in Africa and to analyze its causes. Aristide R. Zolberg, for example, has written a perceptive piece on the process of political conflict in the African context: "The Structure of Political Conflict in the New States of Tropical Africa" offers meaningful although indirect insights into the nature of systemic decline.[5] In addition, two recent works by African novelists offer cogent and provocative comments on the dynamics of devolution. Chinua Achebe's A Man of the People and Ayi Kwei Armah's The Beautiful Ones Are Not Yet Born analyze in depth the stagnation and decay of two major African political systems.[6] Ideology and the type of political framework are not critical variables, for although Achebe examines a multiparty system with competitive overtones and Armah projects from a single-party, authoritarian system, both arrive at the same generalized view of decay. Drawing from these sources and the raw stuff of postindependence events, we can outline a prominent pattern of systemic decay and examine a series of phenomena associated with decline,

[4] Lofchie, "Political Theory," p. 5.

[5] Aristide R. Zolberg, "The Structure of Political Conflict in the New States of Tropical Africa," American Political Science Review (March, 1968) Vol. LXII, No. 1: 70–87.

[6] Chinua Achebe, A Man of the People (London: The John Day Company, 1966) and Ayi Kwei Armah, The Beautiful Ones Are Not Yet Born (Boston: Houghton Mifflin Company, 1968). For an analysis of some deep-seated causative factors see Stanislav Andreski, The African Predicament (New York: Atherton, 1968).

phenomena whose cumulative effect is corrosive, leading to systemic stagnation and devolution. This decline may not be total, that is, resulting in the disintegration of the system, but at the very least means that some previous patterns of political development are reversed and a marked decline in the effective functioning of the system can be noted.

If, as we suggest, the African political systems that are likely to undergo great stresses in the future as the political system is forced to come to terms with its social underpinnings (as well as with the problems of economic development and modernization) are inherently weak, then such a picture of decay will have relevance for the practice as well as the theory of politics in Africa. For this reason, after presenting an analysis of the factors that have contributed to systemic decline in the recent past, we shall point to specific areas of potential decline existent in South Africa, Tanzania, Somalia, and the Ivory Coast and offer operational suggestions as to how such potential decay may be avoided or curtailed.

We do not know enough at this moment to trace directly the causal connections among the various phenomena associated with political decline in Africa, but the following are endemic in many instances of decay. Perhaps the most pronounced and unexpected occurrence has been the deterioration of those "mass" parties that led the way to decolonization and assumed political command at independence. Closely linked to the failure on the part of the political elite to develop a suitable institutional framework for resolving domestic conflict, the decline of mass parties as instruments of political socialization and mobilization precipitated—or at the very least, failed to check—political decay. This is true of those parties such as the Convention People's Party in Ghana and the *Union Soudanaise* in Mali that sought to achieve massive societal transformation and those such as the *Movement pour l'Evolution Sociale de l'Afrique Noire* in the Central African Republic that did not.

The decline of these parties can be traced with some assurance. A major factor in their demise was the ease with which most African countries attained independence. With few exceptions (such as Algeria), the post-World War II struggle for independence was short, nearly bloodless, and rather easily accomplished. The facility with which party leaders were able to mobilize mass support for independence provided them with inaccurate perceptions of their own political causal efficacy. The existence of a common adversary, the colonial authority, and the widespread agreement on the goal, if not the tactics, of independence engendered a sense of "national" unity. Coupled with the substantial participation by the masses in the political arena, such agreement appeared to be of great consequence. Although much of the political analysis of the decolonization struggle in Africa has stressed the elite aspects of the process (by focusing upon such leaders as Sékou Touré, Kwame Nkrumah, Jomo Kenyatta, and Patrice Lumumba), it now appears that there was widespread and meaningful participation by the masses.[7] Even if the masses did not participate in the decision-making aspects of the party (as in the PDCI of the Ivory Coast or the *Parti Progressiste du Tchad* of Chad), they did engage in political activities and were successfully organized during elections. Such mass involvement in politics and the general agreement on the goal of independence undoubtedly gave the political leaders of independent Africa an exaggerated estimate of their ability to mobilize the people after independence.

This helps to explain why there were few attempts to stimulate popular participation after independence, even when the groundswell of identification with the party and the "national" leaders ebbed. Party officials turned their attention from the process of political socialization and became absorbed in the day-to-day affairs of running a country. Most scarce resources, whether trained manpower, capital, or time, were committed to the governmental bureaucracies or allocated to the struggle for economic development. Although there were few positive national symbols prior to independence, the political leaders made only modest attempts to generate them after it was attained. This often coincided with the formulation of single-party regimes (either *de facto* or *de jure*). With the political opposition harassed or outlawed, many political leaders lost interest in the generation of public enthusiasm for politics and because the positions at the apex of the party and government were quickly filled, further political recruitment was discouraged. Elections, which had engendered both excitement and commitment and precipitated political mobilization, were curtailed. In fact, independence often meant less mass participation in politics than in the period just prior to it.

[7] Martin Kilson, *Political Change in a West African State* (Cambridge, Mass.: Harvard University Press, 1966) and Herbert Weiss, *Political Protest in the Congo* (Princeton, N.J.: Princeton University Press, 1965).

For example, from 1957 until 1963 there were three national elections in Kenya. Since independence there has been one. In Chad from 1956 until independence, there were three national elections, but only one after it. In Uganda there were four elections just prior to independence, none afterwards. In many systems even if there were elections, there was no choice and little enthusiasm for them. In November 1965, for example, President Maurice Yaméogo of Upper Volta "received" 99.7% of the popular vote. Two months later he was overthrown by one of the most welcomed coups in postindependence Africa. Elections were either not held (Congo-Brazzaville) or held in such a way as to deny any opportunity for leadership alteration (Upper Volta) or so blatantly rigged as to lose validity (Nigeria). In many instances, political demobilization took place. Political parties that had previously been the major agents of political socialization lost interest in the process and even those systems that had featured genuine mass movements often deteriorated into elite-oriented, oligarchical politics.

The decline in party activity might have been compensated for had alternative national institutions developed which could serve to maintain linkage between the central government and the mass of the population. But with few exceptions, local political structures, national assemblies, and participatory institutions on all levels declined in efficacy right along with the parties. It should be pointed out that in some instances, the growth of governmental bureaucracies and the increase in administrative expertise (as in the Ivory Coast) compensated for the decline in mass political activity. Nevertheless, it is not clear that such developments have totally overcome the decline in political socialization which had previously accompanied the former activity. Further, in many instances the political center lost its power to mobilize the population, its channels of information, and most subnational structures of conflict resolution. In systemic terms, many African governments began to suffer from a progressive hardening of their political arteries and experienced a marked decline in their regulative, symbolic, and rejuvenative capabilities. Thus even when the political leaders subsequently realized the nature of the crisis and the growing danger to the system and made the "right" (i.e. functional) decisions, they were unable to carry them out. Moreover, the failure to develop a set of effective institutional buffers meant that when the euphoria of independence wore off and the societal demand pressures built up, there was no way to channel them away from the political center. Lacking a functional political net to absorb or at least moderate the demands, the system was itself threatened. The stresses that developed and ultimately, the resort to force, impinged directly on the core of the system, in many cases destroying it.

For build up the pressures did. During the decolonizing period, the political leaders had raised the expectations not only of the various interest and pressure groups within society but also of the masses. This may have been due to various factors: a desire to galvanize public support, a set of false perceptions of how difficult societal and economic change would be to accomplish, or a combination of the two. In any case, despite the promises of the political elite, the end of colonial rule did not mean the radical transformation of the socio-economic system. With few exceptions, true, deep-seated revolutions did not take place. In many instances, independence merely meant an alteration of elites and little change in the lives of the average citizen of the country. At the same time, there occurred what Zolberg has called an "inflation of demands." [8] Specific groups such as the military, the bureaucracy, the students, and the labor unions increased the scope and intensity of their demands for opportunity, rewards, and security and often became counterelites. To this were added the not insignificant demands the general population made for welfare, education, and meaningful change in their socio-economic status. Sometimes the political leadership sought to meet some of these demands, but as most systems were distinguished by weak extractive and distributive capabilities in the first place, they were unable to satisfy even a major proportion, let alone all, of the demands. More often, however, the inability or unwillingness to meet the aroused demands were accompanied by rates of markedly conspicuous consumption on the part of the political elite.

When the system did not deliver what its leaders had promised and the political elites asked some groups and the mass of its citizenry to make sacrifices that the elites themselves were unwilling to make, much of the aura of legitimacy gained in the decolonization period was dissipated. Many newly independent African governments lost strength in their symbolic capability, that capacity which was sup-

[8] Zolberg, op. cit., p. 74.

posed to compensate for weakness in other areas. Unable to satisfy the demands rushing in upon it and lacking the mechanisms for conducting an ongoing process of political socialization or conflict resolution, many systems lost their ability to cope with the situation and drifted from crisis to crisis. To the lack of a viable political framework for channelling or muting these demands and the loss of legitimacy was added a general disrespect for the law and, subsequently, an inability on the part of the government to preserve societal order. Particularly vulnerable were those systems where the regime in power had itself ignored or arbitrarily altered the law. In many cases there was a marked increase in civil disorder, communal strife, and political violence, including assassination, as the stresses spilled out of the legal framework and force, whether employed by labor unions, students, mobs, or the military, became the ultimate source of authority. Often the amount of force necessary to overthrow the system was minimal—a few hundred soldiers or striking civil servants. In the Hobbesian situation which developed at the political center, the military, as the most organized group and the one with the greatest available force, found it could easily overthrow the regime and the system.

It is not surprising, then, that within a decade of independence, there were over twenty coups and numerous attempted coups and army mutinies. It is almost impossible to generalize about the motivation behind these coups. Sometimes the military intervened because of a deep-seated conviction that the politicians were destroying the nation; sometimes the army acted because its leaders wished to control the political life of the state. Often it moved because the army felt threatened by the formation of a "popular" militia loyal to individual political leaders or because the armed forces wanted a greater share of the national wealth or an increase in size. In other instances, the army moved to curtail or prevent the outbreak of a civil war. Ideology was seldom a critical factor, for the army overthrew regimes that were regarded as "leftist" in orientation (Ghana, Mali, Congo-Brazzaville), "rightist" (Dahomey, Togo, Upper Volta), and feudal (Burundi). Whatever else this intervention signalled, the wholesale involvement of the military in the political life of Africa and the ease with which it supplanted the political authority in over half of the African states indicated the fragility of most of those systems and the extent to which political decay and loss of control by the political center had already occurred. Despite the dissimilarities between the various systems and the motivation behind the army's intervention, the systems in question had all been enervated by political decay and devolution.

One clear indication of this proposition is the difficulty that the military itself experienced in attempting to regenerate the political system, despite the fact that in many countries its initial intervention was welcomed. Even though the army could maintain societal order by its near monopoly over the use of force, its leaders soon discovered that they could neither meet the demands of the population nor mobilize it. Whether the military took on political mantles (Central African Republic, Congo-Kinshasa, Upper Volta, Burundi, Togo, and Dahomey) or ruled as juntas (Sierre Leone, Nigeria, Ghana, and Congo-Brazzaville), they found it most difficult to rejuvenate or reconstruct the political system. Often the ruling figures could not even control or socialize their own comrades and a second round of coups or attempted coups took place (Sierre Leone, Nigeria, Togo, Ghana, and Dahomey). On occasion, the military recognized the magnitude of the task before them and turned responsibility for the system back to the civilian authorities (Sierre Leone, Dahomey, Ghana).

It is too early to determine whether the African political systems that have undergone military coups have become locked into a depressing cycle of coup and countercoup, mired in a morass of political decay, or whether they are entering a transition phase which will lead to newer, more effective political forms and structures which more adequately take into account the societal groundings of the system.[9] The enormity of the problems facing these systems, however, suggests that those that have already undergone marked political decay cannot quickly or easily be put back on the path to political development. Moreover, some systems—Nigeria,

[9] Claude E. Welch, "Soldier and State in Africa," *Journal of Modern African Studies* (1967) Vol. V, No. 3: 305–322; Ali Mazrui, *Towards a Pax Africana* (Chicago: University of Chicago Press, 1966); and Kenneth W. Grundy, "On Machiavelli and the Mercenaries," *Journal of Modern African States* (1968) Vol. VI, No. 3: 295–310.

Sudan, and Congo-Kinshasa—have already experienced such levels of communal conflict as to make national reconciliation extremely difficult.

Because the onset of a military coup or the outbreak of civil war represents such gross indications of political decay, it is tempting to engage in ex post facto analysis and to enumerate the "might-have-been." Of more relevance, however, is an examination of those systems that are still functioning in order to indicate the potential sources of future decay. Considering the fragility of most African political systems, the inappropriateness of much of their colonial heritage, and the overwhelming problems of nation-building and economic development they face, it is not surprising that so many systems have undergone political devolution. In retrospect, it seems remarkable that so many systems have remained intact. In addition to those reviewed in this work, Mauritania, Kenya, Cameroun, Zambia, Guinea, Niger, Rwanda, the Malagasy Republic, Lesotho, Botswana, Gambia, and Swaziland continue to cope, despite difficulties, more or less effectively with their domestic environment. In terms of the successful future functioning of these and other non-African systems, it is important that political scientists and political practitioners seek to identify and curtail sources of political decay before the process of devolution becomes irresistible. We shall, therefore, conclude this work by examining the discernible defects in the political systems of the Ivory Coast, South Africa, Tanzania, and Somalia, and attempt to evolve strategies for dealing with the causes of political decay, not only in these systems, but in others as well.

In terms of the dangers of political devolution, the Ivory Coast seems vulnerable at the present time. The marked decline in local government, the lack of governmental emphasis on political mobilization, and the increasing rigidity of the system in terms of informational and personnel absorption are all areas of concern. Potentially devastating is the rapid growth of socio-economic groups based on an inequitable distribution process and the current ineffectiveness of the Ivoirien rejuvenative capacity. While these adverse factors do not mean that the system is in imminent danger of collapse, they do suggest that if the system is to survive, it must continue to enjoy two prerequisites for systemic maintenance: the continuation of rapid economic growth and substantial levels of exogenous power, especially during a period of leadership alteration. Should either of these elements be reduced over time, the system would be in serious difficulty.

The socio-economic, even the racial inequalities of Ivoirien society and the neopaternal character of the Houphouët-Boigny regime are tolerated by the population because the Ivoirien system has delivered the economic goods. If the current levels of economic growth can be sustained so that even the lowest socio-economic groups continue to reap some discernible benefits, the system may well endure. But the Ivoirien system remains far more vulnerable to economic slowdown than either Tanzania or Somalia, where the distribution of material rewards is not the principal source of legitimacy and the symbolic capacity of the system is able to compensate for a small pool of goods and services.

The power factor is also of critical importance. The strength of the Ivoirien regulative capacity is based in great part on the presence of exogenous forces within the system and on the assumption that more could be acquired quickly if necessary. We have mentioned why, in the short run at least, this strategy may be beneficial. Nevertheless, the dependence upon outside power does place the system in jeopardy, especially during a period of power transition. In the case of Gabon, for example, the long and predictable illness of President Leon M'Ba and his lack of importance for the legitimacy of the system enabled the French and the Gabonese leaders to find an acceptable successor and insure a smooth alteration of regimes. Given the considerable legitimacy Houphouët-Boigny brings to the Ivoirien system and his tight control over it, the sheer act of passing the political baton may prove difficult if there is not an adequate period of preparation.

There is the further complication of future French interest in maintaining the regime and the system. For the present, there seem to be considerable areas of French and Ivoirien agreement, but should the French decide not to support the system, the political fabric could become unravelled very quickly. The French record of support for African governments has not been unambiguous. Soon after the independence, the French used their power to maintain the regime of Fulbert Youlou of Congo-Brazzaville, but later, during 1963, acquiesced to his overthrow. France moved directly to reinstate Leon M'Ba after his government was overthrown in February 1964. When President David Dako of the Central African Republic was the victim of a coup in January 1966, however, the French did nothing to reinstate him, although in November 1967, French troops were flown in to protect his successor, Colonel-President Jean Bokassa. As late as August 1968, French troops were sent to Chad to ensure the continuation of the regime of President François Tombalbaye. It seems clear that the French are prepared to support, by force if necessary, leaders of black Africa but it is they, not the leaders, who determine the nature, scope, and duration of that support. Currently, Houphouët-Boigny enjoys French favor, but in the future that support could be withdrawn, with potentially disastrous effects on the Ivoirien political systems.[10]

South Africa has somewhat different problems. However illegitimate a government it may be for a majority of its population, South Africa is presently a powerful political system. Thus far it has been able to compensate for the espousal of a costly systemic goal (white supremacy) and gross inequities in the distribution process (especially in the allocation of status) by the maintenance of a strong regulative capability. The system may be pernicious, domineering, and discriminatory but it has demonstrated, in the face of substantial domestic and international hostility, the power to survive. While it is hard to imagine that such an inequitable system could endure ad infinitum, it is also difficult, considering its current strength, to accept the notion that its demise is imminent.

Yet the South African system, too, is vulnerable to economic decline which could reduce its regulative capacity, particularly if this were coupled with the development of an organized military-political opposition with exogenous support and a contiguous foreign sanctuary. Gross societal and economic inequities exist and perceptions of them are widespread. If the discontent generated by these factors could be organized and channeled directly against the system instead of being dissipated and diffused, the system would face its major test. With the development of a political infrastructure, urban guerrilla warfare would prove difficult to combat

---

[10] William Foltz is quite right, however, in indicating that the French government cannot act as a totally free agent since French citizens and expatriot firms present in the Ivory Coast represent pressure groups within the domestic French political system.

and the system might be destroyed in a bloody civil war. At the present time, however, these seem remote possibilities. Decay in South Africa is more societal and personal than political. The process by which Africans are dehumanized and exploited and the pervasive odor of racism which permeates South African life are both signs of moral decay but to date, they have not visibly impaired the functioning of the political system. Moreover, recent tactical flexibility vis-à-vis African states to the north, the destruction of antigovernment groups within the Republic, even the expansion of the Bantustan program to Southwest Africa, all indicate the strength, not the weakness, of the political system of South Africa and it is likely to endure despite a goal espousal that has brought it the professed enmity of much of the international community.

Just as the goals of South Africa represent a potential source of political decay, so systemic goals could ultimately be a factor in the decline of the Somali system. The primary goal of the unification of all Somalis has greatly increased communal solidarity and has given the Somali people a sense of unity and purpose not found in most African political systems. To date, then, this goal has proved highly functional in terms of system maintenance and the development of a strong symbolic capability. At the same time, the frustration generated by an inability to achieve that goal may be a major source of political decay in the future. For example, it may be that in terms of the present power configurations in the Horn of Africa, Somalia might well wish to abandon the goal, at least until conditions change. This seems to be what the present government is suggesting. However, while it would reduce frustration within the system, such a shift would also cut into the preeminent position of the military and could encourage a coup d'etat. Thus the goal espousal which is currently a source of systemic strength could, either by the inability to attain it or its abandonment, prove dangerous to the system.

Political devolution could also result from the process of economic development and modernization. The accompanying demographic and societal changes might well render inoperative the tribal political nets upon which the system relies for much of its political socialization and welfare tasks. Over time, the central government will have to assume more of these functions if the system is to continue to grow. Tension could also develop between the "modernizers" and the "traditionalists" over the future course of the system and, given the Somali tradition of social violence, political fractionalism might spill out of the legal framework and undermine the workings of the system.

Tanzania is functioning quite well. The system enjoys considerable and widespread legitimacy and has demonstrated a capacity for internal conflict resolution, informational accumulation, leadership alteration, and rational decision making. Julius Nyerere has coupled a much needed sense of national unity with a strong accent upon polyarchal decision making and mass participation in politics. The political development already logged could be jeopardized, however, if the country does not move forward economically and the pressure for command decision making builds up. Since the Arusha declaration, there seems to be a growing tension between a desire for unanimity and solidarity and a concern for democratic politics and individual independence. In short, Tanzania has made impressive progress in the area of political development but a continual commitment to it must be maintained if the system is to grow.

Looking beyond the particular problems of the four political systems and drawing upon the extensive devolution experiences of many African political systems, broader questions emerge. Can political decay be avoided? Are there strategies for maintaining political development as there are for insuring economic advance? Can national leaders take specific steps to prevent political devolution? An examination of the process of political decay as it has occurred and an analysis of those systems which have thus far avoided it in the African context suggests that the answer to all three of these questions is yes. Granted that each system has a different pattern of development and decay and its own particular set of socio-economic and political problems it would appear that certain steps can be taken by the political leadership to strengthen any system and curtail the possibilities of systemic decay.

As exemplified by Tanzanian innovations, one approach would be to keep the institutional framework of the system both viable and flexible. Constitutions set down the rules for the game of politics in a particular setting and should correspond as nearly as possible to the way the game is to be played. They should be flexible enough to allow changes to meet new situations but not so flexible as to permit their alteration at the will of a single ruler or regime. They must provide for basic societal order and for a legitimate way to change that order. The political leadership would therefore conduct an ongoing evaluation of the legal framework. Sometimes, the leadership should frankly admit that the existing political framework is inadequate and change it, as in the case of Tanzania, at the same time providing for the future alterations.

Nowhere is this need more clearly felt than in the matter of the power transition. Despite the enormous significance of the act of regime alteration for the political system, there is often little provision made for the process by which political authority may be passed from one regime to another without a loss of systemic legitimacy. Some African systems, such as Ethiopia and Swaziland, have such complicated and confused methods of selecting new political leadership that any interregnum is likely to entail significant dangers for the system. Other systems have made almost no provision for the orderly transfer of power: Guinea, Senegal, and Uganda— to name but three—face uncertain futures when the present leadership departs. Kenya has just witnessed a year of trying to provide a mechanism by which a successor to President Kenyatta can be assured of legitimacy and the preservation of the system. No fewer than four alternatives have been proposed and none has met with overwhelming support. Yet these types of problems must be solved if a situation where force alone insures continuity is to be avoided.

An even more important area of concern is the improvement of linkage between the political center and its constituents. It would seem that if the political system is to maintain itself, let alone develop and grow, it must relate to the rural and increasingly urban masses, drawing them into the political process and galvanizing their support for the system. Given the problems of communication, the low symbolic and regulative capabilities of most systems, the task is a formidable one. But in light of the ease with which the links between the center and its population can be broken and the pejorative consequences for the entire system that accompany such a process, the maintenance and development of those links must be accented. To do so costs time, money, and talent but it must be done. Irrespective of the ideological orientation of the system, the process of political socialization is of overriding significance and perhaps best served by an improvement in the accountability of the system to its population. Some regimes have erred and some systems devolved because they were too responsive to specific interest groups, but few systems have declined for attempting to satisfy the demands of the population as a whole on an equitable basis.

Somalia indicates that one of the ways to improve responsiveness and to mobilize popular support of the political system is periodic elections. Honestly held elections, whether within a single- or multi-party framework, on the local or national level, are excellent homeostatic mechanisms for insuring the accountability of the system. Elections are expensive, time-consuming and, in all systems, developed or developing, difficult to run fairly and honestly. In addition, they are often a nuisance to a leadership bent on economic development or international concerns, and appear to be a waste of time and energy. But, properly conducted, elections can provide maximum payoffs in the process of political mobilization and in the improvement of systemic responsiveness: they stimulate interest in politics, lend credibility to the system as a whole, provide needed informational feedback, and aid in rejuvenation.

Closely related to the problems of personnel alteration, informational flow, and a series of periodic elections is that of dissent protection. No less an advocate of national unity than Kwame Nkrumah has written:

> A serious, well-intenitoned opposition keeps a government alive to its responsibilities, guarantees extensive care in the preparation and formulation of programmes, and underlies the need for sponsors of legislation to be able to justify their proposals.[11]

In fact, "A political opposition is neither a luxury nor a danger. If it performs its functions well, an opposition can be of crucial service both to the government of the day, and to the people of the new nation." [12] This does not necessarily mean an institutionalized opposition, but given the pressures for uniformity and unity in the

[11] Kenneth W. Grundy, "The Political Ideology of Kwame Nkrumah," in W. A. E. Skurnick (ed.), *African Political Thought: Lumumba, Nkrumah and Toure* (Denver, Colo.: University of Denver Press, 1968), p. 77. Ironically, President E. Zinsou of Dahomey cites Nkrumah as a classic example of how dysfunctional can be the "stifling" of all opposition (*Africa Report*, December, 1968, p. 31).

[12] Apter, *Some Conceptual Approaches*, p. 73.

new states, if it is not, the leaders of the system must take steps to preserve the opposition. An active, vibrant opposition within a single-party framework is probably more beneficial in terms of militating against the unleashing of centrifugal forces, but it is difficult to achieve. The political system must, of course, ensure that the opposition is "loyal," that is, committed to the system itself. Often, however, the leaders of the political system engage in a self-fulfilling prophecy by declaring that the opposition is "out to destroy us and national unity." If the political center acts as if this were true, the opposition may well try. The line between a loyal and disloyal opposition is admittedly difficult to draw and there will be opponents of the system as well as the regime. Governments are generally more inclined to draw that line fairly close to themselves, thus depriving the system as a whole of the beneficial aspects of an opposition. If the ruling government sees the opposition as a valuable part of the system and demonstrates by word and deed that politics is not a zero-sum game, the opposition is likely to act far more responsibly than if it is continually harassed and denied a place in the political life of the system. This is not to suggest that an African government ought to encourage or even permit an opposition which urges secession or the demise of the political system. But if the opposition is willing to work constructively within the legal framework of the system, its very existence may well provide supports for that system.

There are at least three functional payoffs to the maintenance of a loyal opposition. In the first place, the existence of such an opposition, either within or without the ruling party, is an effective way of channelling dissatisfaction through legitimate filters, enabling dissident elements within the body politic to let off steam. In this sense, a recognized opposition acts as a safety valve. By offering a legitimate avenue for criticisms and protest—whether of personnel or policies—a loyal opposition can discourage those who are dissatisfied from seeking redress outside the legal framework.

Of even more importance for the system as a whole, an opposition provides useful information, information which the leadership of that system needs in order to make its decisions as objectively and rationally as possible and to evaluate its options on the basis of fact, not fancy. In this regard, the opposition serves as a useful channel of information and provides meaningful feedback on the operation of present policies as well as offering different views of the future. To illustrate, Oginga Odinga, former Vice-President of Kenya, has gone into the opposition. He has formed a competitive party, the Kenya People's Union and published a deeply moving book about the present course of politics in Kenya. *Not Yet Uhuru* places strong emphasis on the dangers of decay inherent in the present political system of Kenya.[13] Without accepting all of its conclusions, or expecting the present leaders of the Kenyan political system to do so, one can argue that the system is richer for the existence of such information. Bad news is still news. Given the kind of ethnic, social, and linguistic fragmentation inherent in most African political systems, one can well sympathize with the political leadership's accent on unity. At the same time, the different points of view that spring from this diversity have to be taken into account, even if they are not agreed with. "Talking until they agree" is of little functional utility to the system if those who don't agree aren't allowed to talk.[14]

For this reason, an opposition serves to prevent the development of a false sense of security. Unity will not be enduring if, in order to give the appearance of it, the political system is allowed to atrophy. Nation-building may prove impossible if the political center lacks feedback on the utility of its approaches to political and economic development. This is not to ignore the potentially centrifugal forces which may threaten the system, but rather to utilize them to help the system function more effectively and insure that the leadership does not make policy decisions in an informational vacuum. We are not, of course, arguing for a Western style, parliamentary opposition. Given the levels of diversity found in Africa, perhaps the best solution lies along lines of the Tanzania system—that is, with a strong, single-party apparatus with meaningful op-

[13] Oginga Odinga, *Not Yet Uhuru* (New York: Hill & Wang, 1967).

[14] Also, as Richard Sklar has written, tribal or ethnic "diversity" is often a "mask" for class privilege and used by individual leaders ("Political Science and National Integration," 6). Thus, politicians say, "the Mossi want" or "the Wakamba want" when what they really mean is "I want." The recent assassination of Tom MBoya is a case in point. While there are undoubtedly strong tribal overtones to the Luo reaction, the fact that many Luo's felt alienated from the present political system greatly enhanced the political repercussions of that reaction.

position and an opportunity for leadership alteration built into that framework. This is difficult to accomplish. Often there is a great deal of appeal to a strategy of defeating the opposition and driving them out of the ruling party, or removing them from the legal political culture. What we are suggesting, however, is that in the long run, such a strategy is more likely to lead to political decay rather than to political development.

If a political system maintains a flexible but sturdy institutional framework, provides for systemic accountability through mass participation in the political process, and preserves some domestic opposition for information and cathartic purposes, it stands a good chance of avoiding political decay. Yet, goal espousal, too, is of great importance: unrealizable goals may generate massive frustration which, in turn, may induce political devolution. We have already delineated the generally weak system capabilities that are such a prominent feature of most political systems of sub-Saharan Africa. Often these handicaps are the direct result of the colonial experience—arbitrary boundaries, Balkanization, a mercantilist legacy which militates against economic development, and dysfunctional political structures thrust upon the states in question. The collective weakness in terms of domestic and international power could be overcome by continental unity. Kwame Nkrumah was correct, "Africa must unite" if it is to avoid what seem like inevitabilities of its situation. Alone, the Togos, the Dahomeys, the Lesothos, and the Upper Voltas are faced with what amount to insurmountable handicaps. Yet, looked at objectively, Pan-Africanism is more honored in the breach than in the observance and the Organization of African Unity, however worthwhile, has not provided a vehicle for supranational amalgamation. It may be—in fact, it is quite likely—that African unity in the sense of a single, organized entity will prove as impossible to achieve as Latin American, European, or Asian unity. In fact, given the a priori handicaps faced by most African states, fragmentation and weakness may well continue into the foreseeable future. This is unfortunate, but a frank realization of the situation and of the difficulties inherent in the positions of the African systems may lead to a more modest— and more beneficial—selection of goals. The international community contains entities—Ireland, Costa Rica, and Iceland—that are weak but satisfied, including some such as Denmark and New Zealand which enjoy high standards of living based not on heavy industry but upon the export of high quality primary products.

Leaders of the political systems of sub-Saharan Africa and interested scholars may well want to reexamine the goals of each system in terms of its present capabilities and the possibility of their future expansion. In view of the difficulties involved, not only in the problems of economic development and political modernization but simply in the maintenance of a viable political system, far more attention needs to be placed on systemic goals. A national policy of *ad astra per aspera* is likely, in many systems at least, to produce substantial frustration, frustration that will ultimately turn back upon the political system and produce a situation where political decay, if not irresistible, is at least probable.

Index

297